Coffee

THE EPIC OF A COMMODITY

Coffee

THE EPIC OF A COMMODITY

Heinrich Eduard Jacob

❀❀❀❀❀❀❀❀❀❀❀❀❀❀❀

TRANSLATED BY EDEN AND CEDAR PAUL

BURFORD BOOKS

Copyright © 1935, 1962 by the Viking Press, Inc.
ALL RIGHTS RESERVED. No part of this book may be
reproduced in any manner without the express written
consent of the publisher, except in the case of brief excerpts
in critical reviews and articles. All inquiries should be addressed to:
Burford Books, Inc., PO Box 388, Short Hills, New Jersey 07078

Printed in the United States of America

10 9 8 7 6 5´4 3 2 1

Library of Congress Cataloging-in-Publication Data
Jacob, Heinrich Eduard, 1889–1967.
    Coffee : the epic of a commodity / Heinrich Eduard Jacob ;
translated by Eden and Cedar Paul.
        p.   cm.
    Originally published: New York : Viking Press, 1935.
    Includes bibliographical references and index.
    ISBN 1-58080-070-X (pbk.)
    1. Coffee. 2. Drinking customs. I. Title.
TX415.J2997   1998
641.3'373—dc21   98-33523
                                     CIP

Contents

Contents

Book Five: Brazilian Dictatorship

Introduction

On the Trail of Coffee . . .

T HE reprinting of *Coffee: The Epic of a Commodity* is long over-due. It stands as a landmark in the evolution of twentieth-century European literature, and its author was among a company of brilliant minds with whom he interacted and correspond-ed. Albert Einstein, Thomas Mann, Franz Werfel (author of *The Song of Bernadette* and *The Forty Days of Musa Dagh*, both classics which were ultimately made into Hollywood movies), the well-known early-twentieth-century German poet Stephan Zweig, German political philosopher Hannah Arendt, and German film director Max Reinhardt, to name a few, were his friends and contemporaries. And his subject was one which has captured the minds and hearts of late-twentieth-century Americans, just as it had captured the attention of Jacob's turn-of-the-century Vienna.

Two years ago, I began working on an introduction to a wonderful book I'd found: *Six Thousand Years of Bread: Its Holy and Unholy History* by German author, Heinrich Eduard Jacob. The book was an obscure classic, originally published in English in 1944. Following its initial enthusiastic reception, it had lain quietly gathering dust in the libraries of dedicated bread lovers and food historians. Laurel Robertson, author of *The Laurel's Kitchen Bread Book*, had drawn my attention to it. Her comments set me on the trail of an adventure which would lead me into the world of Heinrich Eduard Jacob and the political, social, and literary stage of early-twentieth-century Berlin and Vienna.

Introduction to the 1998 Edition

Jacob was well-known and respected in his day as a poet, play-wright, novelist and chief of the Central European bureau (headquar-tered in Vienna) of Berlin's largest newspaper; as such, he socialized and worked with everyone who was "anyone" in the world of German literature, art, and society. I was surprised to learn that not only had he written a thorough history of bread, but he had also written, among other renowned works, an equally comprehensive history of coffee. Jacob was the first to explore the history of a commodity by presenting his information in a dramatic form; thus his "saga of cof-fee" was considered a landmark in European literature.

In 1922, an American author, William Ukers, had written a monu-mental work (800 pages) on the subject of coffee. The Ukers book, with which Jacob was familiar, was a fascinating collection of primary sources: writings, observations, and documents on coffee down through the ages, yet Ukers made no attempt to weave his facts into the fabric of a story as Jacob had done. Robert Barker, who spent his early years hauling pastries to the famed Café Trieste in San Francisco's North Beach, and who is now a green coffee buyer for a specialty coffee roaster as well as the owner of an historic coffee farm in Colombia, thinks that Jacob's dramatic presentation of "that silly goat story"—the legend of how coffee was discovered by a goatherd and his goats—is the first account that sounds even remotely plausi-ble. And the *Deutsches Biobibliographie*, the standard German bio-graphical reference book, claims, ". . .*Myth and the Triumphal March of Coffee* [as it is called in German] is considered the first of the mod-ern nonfiction books . . . in which Jacob meshed mythological specu-lation, historically accurate details and facts with observations on economics and cultural criticism into stimulating reading matter."

How did Jacob conceive this idea? Hans Jörgen Gerlach quotes Jacob in his book, *Heinrich Eduard Jacob: In Two Worlds:*

> "Gerhardt Hauptmann [the foremost German drama-tist of the twentieth-century], Leo von König [one of Europe's most important twentieth-century painters] and I took a stroll over the Island Hiddensee. Hauptmann had been unusually talkative, praising the classical Greeks and their habit of making 'gods

out of things.' 'Such a true god is the god of wine (Bacchus), to whom everyone owes reverence and gratitude,' proclaimed Hauptmann. At this point, von König gave me a sly, amused sidelong glance, for Hauptmann had a reputation as an infamous drinker.

I remained silent. To my mind there existed an anti-Bacchus; namely, coffee. For what was wine to me? Wine may well encourage the creativity of characters like Hauptmann, but it only led me to the vestibule of sleep. To me, it was coffee, the great resurrector, that gave me courage and vigor. So I decided to write its history. The book would be a novel and then some. Something which would require digging deep through entire libraries; a narrative which would be given soul by a coffee-driven euphoria.

My friend Ernst Rowohlt suggested calling it the 'Saga of Coffee.' It would be a documentary novel; the very first of its kind. Oddly enough, the genre became quite popular in America. Odd because it was particularly in the Anglo-Saxon countries where there bloomed a rigid separation between fiction and non-fiction. Today, of course, all that has changed; and writers recognize that scientific books, too, regardless of their serious nature, can be written using epic techniques."

Myth and the Triumphal March of Coffee met with phenomenal success upon its publication in Germany in 1935. Jacob's work had been black-listed by the Nazis since 1933 (Jacob was a Jew, a Mason, and a pacifist), but Jacob's friend, publisher Ernst Rowohlt, in a gesture designed to foster the spirit of literary freedom, had made it his business to publish many works considered undesirable by the Nazis. Jacob's work met with such success in fact, that Josef Goebbels, Hitler's minister of propaganda, allegedly telephoned Rowohlt himself to ask that he "call off his Jew."

Introduction to the 1998 Edition

Coffee: The Epic of a Commodity was eventually translated into twelve languages and published in England, America, France, Italy, Sweden, Greece, Portugal and Spain. In December, 1938, a reviewer in *The New York Times* said, "All this noble arras of adventure, this 'epic of a commodity' one reads in *Coffee* . . . far more a tale from the *Thousand and One Nights* than the sober account of a breakfast necessity." And the *Montreal Daily Star* called it "a book whose flavor is as stimulating as its subject." A reviewer in the *New York Herald* claimed, "Herr Jacob's Coffee kept me awake to the last page." And *The Pittsburgh Press* lauded, "He has produced a book as stimulating and as satisfying as your morning cup of coffee."

Yet I am puzzled by the fact that this book, so very popular upon its publication, has gathered dust on the shelves for over sixty years. Since Jacob's book appeared, no one else has attempted the formidable task of telling the tale and yet the world has gone "coffee crazy," witness the enormous popularity of gourmet coffee vendors and houses on every street corner in America. Jacob's Vienna was renowned for its coffee and coffeehouses: Jacob stated, "Just as in the Imperium Romanum one encountered the military milestones every thousand double paces along the high road, so, throughout Austria-Hungary one encountered the prefectoral headquarters built of yellow sandstone and fitted with green shutters . . . and coffee-houses after the Viennese model." Vienna had, among other things, become "coffee central" in Jacob's day. And he considered living in Vienna to be one of the most important formative aspects of his life. Yet not even Jacob, with his great passion for coffee, could have foreseen the powerful hold coffee would have on the world of today.

What would Jacob think if he could visit the streets of a modern American Metropolis and see his "anti-Bacchus" enjoying enormous popularity side-by-side with its very antithesis? I cannot imagine he would be altogether surprised at the results of this twentieth-century alliance. Alice Lampel, Jacob's half-sister, writing for the *International Herald Tribune* in 1936, said of Jacob, "everything he undertakes aims at reconciling divergencies," so I cannot imagine he would be anything but pleased.

Consciously or unconsciously, Jacob approached this theme of reconciliation, this time between the Arab and the Christian worlds, when he tackled the task of telling the tale of coffee. Just as wine is at the very foundation of the Judeo-Christian European culture, so coffee is the very hallmark commodity of the world of Islam. And just as you find wine wherever you find a Christian-based civilization, so you find coffee wherever the Arab world has made significant inroads. (It is interesting to note that until the most modern times, China remained relatively immune to both of these commodities and religions, testifying to its traditional isolationist stance.) In a sense, just as the Crusaders of twelfth-century Europe returned from the Holy Wars bringing with them an appreciation of things Arab (and forever changing the shape of things to come in Western Europe), so Heinrich Eduard Jacob sought to acknowledge and honor the "wine of Islam" which has had such an enormous impact upon the twentieth-century world.

Inasmuch as wine has long been associated with the feminine (André Tchelistcheff has compared a good Merlot to a "charming, beautiful lady"), relaxation and romance, coffee has long been viewed as masculine and equated with the world of intellectual stimulation. Jacob points out that seventeenth-century English literature was born in the London coffeehouses frequented by Johnson, Dryden, Pope, Swift, Addison and Steele. And the 1960s coffeehouses of New York's Greenwich Village and San Francisco's North Beach spawned a whole "beat generation" of writers. In actuality, coffee and its attendant conversation have often spelt trouble for the status quo. Jacob reports that in 1517, Khair Bey, the new viceroy of the Mecca, forbade the drinking of coffee on the premise that it "led to riots;" and in December of 1675, Charles II of England closed the country's coffeehouses because he considered them "hotbeds of sedition and a breeding ground for subversive movements," all of which was not far from the truth. In 1774, a letter sent by the Committee of Correspondence from Merchants' coffee house in New York to Boston proposed the American Union. Merchants' had been dubbed by some as the "birthplace of the Union" as well as the "true cradle of American liberty," and in 1789, George Washington was officially greeted there as President of the United States. Jacob further describes how, on July 12, 1789, French revolutionary Camille Desmoulins mounted a table outside the Café Foy in Paris' Palais Royale and incited the crowd to

Introduction to the 1998 Edition

storm the Bastille! Likewise, Jacob believed that the French Revolution was born in the cafés of Paris.

When *Coffee: The Epic of a Commodity* first appeared in English in 1935, the "coffee shop" had become an American institution and the country was ready for the saga of its morning wake-me-up. As the millennium comes to a close, there is a specialty coffee vendor on every street corner in America and coffee comes from the four corners of the earth. The country is again crazy for coffee and ready for the retelling of its exciting story.

I am grateful to Peter Burford and his newly-formed Burford Books for having the good sense to recognize and publish this unique book. Its publication would also not have been possible without the generous help of my friend, Dr. Jeffrey B. Berlin, a well-known authority on the subject of early-twentieth-century German authors and keeper of a wealth of knowledge about Heinrich Eduard Jacob, his contemporaries, and his era, who has graciously shared many conversations and many manuscripts with me. In addition, I wish to thank Hans Jörgen Gerlach of Berlin, who is the executor of Jacob's estate, and who has proven himself more than worthy of the confidence bestowed upon him by Heinrich Eduard Jacob's widow, Dora, when she placed her husband's works in Herr Gerlach's care. Without his permission and generous assistance, this book could not have been reprinted in English. Thanks to Beth Hensperger and Helen Mildner for patient proofreading. And most of all, I wish to thank M., who gives heart to all I write.

—Lynn Alley
July, 1998

BOOK ONE

Islam's Wine

Night in the Land of Yemen

T HE ground, which was but a skin of lava and limestone, had little time to cool down at night. The fierce, red sun rose early and set late, so the night was short, hot, and oppressive.

By walking a few miles westward, one could reach the sea. But it was a shallow sea, tepid, and not wide. From time immemorial it had been known as the Red Sea.

Scant vegetation was to be found among the foothills of Yemen. On the flanks of the hills and in the wadies grew dense bushes. Dwarf acacias stood gaunt and motionless in the parched and torrid air. Cushions of golden and brown furze saddled the crests. The aloe was bitter, the date-palm bore sweet fruit. Across them one glimpsed the rust-coloured mountains, the terrible Jebel Shomer from which, of old, fiery streams of lava had descended. Nothing grew on these heights, and men did not visit them. Only the runaway goats, from time to time, climbed the top-most peaks. No one bade them go thither, but thither they went, moved by the lust of adventure and the longing for solitude. After weeks, they would return, lean and out of condition.

The herds of goats belonged to the monastery. The monastery, "She-hodet"—the name means "bear witness"—belonged to Allah, as every-thing on earth belongs to the Creator.

Between goats and men there has, since the dawn of history, been a bargain. Such was the case here. The goats supplied the monastery with milk and goat-hair; in return, the monastery provided the goats with herdsmen, watchdogs, and protection. Often enough, however, the monks broke their side of the contract. Then the goats were, in part, elaborated into morocco or cordovan. Sometimes, as parchment leaves of the Koran, they testified to the greatness of Mohammed, the Prophet of Allah—after their flesh had been devoured and their skins thoroughly dried in the baking air. Nevertheless most of the goats continued to dwell among the foothills, though they could easily have wandered beyond the reach of dogs and men.

Goatherds have little to do. That is why they have always been liars, braggarts, and intriguers. Was not Melantheus, the goatherd in the Homeric saga, a busybody; did he not reflect the covetousness and disquiet of the beasts under his care? Exceptionally false-tongued must have been those goatherds who misled Claudius Aelianus, the writer of classical Rome, into believing a quaint item of natural history: "One of the peculiar merits of the goat is the strange way in which it is able to breathe. For this animal can breathe through its ears as well as through its nostrils, and is, speaking generally, the most sensitive of all cloven-footed beasts. I do not know why they breathe thus, but merely record what I have learned. Since the goat was created by Prometheus, he alone, I presume, knows why he created it no otherwise. . . ."

The goatherds of Shehodet Monastery knew their charges well, as was meet; knew the creatures' Promethean disinclination for peace and quiet; their fondness for climbing, for butting, and for gnawing the bark off trees; their perpetual craving for salt. The goatherds knew that goats would often take to the high mountains for a week or more, and be slow to return. But now the beasts were displaying a new characteristic, one which was troublesome to their keepers. Hitherto a goat's day had been, like a man's, a day of twelve hours. At sunset, they were wont to go to sleep, lying with outstretched limbs, as motionless as stone. But now the goats were affected with sleeplessness.

All night, for five nights in succession—nay, for seven or eight—they clambered over rocks, cutting capers, chasing one another, bleating fantastically. They turned their bearded heads hither and thither; with reddened eyes they gambolled convulsively when they caught sight of the goatherds, and then they darted off swift as arrows speeding from the bow.

"The goatsucker has been plaguing them," said an old herdsman. This bird takes its name from its supposed habit of pecking at goats' teats in the night-time, and thus driving the animals crazy.

"There is no goatsucker," said young Hassan with a contemptuous laugh.

"What, didn't you hear it churring out of the darkness four nights ago?"

"Certainly. I heard the call of the nightjar, but that bird drinks no milk. A fable for children! The creature is no larger than my hand. What would it stand on to pluck at a goat's teats with its bill?"

"Idiot, could it not cling to the beast's hair with its claws?"

Already the two men were raising their staffs against each other in their anger. Old Abdullah parted them, and said:

"Let us fetch the imam from the hill!"

The chief of the monastery came. He looked rather like a goat himself, as he sat among the goatherds: lean, with a tremulous beard, large eyes peeping forth from reddened lids, and a leathery skin. Two of the animals were brought. There was nothing amiss with their teats, no sign that a bird had been pecking.

"Your goats must have eaten poison."

"What poison could they have found?"

"Follow them, and keep them under close watch."

But the goats, as usual, nibbled coltsfoot, sage, mimosa leaves, broom; plundered the caper bushes. Their udders swelled with milk. All the same, they did not sleep.

"We've found the plant that has bewitched them!"

The imam, who was resting in the shade with his chief assistant, Daood, beside him, looked up. Before him stood one of the goatherds, holding out a spray.

It was a moderate-sized, flexible spray, that of a shrub rather than a tree, with the dark-green, firm, and shiny leaves, somewhat resembling those of a laurel. From the axils of the leaves projected short, white blossoms, closely set like those of jasmine. Some had ripened and fallen, leaving their fruit, little berries of a strange magenta hue. If you grasped one of these between finger and thumb, you could feel that it had a thick, hard kernel. The imam turned the spray over and over, much astonished. What he held resembled a *Planta universalis*, with the characters of many plants he knew, but in its assemblage of characters unknown.

"Your goats have been eating this?"

The goatherd replied that there could be no doubt of it. A coppice of this unknown shrub had been discovered, obviously devastated by the goats in their search for food.

"In what direction?"

"Towards the north."

After climbing for more than three hours, over screes and smooth boulders, through gorse and agave and brambles, the imam and Daood, guided by the goatherds, reached the coppice. It was in a wadi, damp and hot. What remarkable trees! They ranged in height from six to twelve feet, and looked more like overgrown shrubs than trees.

No one had ever seen anything of the kind before. The imam, who wanted to try the effect of the leaves and blossoms, plucked some and chewed them, but soon spat them out. The taste was neither bitter nor sweet, neither salt nor sour nor oily—they had no taste worth speaking of. Nor had they any scent that could have allured the goats.

On the way back, Daood said that perhaps a description of the unfamiliar plant might be found in a herbal. The monastery was well provided with parchment volumes, among which were some containing all that the Arabs knew about plant lore. But the herbals were searched in vain.

"To my way of thinking," said the imam, "this shrub is not a wild one, but a cultivated one that has escaped from a garden and run wild."

Daood protested.

"How could there ever have been a garden in or near so desolate a spot? Even the jinn would hardly have established one in a place as inaccessible!"

"I was not thinking of a garden planted either by true believers or by the jinn," replied the imam. "You must have heard that, centuries back, our land was conquered by the giaours. I do not mean the white Christians of the North, the Roumis and the Feringhees, those who call themselves Romans and Franks; but Christians from the West, black Christians from Africa, subjects of the monarch of Ethiopia. They crossed the narrow waters of the Red Sea, coming from the territory known as Kaffa. They brought with them domestic animals, and also their favourite vegetables and flowers. I think this is a Kaffa tree. . . ."

"If the tree has magic virtues, surely we should have heard of it?" said young Daood, dubiously. "It is but a tree like many another, and

I can hardly believe that Allah would have equipped it with powers peculiar to itself."

The skies had flushed red while Daood was speaking. A large green beetle, metallic and burnished, flew into the room from the courtyard. It circled desirously above the blossoms on the sprays the monks had brought back with them.

"The goatherds," the young man went on, "have probably lied to us. They are habitual cheats, up to every kind of dodge. Who can tell whether they may not, wishing to humbug us, have filled the goats' hair with stage-beetles and poisonous ticks, and whether these pests may not have kept the poor beasts awake. Now the rascals are laughing at us up their sleeves because we have swallowed their fable about Allah having made a plant which can render his creatures sleepless. It amuses them to fool the learned and the pious!"

Daood said good-night and departed. The imam prayed. Daylight quickly faded, the red sky turning to a peaceful green, which became a blue that darkened apace. The evening star shed its silvery beams into the courtyard. Deliciously soothing were its cool rays after the heat and glare of the tropical day.

Donkeys laden with goatskins full of water were being driven up the hill. They brayed as they clattered into the yard. The monastery possessed no well, and its pitchers had to be replenished every morning and every evening. The monks issued from their cells carrying vessels of unglazed earthenware, in which the water would remain fresh and sweet for hours, whereas it would soon begin to stink if stored in goat-skin sacks.

The imam, too, went out into the yard to fill his pitcher. He was much exercised in his mind as to whether Daood was right in the surmise about the goatherds' trickery, or whether the strange plant could really have mysterious powers.

"I will make an infusion," he thought, throwing some of the leaves and flowers into a glass vessel, and crushing them with a spoon. There were berries as well, and his spoon encountered the kernel of the fruit. The beans were hard and firm. Cold water could have no effect on them. With a twist of the container he ejected water, flowers, leaves, retaining only the kernels. Eagerly pursuing his investigation, he heated these in a chafing-dish over the embers on the hearth. They sweated, dried, and darkened. He crushed them in a mortar, and, having boiled some water, while it was still bubbling from the fierce heat, he threw a fair quantity of the dark-brown powder into the vessel. The result was a brew dark as the lowermost sea in Gehenna, while an aroma such as had never before filled his nostrils rose from the pot.

The imam poured out for himself a beaker of the steaming decoction, and drank. It was bitter to the taste, savouring of forbidden pitch, of charred wood, of the droppings of Eblis. Then he lay down and composed himself for sleep.

Within a few moments, the imam of Shehodet Monastery was as if under a spell. He was in a state of intoxication differing from all other intoxications hitherto known to his people. The imam, indeed, being a fervent Moslem, had had no experience of drunkenness.

He was somewhat painfully aware, on the left side, between the fifth rib and the sixth, of the quickened beating of his heart, as it rhythmically expanded and contracted. Was not the rhythm somewhat disordered? He was sweating a little, and had a wondrous sense of lightness in the limbs. This was the hour when, ordinarily, night began to take possession of his frame, and to slacken his joints with the first promptings of sleep. Now, however, though he had almost ceased to be aware of his body, his mind was unusually active, cheerful, and alert. He was not merely thinking; his thoughts had become concretely visible. He watched them from the right side and from the left, from above and from below. They raced like a team of horses. A hundred details, ordinarily blurred, became meticulously clear. Although the team was covering the ground faster and faster, there was no confusion. Far from it, he was thinking five times or ten times more clearly than ever before. In the time normally requisite for one thought, the imam could now, without effort, think a dozen thoughts, and yet keep them absolutely distinct. The members of the racing team did not get their harness tangled. The ideas were luminously clear, and sped onward towards the distant horizon. But, having reached that horizon, they were as plainly visible as if they had been close at hand.

Thus the imam lay, sweating a trifle, and panting gently as he breathed. He found that something unusual was going on in his consciousness besides the way in which his inward eye contemplated his racing thoughts. With his outwardly directed vision, too, he saw other things than the normal. The parchment tome close at hand had an unwonted length, breadth, and thickness, and an unusual lustre. His "chalat" (an outer garment for daily use), though hanging empty from a peg on the wall, looked as if it were filled out with the curves of his figure. His gaze darted briskly hither and thither in the room, which was dimly lighted by a floating wick. The objects he contemplated were not flat, but full-bodied. He himself was as lively and vigorous as if he had been refreshed by thirty hours' sleep, had been strengthened by heavenly food brought to him by the angels of Paradise, and would never need to sleep again. . . . Thus did the imam feel as he lay on his pallet; thus did he feel thereafter when, having sprung to his feet, he paced the chamber un-tiringly.

When midnight came, the hour for the prayer which is called "ishe," he went along the corridors to awaken the brethren in their cells. Heavy with sleep, they reluctantly sat up and yawned. They yawned to get the sleep out of their throats and lungs, yawned and stretched. Heavily and unwillingly they began, as commanded by the Prophet, to invoke the blessing of the Allah of midnight.

As they did so they felt, as they felt night after night, that this particu-lar commandment of the Prophet was grievously unnatural. Was it true, as they had so often heard the muezzins call from the minarets, that prayer is better than sleep? When the world was created it had, by a wise ordinance, been divided into a white half and a black, into a day-side and a night-side—that is, into waking and sleep, which must not be allowed to encroach upon or jostle each other. What wonderful will-power must Mohammed the Prophet of Allah have had to be able to wake up, in order to pray, after four hours' sleep! The monks found it a great hardship, for they were ordinary mortals.

But the imam, coming to each of them in turn, gave them to drink of a black, bitter drink, which had an unpleasant taste though the odour was pleasant enough. This beverage instilled into them the will to wake. It seemed that one who swallowed a sufficiency of it forgot that he had been prematurely aroused from slumber. The sense of fatigue departed from his knee-joints, and he felt not the dead weight of his arms hanging from his shoulders. He was freed from the insistent pull of gravitation.

Night after night, when the hour of the "ishe" arrived, the imam and his monks refreshed themselves with the decoction of the Kaffa-seeds. In their thankfulness they gave the elixir a name with a twofold meaning. They called it "k'hawah," the stimulating, the invigorating; this was with reference to the magical qualities of the coffee-bean, as well as to the supposed original derivation of the shrub from Kaffa. They thought also of Kawus Kai, the great king of Persia, who had conquered the force of terrestrial gravity and had ascended into heaven in a winged chariot.

The Fight Against Bacchus

T HE essentials of this tale were related by Antonius Faustus Nai-ron, a Maronite monk and scholar, who ultimately became pro-fessor of theology at the Sorbonne in Paris, and died in the year 1710.

Is the story true? Beyond question it has been widely related in the West. It is to be found, with similar imaginative embroidery, in an old encyclopædia, Hübner's *Natur-Kunst-Berg-Gewerk-Handels- und Zeitungs-Lexikon*, published in 1717. It bears the manifest stamp of an Oriental apologue. The fact that the excrement of goats looks very like coffee-beans may have given rise to the fable. The famous doctrine of similars, the belief that objects that resemble one another must have a mysterious connexion, had an even stronger hold upon the Oriental than upon the medieval Western mind. That led to a supposition of some link between goats and the coffee-shrub.

The important core of the legend is not the discovery of coffee by goats (although in early days the behaviour of domesticated animals often guided human beings in their researches) but the speedy recogni-tion of the magical qualities that reside in coffee-beans. More important, therefore, than the goat story is another myth as to the origin of coffee. According to a fairly modern Persian saga, when Mohammed, the Prophet of Allah, was suffering from excessive somnolence verging on stupor, the angel Gabriel appeared to him at the command of the Al-mighty, bringing him for his relief an unknown beverage. This drink was black, as black as the Black Stone built into the corner of the Ka'ba at Mecca. The Black Stone is meteoric, of heavenly origin, and is venerated by all true Moslems. The name of the elixir brought to Mohammed by the angel Gabriel, a bitter fluid, was "kahveh," or "k'hawah," the stimulating, the invigorating.

This much is true, that when the use of coffee began, the world was dowered with a magical force unknown to classical antiquity. Wine had played a leading part in the history of the ancient world. The ancients were familiar with the Bacchic stimulation obtainable from the juice that issued from the wine-press when once that juice had been fermented, but they knew nothing of the anti-Bacchic influence of the no less exciting and mysterious caffeine, the active principle of the coffee-bean. It was Arabic civilization, a vigorous rival knocking at the door of medieval Europe, that brought coffee as a sustaining companion to man on his way through life.

Coffee has sometimes been spoken of as the "wine of Islam"; and, in actual fact, Mohammedan civilization, the Moslem love for drawing fine distinctions, for hair-splitting, for disputation—all the "cold heat and flaming sobriety" of Arabic civilization, are closely connected with the effect of coffee upon the human brain. The Stoics of Hellas had taught "ataraxia," passionlessness, resignation to the will of destiny; but it was left for the conquering Arabs, paradoxically, to inculcate these virtues at the point of the sword. Anti-Bacchic stimulation, the idolization of reason, the religio-intellectualist doctrine of salvation that has always been characteristic of Mohammedanism, are cousin german to the aroma of coffee. The peculiar style of architecture that spreads across the sometime empire of the caliphs, from the Alhambra to the mosques of Baghdad, was devised by coffee-drinkers and never by wine-bibbers; it talks the language of Moorish dialectics, and lifts minarets skyward like pointing index fingers. It resembles the conversation of the men who inhabited these buildings—they and their talks being rich in arabesques, wide awake, and yet perpetually elusive. This style of architecture is of the same family as the bold philosophical systems of Avicenna and Averroës.

Coffee is, indeed, "the wine of Islam." To become this, however, it had to present itself as an anti-Bacchic, and to overthrow the classical culture, which was a Bacchic culture. No matter whether, as the aforesaid legend tells us, Mohammed the Prophet knew coffee or whether the angel Gabriel revealed its use to some of the latter caliphs; Mohammed, with his fulminations against wine, changed the human heart before coffee had changed the human brain.

In the chapter of the Koran entitled "The Table," the Prophet inveighs against the use of wine. He prohibits the enjoyment of that drug, that intoxicant, which for several thousand years had furnished man with his only possibility of escape from himself and from the weariness of everyday life. He rejected any enchantment, any expansion of the ego—that without which the life and literature, the civilization and the art of the ancient world would never have come into existence. Wine had been the very mortar of the edifice of classical culture!

Why did the founder of Islam come to this epoch-making decision? There is nothing comparable to his prohibition of wine in religious systems earlier than his own. Above all, neither Judaism nor Christianity, which Mohammedanism synthesized into Islam, had adopted a hostile attitude towards wine.

According to Jewish legend, Father Noah discovered wine shortly after the Deluge. The tale is related in the twentieth and subsequent verses of the ninth chapter of Genesis. Simultaneously, indeed, we are warned of the disastrous effects of drunkenness! "And Noah began to be an husbandman, and he planted a vineyard: and he drank of the wine, and was drunken; and he was uncovered within his tent. And Ham . . . saw the nakedness of his father, and told his two brethren without. And Shem and Japheth took a garment, and laid it upon both their shoulders, and went backward, and covered the nakedness of their father; and their faces were backward, and they saw not their father's nakedness." Wherefore Shem and Japheth were blessed, but Ham received his father's curse. This anecdote is a parable against the immoderate use of wine, but the reasonable use of it is not condemned.

Nor, with one exception, is the reasonable use of wine forbidden anywhere in the Old Testament. The exception stands apart so clearly that it has no bearing upon the normal, everyday life of the ancient Hebrews. I refer to the description of those who are styled Nazarites, in the sixth chapter of Numbers. There we read: "When either man or woman shall separate themselves to vow a vow of a Nazarite, to separate themselves unto the Lord: he shall separate himself from wine and strong drink, and shall drink no vinegar of wine, or vinegar of strong drink, neither shall he drink any liquor of grapes, nor eat moist grapes or dried. All the days of his separation shall he eat nothing that is made of the vine tree, from the kernels even to the husk. All the days of the vow of his separation there shall no razor come upon his head: until the days be fulfilled, in the which he separateth himself unto the Lord, he shall be holy, and shall let the locks of the hair of his head grow. All the days that he separateth himself unto the Lord he shall come at no dead body. He shall not make himself unclean for his father, or for his mother, for his brother, or for his sister, when they die: because the consecration of his God is upon his head." Even this passage is not so much a diatribe against wine as against the disturbance of concentration that might result from the enjoyment of wine, thus threatening the "separation," that is to say, the fulfilment of a vow to go into retreat. The old scribe has in mind the paralysing force of wine, the way it breaks down inhibitions. This influence is compared with the working of the razor, which removes the primitive energy of the growing hair, shown by the legend of Samson and Delilah to be one of the most important emblems of virile strength. The mental derangement that results from excessive wining is, in the passage quoted from Numbers, put on the same footing as the paralysis caused by the contemplation of the dead and of organic decay—which, according to the Jewish hygienists, was readily transmitted from the dead to the living.

Still, there is no talk here of the danger of wine in ordinary circumstances. The Nazarites were exceptional persons, who had "vowed a vow," and, on the expiry of the vow, they were liberated from the prohibition against wine. The account of the Nazarites may be contrasted with many passages from Holy Writ which are in full conformity with the joy of life characteristic of the Jews, who regarded wine as one of the most splendid gifts of God to men. This account of the Nazarites and that of the Rechabites in the thirty-fifth chapter of Jeremiah and the warning references to drunkenness in the twenty-third chapter of Proverbs notwithstanding, the Old Testament is full of the glorification of wine. Wine was plentifully used by the Hebrews at wedding festivals and at the Seder, the home feast on the first night of the Passover. All Palestine, in those days, was a vineyard. "Go thy way, eat thy bread with joy, and drink thy wine with a merry heart," saith the Preacher. We read in the Talmud: "In the world to come, man will be called to account for every permitted pleasure which has been offered to him and which, without good cause, he has shunned."

Thus among the children of Israel wine was greatly prized as a popular article of diet and as the furtherer of sociability, being forbidden only to priests and judges when engaged in the performance of their official duties. Thus in the sacred writings of the Jews the founder of Islam could find nothing in the least analogous to the prohibition against wine he introduced into the Koran. Nor could he find anything of the sort in Christian teachings.

On the contrary, Christianity went a step further in the apotheosis of the civilizing and uniting qualities of the vine. In the mystery of the Last Supper, the blood of the grape became the blood of Jesus. Asceticism and abstinence, though essential elements of Christianity, were not applied to the use of wine. It seemed to the early Christians as innocent as bread, for otherwise it would not have been made symbolical of the holiest of sacrifices. Even a religion that sedulously preached the mortification of the flesh, a religion in whose name Tolstoy seriously recommended that we should abstain from procreating our kind—even Christianity held in honour the cordial, brotherly, intellectualizing and spiritualizing effect of wine. Christ was no anti-Bacchus.

But Mohammed was an anti-Bacchus! With an impulsive energy that outsoared anything that Jew or Christian before him had said against wine—in essentials, his predecessors had done no more than recommend temperance and decency—Mohammed uprooted the vine. Wherever Islam set its foot, vineyards were turned to other uses and the cultivation of the grape came to an end. All round the southern shores of the Mediterranean, from the days of the Hegira onwards, viticulture was abandoned.

The German traveller Gerhard Rohlfs, who, in 1868, travelled through the region known to the ancients as Cyrenaica, sometimes called Barca by modern geographers, saw the ruins of the temples of Bacchus. Among the imports from which were derived the revenues of what was then a Turkish vilayet, wine was mentioned, for none was grown locally. When, in northern Africa, Bacchus still held sway, there was no need to import wine!

Thus, from the outlook of the economic geographer as well, the revolution wrought by Islam was enormous. With the coming of Mohammed and his prohibition against wine, after the great days of the folk-migrations, along the southern part of the Mediterranean basin classical culture had come to an end. For the culture, the civilization, of the Greeks and the Romans had been fundamentally Bacchic.

Lewin, the toxicologist, writes: "There was not only one Noah, to discover the uses of wine; there have been many such innovators on our globe, led by chance observation or by deduction to the preparation of alcoholic beverages."

Only one branch of civilization, the Hellenic, thought fit to deify the spiritual expansion that results from the witchery of wine. For the Jews, Noah remained a man; Bacchus-Dionysus became a god. A very large part of Greek mythology relates to the spread of the worship of Bacchus. Ere long the cult of Dionysus overshadowed and outweighed the service of other gods, though these latter from time to time came into their own once more. The final conquest of Bacchus, as we learn from Greek tragedy, led to tremendous upheavals in the human mind and in social order.

Strangely enough, the founder of Islam, who, in the fierce campaign he directed against wine, could find no support in Jewish or Christian authorities, could get what he wanted from Hellas! The foundations of the abstinence movement were undeniably laid by the Greeks. It seems as if the temperamental harmony and moderation of the Hellenic mind had reacted against the extravagances of the worship of Bacchus. The Pythian Apollo was at enmity with Bacchus until he struck up an alliance by which Bacchus was brought under control.

Nietzsche has pointed out that the original theme of Greek tragedy was the woes of Dionysus. Woes? That seems strange. Are we to suppose that the primitive Hellenes had already come to regard Dionysus as a god mishandled by the Puritans? Certainly one of these anti-Bacchic enthusiasts, Pentheus, who succeeded Cadmus as king of Thebes and who resisted the introduction of the worship of Dionysus into his kingdom, came to a bad end. He was torn to pieces by his mother and his two sisters, Ino and Autonoë, who, in their Bacchic frenzy, believed him to be a wild beast.

Had not Pentheus refused to come to terms with Dionysus, he would have saved his kingdom and his life. The United States would, by such an alliance, have been saved many of the troubles that prevailed during the dozen or so years in which the Eighteenth Amendment to the Constitution was in force: assassinations, bootlegging, gangsterism, corruption, social disorganization on a large scale. This experience has shown that the Hellenic myth may counsel a recognition essential to human nature.

A temperance movement, certainly, existed among the Greeks. In the circle of Socrates, for example, moderate drinking prevailed. The Pentheus tragedy was aimed only at those who demanded the absolute prohibition of wine, the "teetotallers" of that day who desired asceticism for its own sake. Indeed, the very word "tragedy" meant primarily "goat-singers" (perhaps because the singers were clad in goat-skins, or because a he-goat was the prize); but it is certainly remarkable that the persistent excitability of these cloven-hoofed creatures, which plays so great a part in the Arabian fable of the discovery of coffee, should, in Hellenic mythology, have made them the totems of wine. Goats are always represented as drunken; sometimes under the inebriating influence of wine, and at other times exhilarated by its opposite, the stimulant coffee.

"We shall have won a clue to the mystery of æsthetics when we have realized that the progress of art is associated with the twofoldedness of the Apollonian and the Dionysiac." Such are the words with which Friedrich Nietzsche begins his great study *The Birth of Tragedy*. "To bring these two impulses into closer approximation," he continues, "let us contemplate them as the discrete artistic worlds of dreams and intoxication. . . ." Here I will cut my quotation short. For, though it is true that Dionysus was the god of intoxication, it remains uncertain, as far as our present knowledge goes, that Apollo was the god of dreams. Clear, thoroughly wakeful images, such as are appropriate to Apollo, and the sharply outlined and lucid Dorian art of which he was the alleged originator, have nothing to do with the phenomena that belong to the field of what we now understand as dreamland. That is why we balk when we read that Nietzsche assigned dreamland to Apollo as the god's spiritual abiding-place.

The truth is that today, differing from Nietzsche, we look upon dreams and intoxication as twins and not as opposites. The imagery of our minds during sleep, the invasion by the unconscious of the land of dreams, is not by us contrasted with the ramblings of the spirit under the influence of alcohol. Besides, in the end drunkenness leads to sleep, and by way of sleep to dreaming. Things that are on the same staircase, and differ only by their being on a higher or lower step, cannot be polar opposites. Nietzsche's Apollo and Nietzsche's Dionysus are not really antagonists as are wine and coffee.

Nietzsche's Apollo does not carry a charm that can rival the magic of wine; that is why the German philosopher's Apollo resembles Bacchus far more closely than he thinks. The undermining of early Hellenic culture by hyper-logicality, enlightenment, "Socratic thought," did not, as Nietzsche opined, occur in the days of Euripides, but much later. It occurred in the hey-day of the Arabs, and their powerful black potion, which made an end of Hypnos as well as of Bacchus, dispelled dreams as well as drunkenness. Coffee became a far more powerful enemy of Bacchus-Dionysus than the Pythian Apollo had ever been. In the end, indeed, coffee became an enemy of the Pythian Apollo as well. The goal of a brain spurred onward by coffee is anything but Apollonian. The runaway chariot of logic, the furious gallop of the steeds of thought, has nothing in common with the harmonious and restful clarity with which Apollo, the "dreamer," develops his imagination. Nietzsche on one occasion drew a distinction between the Dionysus of the Greeks and the Dionysus of the barbarians. Are we to suppose that, in the history of civilization, coffee may have been the "Apollo of the barbarians"?

It is not idle to inquire what would have blossomed out of Greek civilization if a barbarian Apollo had taken the place of the Hellenic. It is not idle to imagine what the life of the classical world might have been like if coffee had come into daily use side by side and on equal terms with its adversary wine. Diderot and d'Alembert, the founders of the *Encyclopædia*, would seem to have toyed with the notion that at least one person originally a Hellene had known of coffee, namely, Helen of Troy. They referred to the passage in Homer's *Odyssey* in which there is mention of a magic draught which, as described, certainly has an effect similar to that of coffee. This is the episode in the fourth book, when Telemachus, son of Odysseus, searching for his lost father, is sitting at the board of Menelaus. The company are weeping, and no one can make an end of lamentations: "Then Helen, daughter of Zeus, turned to new thoughts. Presently she cast a drug into the wine of which they drank, a drug to lull all pain and anger, and bring forgetfulness of every sorrow. Whoso should drink a draught of it when it is mingled in the bowl, on that day he would let no tear fall down his cheeks, not though his mother and his father died, not though men slew his brother or dear son with the sword before his face, and his own eyes beheld it. Medicines of such virtue and so helpful had the daughter of Zeus, which Polydamna, the wife of Thon, had given her, a woman of Egypt, where earth the grain-giver yields herbs in great plenty, many that are healing in the cup and many baneful. There each man is a leech beyond all human kind."

Is not that an almost exact description of the clinical effect of trimethyldioxypurin upon the nervous system? Whereas alcohol has always promoted the onset of "maudlin misery," a dose of caffeine promptly inhibits the lachrymal secretion. As is well known, it is impossible to shed tears after drinking a strong cup of coffee. Whence, moreover, did Helen procure nepenthe, which for a whole day dried the tears of the drinkers? We are told it came from Egypt, perhaps from upper Egypt and Ethiopia, from that territory known as Kaffa where—is it too bold an assumption?—in the days before the rise of Islam the coffee-tree was already known and cultivated.

Diderot and d'Alembert got their idea from Pietro della Valle, who supposed that Helen's drug might have been a mixture of wine and coffee. The effects of what she administered might also be those of Indian hemp, or hashish. Pietro della Valle was an Italian traveller who visited Turkey, Egypt, Palestine, Persia, and India, his journeys lasting from 1614 to 1626. At the beginning of the eighteenth century it seems to have amused scholars to speculate concerning how far the ancients may have been acquainted with our modern intoxicants, stupefacients, and stimulants. Paschius, for instance, declared that coffee was among the gifts that Abigail brought to David, to appease his anger against Nabal—which is, of course, absurd, since the five measures of parched grain referred to in the eighteenth verse of the twenty-fifth chapter of the first book of Samuel were obviously wheat.

However that may be, Helen of Troy alone is mentioned in Homer as having this remarkable drug at her disposal. It was an isolated philtre, which could not seriously compete with the energy of wine. Not then. Not to the men of the days concerning which Homer wrote. That could not happen until heaps of coffee-berries were collected from the hot wadies in the land of Yemen.

Coffee and wine! Wakefulness and sleep! For the last effect of wine is sleep, whereas the last effect of coffee is wakefulness.

The antipode of sleep is not, as Nietzsche thought, the dream, but wakefulness. It was the mission of the Arabs to extract wakefulness from the coffee-bean, and decoct it into a magic potion for coming centuries. It was the children of Mohammed who were the first, with Apollonian clarity, to venture the decisive thought of protesting against sleep: "He who sleeps away half his life, lives only half his life."

The Arabs led the attack upon unconsciousness and darkness, upon the fettering influence of gravitation; they led the attack but for which modern civilization would be unthinkable; and a strange thrill affected those who for the first time read in the book of *The Thousand and One Nights* the bold utterance: "Well is it for him who never sleeps!"

Trimethyldioxypurin

W HEN the imam and his monks in Shehodet Monastery tasted coffee for the first time, did they know the nature of the substance that was its active principle? They did not know, and not until many centuries had elapsed did chemists isolate the drug and give it a name. In the year 1820, a German chemist, Runge, extracted it for the first time. It belongs to the class of bodies known as alkaloids, and its chemical composition is expressed by the name of trimethyldioxypurin, known for short as caffeine. It presents itself in the form of shining, white, needle-shaped crystals, reminding us of swansdown and still more of snow. They have a faintly bitter taste, but are odourless.

Pending its discovery by man, this drug was slumbering in various habitats other than coffee-beans. Nature is a huge masked ball, which we are privileged to watch; and trimethyldioxypurin is hidden under many disguises. Probably plants containing it are found in all parts of the world. The Sudanese Negroes get the effect of coffee from an extract of the cola-nut; the bushmen of South Africa, from a decoction of cyclopia leaves (bush tea). From the roasted seeds of *Paullinia cupana,* the Indians of the Amazon region prepare a caffeine paste which they name "guarana." The Brazilians and Paraguayans, from of old, have been accustomed to prepare a caffeine-containing infusion from maté, the leaves of a species of ilex.

Amazing is the way in which, throughout the world, people have discovered this odourless chemical, which exists nowhere in the free state and never cries out to them, "Here I am!" A bodily and mental urge must have guided them in their pursuit of trimethyldioxypurin when, without the help of science, they set themselves to find it. But in no other form has caffeine had so determinative an influence upon civilization as in that of the beverage known as coffee. Not the *Cola acuminata*, the cola-nut of the Sudanese, although it contains more caffeine than does coffee, has transformed the civilized world, but *Coffea arabica*, originally derived from Ethiopia, from which coffee was first prepared by the Arabs.

The Russo-Swiss expert, Gustav von Bunge, professor at Basle, considered that the longing for caffeine arose from the fact that this substance is akin to a highly nitrogenous substance known as xanthin, small quantities of which are found in all tissues of the body. In his view, therefore, the caffeine craving of human beings is the expression of an unconscious longing to increase their store of xanthin as one of the substances of which the tissues are built.

No matter whether caffeine be really summoned into the fortress of the body as an ally; as soon as it has crossed the threshold it induces a remarkable condition which, in the true sense of the word, is an "ecstasy," a "being put out of place," a marvellous disturbance. Promptly it brings about dilatation of the blood-vessels. The drawbridge is lowered. The central nervous system, the brain and the spinal cord, are invaded by its stimulant action; they are "occupied" by the intruder. . . . The great awakener, caffeine! It influences the respiratory centre in the *medulla oblongata*, and bestows upon the entire organism the advantage of an accelerated interchange of gases. Its powerful elixir facilitates the labour of the heart-muscle. In the joints of the arms and legs, it dispels the paralysing accumulation of the products of fatigue, the body's auto-intoxicant poisons. It increases the vigour of the skeletal muscles. It promotes intestinal peristalsis and the activity of the kidneys. Every cell of the human body is, as it were, renovated, so soon as caffeine reaches it.

The American physiologist Horatio Wood has studied the effects of caffeine upon the circulation and the muscles, and Hollingworth has investigated the curves of the intelligence under the stimulus of coffee. Both these authors had access to abundant material. In the year 1912, Hollingworth made some seventy-six thousand measurements and other experiments. Wood describes the promotion of muscular energy by caffeine as follows: "Caffeine works as a stimulus upon the reflex centres of the spinal cord. It enables the muscles to contract more vigorously, without any subsequent depression, so that the total muscular work performed by a man who has had a dose of caffeine is greater than he could have done in default of it."

Wood goes on to draw the following momentous conclusion: "If the caffeinized muscle always does better work, without having to pay for this in any other way than by the natural onset of fatigue in due course, we are compelled to recognize that caffeine does not merely intensify the vigour of muscular contraction, but also enables the muscles to act more economically—in a word, to do more work with the same expenditure of energy."

This law, a definitive gain in the economics of the human labour process, was supplemented in 1925 by the work of Allers and Freund, who showed that coffee is an energizer of the brain no less than of the muscles. They found that the processes of acquiring knowledge were greatly facilitated by the drinking of coffee, but, on the other hand, that the reproduction of what had previously been learned was nowise furthered. (This reproduction is, rather, interfered with by a superfluity of new images and ideas.) The experiments also showed that in abstract thinking the visual elements of thought became more conspicuous. Furthermore, the intellectual elements of thought grew more pregnant, while the power of detailed expression was facilitated. The description of a movement, for instance, contains a larger number of optical subsections. "Sensory and conscious associations moved into the foreground while automatic associations passed into the background. Thus coffee is able to promote the brain's power of effecting combinations. Where we have to do, however, with the reproduction of data previously stored in the memory, with the recalling of matter already learned, coffee would seem to be a hindrance rather than a help." It would be hard to give a more vivid description of the "creative and liberative" power that coffee exerts upon the brain. This brilliant, rebellious, anti-conservative influence has made coffee, throughout its history, a harbinger of storms.

What, however, are the hundred thousand human beings studied during the twentieth century by Hollingworth, Wood, and others, in comparison with the countless millions who, since the beginning of the modern age, at first on the coast of Araby and thereafter in all quarters of the world, have been drinking coffee? Coffee has changed the surface of the globe! The muscular and cerebral stimulation and transformation produced in mankind by coffee have transfigured the visage of history.

For this remains unquestionable. If today the city of New York, with its skyscrapers and its indefatigable swarms of human beings, differs so greatly in aspect from Rome in the year 1300, there are, no doubt, many reasons for the contrast; but one of the most important is this, that since the discovery of coffee the human working day has, theoretically, been expanded from twelve hours to twenty-four.

Throughout classical antiquity and the Middle Ages, the only drugs known to have a powerful action upon the nervous system were narcotics and depressants. (Physiologically considered, alcoholic beverages are essentially narcotics, or stupefacients!) "Denarcotizers" had not been discovered. No pure stimulant was known to those who sustained the civilization of classical days and of the Middle Ages; nothing that could keep the body bright and alert when it was craving for sleep.

The discovery of coffee was, in its way, as important as the invention of the telescope or of the microscope, without which we should know little of the incredibly vast and nothing of the incredibly small. For coffee has unexpectedly intensified and modified the capacities and activities of the human brain. For thousands of years, until the discovery of coffee, work always stopped when the worker's body grew tired. But the cæsura of sleep, which ensued upon fatigue, changed the essential nature of the work; it was no longer the same man who resumed work after the interruption of sleep, not the man who had begun the labour process. Before the discovery of this stimulant, every kind of "differential" work, every task that needed extreme accuracy, extraordinarily minute measurements, was impossible, except for those few persons of altogether exceptional will-power who have existed in every century.

This is the marvellous fact, that since the discovery of coffee vast masses of persons who are far from being geniuses have found within their own brain-boxes a "docile domestic animal which has many of the capacities of genius." Mathematics, chemistry, physics, the whole group of sciences belonging to the philosophico-mathematical category—above all, medicine and its ancillary disciplines—were, in classical antiquity, studied and practised, furthered and understood, only by a restricted number of persons, because, when human society was under the influence of wine, "the anteroom of sleep," a great majority of cultured persons were averse to intellectual research. Bacchic civilization, the cult of eloquent drunkenness, switched most persons of culture on to a different road.

Analytical thought, which, in contrast with synthetical thought, has been the main characteristic of civilization since the opening of the modern era, is mainly attributable to the generalizing influence of coffee upon thought itself. Without effort, today, countless persons, in numberless professions, are engaged in "differential" activities, which in antiquity were possible only to such outstanding geniuses as Archimedes and Hero of Alexandria.

A cup of coffee is a miracle.

A miracle like a musical harmony, a wonderfully compounded assemblage of relationships.

Although our sense of taste is no less acute than our hearing, our gustatory nerve would react to pure caffeine, the chemical substance with the formula $C_8 H_{10} N_4 O_2$, not at all or only to report a faint and uninteresting bitter sensation. It is the fats and the mineral substances that impinge upon the taste-buds, and those that, volatilized, assail the endings of our olfactory nerve—the ethers, phenols, furfurals, acetones, ammoniacal substances, and twenty lesser satellites—which combine to produce the enthralling aroma and taste of a well-made cup of coffee.

The ratios must be carefully maintained. Otherwise there will be crude disharmony, and the general result will be nauseating. Trimethylamin, for instance, which plays so important a part in producing the agreeable flavour of coffee, is the substance which predominates in putrefying fish. It is thus something more than a possibility of discord; it is a vegetable poison. But, in the minute proportions in which it is found in a well-roasted coffee bean, it combines to produce the attractive harmony of the flavour.

There is a perpetual dance of the various ingredients. "Dance is universal." By this proposition of the romanticist physicists and natural philosophers, a proposition which recalls the teachings of Oken and Schelling, we are reminded of what happens when we analyse the little planetary system of the coffee-bean. Attraction and repulsion, affinity and the harmony of numbers! Mankind is not made up simply of human beings, but of what individual human beings eat and drink. It consists of the demons that enter us through our mouths. Insoluble is the riddle why, in certain epochs, the demons of sleep predominated in what we put into our mouths, whereas in other epochs the demons of wakefulness have predominated.

Coffee has strange kinships; it has clansmen who march side by side with the chief. In chemical laboratories today remarkable discoveries are being made. Professor Nottbohm of Hamburg, for example, has discovered that in coffee there is another active principle, another alkaloid, besides caffeine, namely trigonellin. But this substance, as Hantzsch has proved, is one of the main constituents of nicotine, the active principle of tobacco.

The first time I heard that coffee and tobacco, the two great quellers of fatigue in contemporary civilization, stand chemically side by side, I was reminded of an exciting discovery of the geologists. It appears that in Swabia there is a region where, underground, the waters of the Danube and the Rhine mingle, before one river sets forth on its eastward and the other on its northward flow. Thus is it with coffee and tobacco, the magical elements join hands for a moment before they separate.

Dance is universal.

4

Persecution and Victory

WHEN was it that, in Shehodet Monastery, the monks had their first taste of "k'hawah"? The date is hard to ascertain.

This much is unquestionable, that Avicenna, the famous Arabian philosopher and physician of Bukhara, often styled the Prince of Physicians, was acquainted with coffee by about the year A. D. 1000. He did not call it "k'hawah," but "bunc"—the name by which coffee is still known in Ethiopia.

It was not then a beverage widely consumed by the people. True, both the Arabs and the Persians drank coffee, but we have no reason to believe that the coffee-plant was systematically cultivated either in Arabia or in Persia. Coffee was brought from Ethiopia and Somaliland by caravans; then it was shipped across the Red Sea for a further long journey by land. This made it a high-priced commodity, available only to the wealthy. Even so, it probably did not become a daily beverage, but was employed medicinally, for the relief of certain ailments.

Such a use of coffee may have continued inconspicuously during the eleventh and twelfth centuries. In the French national library there is preserved a manuscript by Sheikh Abd el Kader wherein we are informed that coffee was not known in Yemen earlier than the year 1450. This statement is certainly incorrect. The probability is that a certain Jemal Eddin, also known as Dhabani, who had travelled in Ethiopia, introduced the cultivation of the coffee-shrub and the use of the beverage into Yemen, so that, being locally produced, the expensive import was no longer needful, and coffee became much less expensive.

Even then, however, it had not become an article of widespread daily consumption. That did not happen until a religious dispute attracted general attention to it. People began to try the beverage as soon as it was forbidden. There was a prohibitionist movement, and the average man is likely to lust after forbidden fruit! In the holy city of Mecca, a zealot of high rank declared war to the death against coffee, with the result that its influence quickly spread wherever the Turks held sway.

In the year 1517, the sultan of Egypt appointed a new viceroy in Mecca. His name was Khair Bey, a proud and extremely ambitious young man. He found it vexatious that the world was so old. "A worn-out slipper is no longer a slipper," he was accustomed to say to his servants. For this reason, he was mockingly spoken of as the "slipper philosopher." Lampoons in verse were composed about him, making fun of his zeal for purifying public morals. Enraged thereat, he sent forth spies to find out who were the writers. Always they were coffee-drinkers, who sat beneath the colonnades of the mosques, giving their fancy free rein.

It was not the poems or the poets whom Khair Bey, the viceroy, wished to attack. They were too small game. His target was the "stimulant" that endowed ordinary persons with shrewdness and wit, and made their minds sparkle.

He concealed the true reason for his campaign, a personal one he would have been ashamed to acknowledge. He professed a determination to pass judgment upon coffee, coffee-drinking, and coffee-drinkers, in accordance with the dictates of the Book of Books. "Little do I care," said he, "if people say that coffee has been drunk for centuries. The Koran has no concern with venerable customs. The Word of the Prophet is timeless; it is a sword of judgment in the hands of him who knows how to make distinctions."

He assembled in his divan a number of Ulemas, muftis, military officers, philosophers, and men learned in the law. His brow was clouded with wrath, for he was a passionate youth.

To begin with he ordered the preparation of the beverage which was to be the subject of inquiry. Two slaves made coffee in the presence of the company, roasting the beans, pounding them in a mortar, and seething them in water. The coffee thus prepared gave off a pleasing aroma, which ran counter to Khair Bey's intention. He said: "No matter if the odour be delightful. We read in the Koran that the devil can assume a seductive mask."

The company preserved a respectful silence. Now the viceroy, taking a bean between finger and thumb, lifted it high in the air, showed it to all present, and continued: "We read in the chapter entitled 'The Table' that wine, gaming, pictures, graven images, and casting lots, are among the most evil devices of Shaitan!"

"That is not wine!" said one of the muftis. "It is more of the nature of charcoal. Grind it between your teeth, and you will realize that it is like wood charcoal."

"You say, then, it is an ash?"

"Certainly it resembles ashes."

"In that case it is as earth, and you know well that earth is one of the articles of diet forbidden by the Koran."

"You are mistaken, lord!" said one of the masters of the law. "That roasted seed is not earth in the sense in which we apply the term to the earth of our fields. It is a dead portion of a plant. Even if this plant were forbidden—we do not know, as yet, for we are assembled to decide that point—it would be permissible in the condition of the bean you hold, for it has passed through the fire."

"Yes, I agree," said an old, white-bearded Ulema. "Fire, 'atesch,' purifies everything. It purifies by transforming. Even though the blossoms and the substance of the coffee-berry were unclean—which we do not know as yet, since that is what we are gathered here to ascertain—the condition of the bean you now hold is one transformed. An unclean article can be purified through the instrumentality of another. Bear in mind Abu Bekr's dog. Being a dog, the beast was unclean. But when it fell into a salt lake and became petrified, it was cleansed."

The viceroy grew angry, but contained himself. Those whom he had assembled in council were the wisest of the land. He dismissed them to think the matter over, enjoining on them to return at the same hour next day.

"Bismillah!" he said piously, to open the conversation. "In the name of Allah, the all-merciful, we have set out from false premises. We are not concerned with passing judgment upon the plant, but upon its effect. I consider it to be 'buzeh,' intoxicating, like brandy or mead. There are two hakims among the company. Let us hear what they have to say about the matter."

"That is not so easy," replied the elder of the two physicians. "One who is to know what is 'buzeh' must be an infidel! I have never partaken of mead or brandy, but I have been informed by others that he who has consumed a sufficiency of strong drink becomes, in the end, in-sensible. When I have drunk coffee, the power of my senses has been redoubled."

"If Allah," rejoined the viceroy pithily, "had wished to redouble your intelligence, he would have done so himself, without this artificial aid."

"True," said some of the muftis. This seemed to most of those present a strong point against coffee. If it conferred supernatural powers on one who drank it, it must be a devilish potion. A man had only two hands, although he might fancy that it would have been more convenient for him to have four.

"Not one of us knows what an intoxicant is," said the viceroy, whose temper had improved. "Still, which among you can deny that coffee banishes sleep? What do you think of that in the light of the sixth chapter of the Koran, the one entitled 'The Beast'? Do we not read therein: 'Allah sends us the morning, having ordained the night for repose, and provided the sun and the moon for the determination of time'? Remember that the Koran proceeds as follows: 'Such is the ordinance of the Almighty!' "

All present sprang to their feet. With one exception, they pointed meaningly, with the exclamation: "Forbidden! We have decided!"

"Not so fast," put in the younger hakim. "Our ruler asks my opinion. As that of a practising physician, may I utter it?"

"Say on."

"No more than the rest of you do I know from personal experience the effects of wine, being a true believer. But there are other things than wine that can produce insensibility. There is, for instance, opium, the juice of the poppy plant. This puts the senses to sleep."

"As I listen to your words, hakim," said the viceroy sourly, "I recall the thirty-eighth verse of the sixth chapter of the Koran: 'God leads astray whom he wills, and leads whom he wills into the right path.' "

"May I be allowed to continue my argument?" asked the hakim. "I will elaborate. If coffee is a magic potion, so is that prepared from the opium plant. If we are not permitted artificially to induce wakefulness, neither may we artificially induce sleep. In the ninety-sixth verse we read: 'Allah has appointed the night for repose.' The scripture does not say that He has appointed the day for repose! But those to whom opium has been administered sleep by day as well as by night. Why then, lord, should we be forbidden to drink coffee so as to keep awake at night?"

The assembly of the sages was agitated like a sea. Their green silken robes rustled. The wearers, with lean faces, aquiline noses, eloquent lips, disputed acrimoniously. Some agreed with the older physician, others with the younger. Impotent in his wrath, the viceroy looked on. He did not venture to utter anything authoritative that might tip the scales one way or the other. All he could say was: "I look to you for a truthful decision. Such is the will of Allah!"

The dispute went on for hours. The parties to it swayed, now to the right, and now to the left, differing from one another as much as is possible among pious Moslems. One of the army officers went so far as to compare the dark, roasted coffee-beans with the brilliant eyes of the houris of Paradise. This infuriated a mufti who, foaming at the mouth, shouted words from the forty-fourth chapter of the Koran: "The tree sakum is the sinner's food! It will scald the belly of those who consume it, like molten brass or boiling water!"

Thus did they argue more and more fiercely, until peace was restored by sunset and the summons to evening prayer. Then, when devotions were finished, lest the debate should be resumed, an old man of ninety said: "When I look at you, I am reminded of those soldiers who engage in a sham fight, twenty marching towards the west and twenty towards the east. I also recall the words of the learned Muktassi, who visited many lands, and, who at the close of his life, wrote: 'It seems to have pleased Allah that I should be both holy and unholy. I have swallowed broth with the Sufis, eaten porridge with monks, and have consumed the rough diet of seafaring men with sailors. Sometimes I observed all the rules of piety; and at other times I ate forbidden victuals, against my better judgment and without any absolute necessity. I have lain in prison; I have been highly honoured. Mighty princes listened to my words; at other times I was chastised with rods.' Since, my lord viceroy, we cannot, at your divan, decide as to the qualities of coffee-beans, let us break up our assembly. Some will avoid coffee, regarding it as forbidden, others will drink coffee, regarding its use as permissible."

"You do not speak like a true believer," said some of the company, critically, before departing.

The upshot was, however, that coffee was declared to be "mekruh," neither forbidden nor permitted, thus merely "undesirable."

At midnight Khair Bey stood on the roof of his house looking down on the Holy City. There are larger towns than Mecca, but none more sacred. Here the footprint of Father Abraham is eternally preserved in stone. Here is the hallowed Ka'ba, with the Black Stone built into one of the corners. From all parts of the world, a polyhedron with multitudinous sides, the bodies and souls of men fly hither like pious arrows. They wander unceasingly round the sacred edifice, and contemplate the Black Stone.

Khair Bey contemplated the sleeping city, or what should have been the sleeping city. The constellations Aquila and Swan sparkled in the sky. Betelgeux and Aldebaran were writing the glories of Allah in the firmament, and the minarets, the stony fingers of the mosques, were dumbly tracing the record of the heavens.

Here and there, however, in the town, there was light where darkness should have reigned. Torches moved near the walls, and noises from the distance reached the viceroy's ears. He could even hear the sound of fiddles!

Khair Bey was in a rage. "They are wounding the night," he thought. Summoning the watch, he issued his orders, and his men hastened to the coffee-houses, where the copper utensils were flung ruthlessly to the floor. Few among the drinkers ventured to resist, and they were bound that they might be haled to prison. Their friends and relatives assembled to attack the watch. Wounds were inflicted; two men lay dead upon the ground. Three of the coffee-houses were burned.

Next day coffee was prohibited. Not because it was contrary to the sacred words of the Koran, but because it "led to riots." There followed a reign of terror lasting a whole week. Those who persisted in drinking their favourite beverage were bound, face to tail, on the backs of asses, and driven through the town, being flogged the while. It is recorded that many of the women forsook their husbands from jealousy of coffee, since he who sat awake enjoying the stimulation of the draught had no desire to lie down beside his wife.

The viceroy sent a report of these happenings to the sultan at Cairo. He described what measures he had taken, and asked the monarch's approval. The sultan was in a quandary. He himself, and all his courtiers, were habitual coffee-drinkers. His reply to Khair Bey took the form of an advice to withdraw the prohibition of coffee. None of those, said the sultan, who were most learned among the interpreters of the Koran could find any ground for forbidding the use of coffee. Besides, if there had been riots, they had not been due to coffee, but to the steps taken to prevent its enjoyment.

Mecca is the centre of the world. What happens in Mecca speedily becomes known in Afghanistan, Persia, Egypt, Libya, Mesopotamia, Syria, Asia Minor. The news that Khair Bey had sustained a defeat in his attack upon coffee was borne by returning pilgrims on swift camels to all parts of the Mohammedan world. "K'hawah" had become a stimulant in more senses than one. It played a great part in religion and in politics. The spirit of wakefulness and alertness hidden in the shining bean was not a spirit of evil! Khair Bey was forced to restore the utensils he had impounded in the raid on the coffee-houses. The export of Mocha from the wadies of Yemen to the seacoast towns was considerably increased.

Enthusiasm of the friends of coffee was, however, countered by the fervour of its adversaries. No one could deny that the drinking of this beverage made people contentious, and that their contentions led to the use of knives and sticks. In the year 1521, at Cairo, there were riotous affrays among those who tarried long at the coffee-houses. For at the refreshment houses in the lands where Islam was dominant, the beverage on sale was not wine but coffee. Quarrels took place between coffee-drinkers and those who wished to lead pious lives and to retire seasonably at night. There were not wanting persons who declared that coffee promoted a critical spirit, and who maintained that the sultan was guided by the voice of his own lusts and had listened to evil counsellors.

Thus in the land of Egypt, where, twenty years before, the prohibition of coffee in Yemen had been remitted, the drug was for a second time prohibited in places of public entertainment. In private houses, however, people continued to drink as much as they pleased, so that the law was a dead letter.

Besides, what was drunk in Egypt, though in private, was drunk openly and without shame in Aleppo, Damascus, Baghdad, and Tehran. A hundred reasons, good, bad, and indifferent, were given for drinking coffee. During the heat of the day it promoted coolness of body and deliberation of mind, whereas during the cold hours of the night it fostered warmth both physical and mental. Especially was its use recommended in the foothills, because it counteracted the evil effects of the *tramontana*, the cold wind from the mountains. Then, as now, it was the sovereign remedy for migraine.

From time to time, religious zealots took up their campaign against coffee. The dervishes raged whenever they saw the black drink boiling in copper vessels over a fire. Many fanatics declared that, at the Day of Judgment, the faces of coffee-drinkers would be as black as the beverage itself. Of course this did not matter to the Ethiopians and other Africans, who were now being won over to Islam, since they were blackavized by nature.

It was the period in which the power and greatness of Islam were spreading far and wide. Vengeance was being taken against Christendom for having unchained the horror of the Crusades against Syria and Palestine. The aims of Islam were more than half fulfilled. In 1453, Constantinople fell before the onslaught of the Turks; the Byzantine empire was partitioned; the Balkan peoples had been largely exterminated or forcibly converted to Mohammedanism. Within the boundaries of the state, the Turkish impetus unified the Moslem realm, destroying the petty sultanates, so that Islam and the Ottoman Empire had come to mean the same thing. In the year 1517, Selim I annexed Egypt and Arabia to the northwestern portion of the Ottoman dominion.

In the unified Turkish realm, the importance of coffee was greatly enhanced. In camp and on the battlefield, it refreshed the Turkish warriors, and at home it performed the same service for the members of philosophical circles. Even women, now, had begun to drink the beverage. It was found that coffee eased the pains of labour, and in Turkey a law was actually passed making it a valid ground for divorce that a husband should refuse coffee to his wife. By now the national drink had become a regular article of diet, declared to be nutritive and of equal importance with bread and with water.

In view of this widespread popular sentiment, the attacks of the zealots and the dervishes had no more than a sectarian significance. Yet they were right enough in contending that coffee, "reduplicating the ego," was really being idolized, for people thought more of their coffee than they thought of Allah. To the ultra-faithful, this seemed as intolerable as the deification of the vine in the Greek worship of Bacchus.

Moreover, just at that time, a fierce struggle was going on between

Tumbledown Arab coffee-house near Port Said

Arab coffee-house in Jidda

Arab coffee-house in Cairo

Constantinople coffee-house

coffee and wine. In the newly conquered provinces, which had so recently been Christian, viticulture naturally prevailed. Coffee-drinking was advocated with missionary fervour as against wine-bibbing. In Constantinople, more particularly, wine-shops were closed. Thus the "Black Apollo" became once more one of the most successful champions of Islam.

"Now, at length, the coffee-bean is victorious!" sang the poet Belighi. Coffee had conquered, for, after long splitting of the cadis and the devotees of the Koran into parties, the learned became unanimously convinced of its virtues. In Damascus, Aleppo, and Cairo, it won the battle; and on the Golden Horn, whither a breeze from the Bosporus blew, "the aroma of wine, the forbidden drink," had been dispelled.

Since then, the pleasant reek of coffee has been inseparable from the thought of Constantinople. Approaching Istambul seawards shortly after sunrise, as did James Baker, "catching sight of cupolas and minarets thrusting upwards out of the mist, like jewels lying upon cotton-wool," one's nostrils are assailed by the aromatic odours of coffee being roasted and brewed. Invisibly it presides over Pera and Galata, mingling with the warmth of morning and helping to dispel the chill of night.

The first coffee-houses in the town on the Golden Horn were opened in 1554 by two merchants, Hakim from Aleppo and Jems from Damascus. They were termed "mekteb-i-irfan" (schools of the cultured). Coffee itself soon came to be called "the milk of chess-players and of thinkers." For then as now, day after day and night after night, men in white silken robes with wide sleeves sat facing each other across the chessboard, moved their pieces with one hand while they stroked their chins with the other.

5

Kolshitsky's Valiant Deed

THE growth of the Ottoman Empire continued. From its new centre, Constantinople, which, under its old name of Byzantium, had been the focus of widespread Christian dominion, it radiated towards the four winds of heaven, east, south, west, and north. Somewhere about 1460, Serbia and Bosnia were conquered; two years later, Walachia; in 1517, Syria, Mesopotamia, Hejaz, and Egypt. Two years later, Algeria; five-and-thirty years afterwards, Tripoli, and later, Tunis. By this time, the Crimea, Moldavia, Transylvania, and Hungary were allied or vassal States.

Thus Islam became a great power which, despite the loss of Spain, the headquarters of the western caliphate, to the Christians, became a graver and ever graver menace to western Europe. All the more dangerous because, this time, the impetus of the Tartar thrust came from the east, and not from the south, which had no hinterland.

With the conquest of the greater part of Hungary, however, victorious Islam reached the zenith of its fortunes. Progress was arrested at the gates of Vienna in 1683, Buda was recovered from the Turks in 1686, and thenceforward there began a slow decline in the power of Islam. The decline lasted until the close of the World War in 1918.

The repulse of the Turks from Vienna, this strange turn in the fate of what had for several centuries been a conquering nation, was mysteriously associated with the history of coffee. The story of the rise and fall of the Turks cannot be treated apart from the saga of coffee.

Leopold I, Holy Roman Emperor, had foreseen the attack of the Turks on Vienna, having been kept well informed by his ambassador in Constantinople. Nevertheless Leopold had reason to hope that war might be avoided, for he knew that the sultan did not want war. But

Kara Mustafa, the ambitious grand vizier, whose position at the sultan's court was shaky, needed the war to restore his prestige. He began it. The emperor fled to Linz. Thence he negotiated with the electors of the Holy Roman Empire, with the estates, and with the king of Poland, in order to assemble an army able to cope with the Turks. Vienna, which had been hastily fortified, was invested by the huge army of Kara Mustafa, and the siege began. The fall of the city was imminent on the very first day, when a fire broke out close to the arsenal. Panic among the citizens was only prevented by the presence of mind of Liebenberg, the mayor, and Starhemberg, the chief of the armed forces of the city. In trenches and in mines, the Osmanlis drew nearer and nearer. Not a day, not an hour, passed without bombardment. The dead and wounded lay in heaps before the wall; but, as the crescent moon returns with unfailing regularity month after month in the skies, so unceasingly was renewed the crescent-shaped order of battle of the besieging Turks.

Matters had still been bearable in July, but in August the hospitals of the city became overcrowded, for an epidemic of dysentery then broke out. The morale of the besieged was being undermined, and short of a miracle they could not maintain their resistance.

Had Vienna fallen, the way up the Danube to Linz would have been opened to the Turks; Passau and Ratisbon, now known as Regensburg, would have fallen; Bavaria and Swabia would have been conquered. In that case, maybe, the Turks would have been established on the Lake of Constance. For several centuries the history of Europe would have taken a different course. Thus the resistance to their advance at Vienna was a second Battle of Poitiers, when Charles Martel, defending the soil of France, saved the whole western world from the rule of the Saracens.

The man who gave the Viennese courage to hold out until the arrival of the relieving forces was Georg Kolshitsky, a Pole. Born at Sambor in Galicia, he had for a long time been a Turkish interpreter, and had lived among the Osmanlis. He offered to carry a letter to the Duke of Lorraine, the leader of the relieving force, although for this purpose he would have to pass through the Turkish lines.

He and his servant Mihailovich, both disguised in Turkish dress, slipped out of Vienna on August 13, 1683, and made their way among the Turkish tents. Although it was raining in torrents, Kolshitsky sang merrily in Turkish. As if fortuitously, the two men halted in front of the tent of a distinguished aga. The aga, who was a pious and benevolent man, came forth from his tent, commiserated his two supposed fellow-countrymen for being drenched to the skin, and asked them where they were going. They answered that they wished to leave the camp towards the west, where there were vineyards, in order to satisfy their hunger with ripening grapes. The aga warned them against this forbidden fruit, and warned them even more emphatically against the vine-dressers who, being zealous Christians, would be eager to cut down two isolated Moslems. He gave them big bowls of coffee to drink, saying that this beverage was far more pleasing to Allah than the wine prepared by the Christians. Then, granting their request, he had them conducted beyond the western side of the camp.

The pair made their way undisturbed through the vineyards, first to the Kahlenberg, then to Klosterneuburg, and on to Kahlenbergerdorf. On a wooded island in the river, they caught sight of a number of people, but could not at first make out whether or not these were Turks. At length they perceived that the women were unveiled, and were bathing in the river, and must, therefore, be Christians. They waved their hats. The Christians, believing them to be Turks, fired at them with harquebuses. One of the bullets passed through Mihailovich's long Turkish sleeve.

Kolshitsky, however, shouted that he was a Christian, and an emissary from Vienna. Thereupon the others sent a boat to convey him across the stream into the German camp. Early on August 15, he handed Duke Charles of Lorraine the dispatches which had been entrusted to him. With a written answer, supplemented by oral messages, he and Mihailovich set out on their return, once more under heavy rain. They went by way of Nussdorf. Here the danger they ran from sentinels was exceedingly great, so they determined to separate, after a brotherly embrace and commending one another to God's care. Soon, however, Mihailovich, feeling timid alone, rejoined Kolshitsky, and the two went on together, much depressed, through the dawn. By way of Rossau, which had been burned to ashes, they reached the Alserbachstrasse. Five Turks were now following them, moved partly by curiosity, but also by suspicion. The two spies hid among some rubbish, where they found a cellar-flap, opened it, and tumbled down the steep steps. Kolshitsky, who was tired out, instantly fell asleep. Towards noon, by chance, a Turk made his way into the cellar. Finding two men there, he was stricken with terror, and ran away. Since the Christians did not know whether he might not seek reinforcements, they, too, quitted the cellar. What would they not have given to encounter another benevolent aga who would refresh them with the "magic drink"! No such luck! Half dead with hunger and fatigue, at nightfall they reached the Schottentor of the city of Vienna.

Kolshitsky's bold sally and fortunate return gave fresh courage to the beleaguered Viennese. All and sundry felt once more that, beyond the Turkish forces, there were Christians ready to help them, that a formidable relieving army was assembling in the west, and that the hour of liberation was at hand. As prearranged, to acquaint the Duke of Lorraine with the fact that Kolshitsky had got back safely, Starhemberg, the chief of the defending forces, sent up three rockets, that same night, from the tower of St. Stephen's.

Kolshitsky and Mihailovich were handed a gratification of two thousand gulden. Through the instrumentality of the mayor, the municipality of Vienna promised to grant Kolshitsky the freedom of the city, to bestow on him a domicile (8, Haidgasse in the Leopold quarter), and to give him a charter to pursue any occupation he pleased.

It was not until towards the middle of September, a month after Kolshitsky's bold penetration of the Turkish lines, that the allied German and Polish armies at length began the attack that was to relieve Vienna.

On September 12 the Viennese, after long and weary waiting, at length saw the lances and banners of the Poles on the heights of the Kahlenberg. At this moment, too, the leaders of the Christian army first glimpsed the immense hosts of the enemy.

"God in heaven, what a sight!" wrote Dupont, a Frenchman in the Polish service. "A wonderful spectacle awaited us when we reached the crest of the hill. The whole plain, including the Leopoldstadt Island, was thickly beset with them. The thunder of Turkish artillery was answered by firing from the walls of the town. Flames and smoke enveloped the capital to such an extent that only the tops of the towers showed above it. In the camp of the Osmanlis were two hundred thousand men in battle array, stretching from the Danube to the hills. Farther to the left, beyond the Turkish flanks, were disorderly hordes of Tartar cavalry making ready to attack the forest. All was in lively movement, directed towards the Christian army."

This was on the twenty-fifth day of the Mohammedan month of Ramadhan. Slowly the army of liberation thrust forward a wedge of pikemen and riders. At Sievering and Pötzleinsdorf, and also in the long semicircle between Dornbach and the Danube, the adversaries came into contact. The Christian artillery drew so close to the Turkish army that sometimes the guns fired at a range of only forty paces at foes who were manning the vineyards. Then, as Vaelkeren relates, there began "a skirmishing with men in full armour, men armed with swords and daggers, with harquebuses and pistols." Under difficulties, however, because the contesting warriors were hidden among the vineyards, so that often only their headgear could be seen. King John Sobieski commanded that the Polish infantry, to distinguish it from the Turkish and lest the Christians attack their own men, should wear aprons of plaited straw.

Now, while the battle raged fiercely, in the midst of the Turkish lines, when the smoke parted for a moment, there was visible a red tent, over which had been hoisted the green flag of the Prophet, the sacred banner brought from Mecca. It signified "victory or death." In this case it signified death. The valour of the Turks was of no avail. Badenese, Franconians, and various others of the Christian troops had already made their way among the Turkish tents, and Count Mercy's dragoons were close to the walls of Vienna. They shouted to Starhemberg that the time was ripe for him to make a sally, but—wonder of wonders!—in the trenches that faced the wall there was hardly a living Turk left. By the time Charles of Lorraine had led his forces as far as Währing, some of the besiegers had already fled headlong towards the east.

This flight of the Turks was so sudden, and so unexpected after their valiant resistance, that Sobieski thought it might be a ruse. Under pain of death, he forbade any of his men to leave the ranks or give themselves up to pillage. But no further attack came from the Turkish side.

A vast amount of booty was secured from Kara Mustafa's camp. "The Turkish generalissimo," wrote Sobieski to his wife, "was in such a hurry to escape that he fled with only the horse on which he was riding and the clothes on his back. The area of the camp is as big as that of Warsaw and Lemberg put together." Five-and-twenty thousand tents were taken uninjured; twenty thousand head of beef, camels, and mules; ten thousand sheep; and two hundred and fifty thousand quarters of grain. The famine in the beleaguered city thus came to an end. The burgesses streamed forth from the town, and, with tears in their eyes, embraced one another as they saw the mountains of honey, rice, and dripping. The prices of comestibles, which, during the last days of the siege, had risen to dizzy heights, came down with a rush. A pound of beef could now be had for sixpence.

Amid the spoil there was so much unfamiliar to the Christians that they were inclined to make fun of it or even to destroy it. For instance, there were parrots; and in the tent that had belonged to the pasha of Damascus was a tame monkey, fettered by a silver chain. The civilians of Leopoldstadt and the Bavarian dragoons came to blows that night when they discovered five hundred sacks full of a black, dry, agreeable-smelling substance that seemed to them to be some sort of fodder. The sacks were enormous. As to their contents, no one had ever before seen the like.

They were beans or grains, and a Bavarian cavalry lieutenant said he had heard of them. They were used as camel-fodder. Well, there were plenty of camels among the spoil: long-necked, two-humped beasts, of no use as mounts for Christians. The troopers were disposed to empty the sacks into the Danube.

The Leopoldstadt men objected, since the Bavarians had found these sacks of "fodder" upon their ground. The dispute went on for some time, and the dragoons set fire to one of the sacks, contents of which, as they burned, gave off a pleasant odour. With a servant holding a torch to light him on his path, Kolshitsky, the new citizen of Vienna, now arrived upon the scene. He was no longer wearing his Turkish dress, and, as promised, he had been provided with a residence on Leopoldstadt Island. But he had not yet applied for his charter to practise some specific occupation.

Kolshitsky's nostrils dilated as he inhaled the reek from the burning sack. "Holy Mary!" he shouted to the disputants. "That is coffee that you are burning! If you don't know what coffee is, give the stuff to me. I can find a good use for it."

Nothing could be refused to the stalwart Pole who had done the beleaguered Viennese such good service, so the "useless fodder" was bestowed on him to do with as he liked.

During the next few days, Kolshitsky had a private conversation with some of the town councillors of Vienna, and he found the desired occupation.

Of course, Kolshitsky was not the first inhabitant of Central Europe who, at that date, had heard of coffee and partaken of the beverage. Christian travellers in the East brought news of it much earlier, but the news had remained unheeded. Many such travellers, strangely enough, ignored it: for instance, Antonio Menavino, in his enumeration of the beverages drunk by the Turks in the year 1548; nor did Pierre Belon refer to it when, ten years later, he listed the important shrubs of Arabia. Belon probably regarded coffee as an African plant.

The first book of travel in which a German alludes to coffee is that of the Swabian, Leonhard Rauwolf. This distinguished Augsburg physician published his *Reis' in die Morgenländer* in 1582, a whole century before Kolshitsky opened the first coffee-house in Vienna. Rauwolf lived in the Near East from 1573 to 1578, and travelled as far as Persia. Everywhere he found the population drinking coffee, and was told that it had been a familiar beverage for hundreds of years. "Among others there is an excellent drink which they greatly esteem. They call it 'Chauve.' It is almost as black as ink, and is a valuable remedy in disorders of the stomach. The custom is to drink it early in the morning, in public places, quite openly, out of earthenware or porcelain cups. They do not drink much at a time, and, having drunk, walk up and down for a little, before sitting down together in a circle. The beverage is made by adding to boiling water the fruit which they call 'bunnu,' which in size and colour resembles laurel berries, the kernel being hidden away between two thin lobes of fruit. The use of the drink is so general that there are many houses which make a practice of supplying it ready prepared; and also, in the bazaars, merchants who sell the fruit are plentiful."

An important thing to notice in this report is that Rauwolf mentions, besides the Arabic name of coffee, the Ethiopian name of the fruit, for his "bunnu" is obviously the same word as "bunc." Indeed, Hübner's encyclopædia, published in 1717 and one of the earliest works of the kind, actually informs us that the German word "Bohne," bean, is derived from "bunc." Of course this is absurd, for there is an old Teutonic root, "Baûna," from which "Bohne" and bean are both derived.

The next person in Europe to describe coffee was the remarkable man Prosper Albanus. Like an Italian of similar name, Pietro d'Abano, the medieval "sorcerer," he was professor of botany in Padua. From the home of magic, from contemporary Egypt—which for many Europeans in 1592 was as magical a land as it had been for the Greeks of Homer's day—Albanus compiled a herbal. Naturally he mentioned the "arbor bon," "cum fructu suo buna." This scholar writes: "In the pleasure-garden of a Turk, my distinguished friend Hali Bey, I saw a fine tree which produces grains of an ordinary aspect. They are called 'bon' or 'ban.' From this the Arabs and the Egyptians prepare a black beverage, which they drink instead of wine, and which, like wine in our own country, is sold in public-houses. They call it 'caova.' The beans of the 'ban' tree are imported from Arabia Felix. I have seen one of these trees, whose leaves are extremely thick, and have a strong lustre. It is an evergreen."

Prosper Albanus the botanist having said his say, Prosper Albanus the physician continues: "The Turks use the decoction from these beans to relieve ills of the stomach and to dispel constipation. They also find it most useful when the liver is congested or when they have pains in the splenic region. Nor can there be any doubt that 'caova' is a valuable remedy in inflammations of the womb. The women of Egypt drink a great deal of it, very hot, during menstruation, in small sips at a time, being especially inclined to use it when the menstrual flow is suppressed. This use of the remedy has been well tested; 'caova' purifies the body."

Bellus, the humanist, was the first to send coffee beans to Europe, doing this in the year 1596. The recipient was Clusius, the physician and botanist whose unlatinized name was Charles de Lécluse, who was instructed by Bellus to "roast the beans first over the fire, and then crush them in a wooden mortar." De Lécluse, who was for many years resident in Vienna as director of the Imperial Gardens, and who spent the last days of his life in Holland, gave an account of coffee in two of his works: *Rariorum plantarum historia* and *Exoticorum libri decem*.

The humanist Pietro della Valle set sail in 1614 upon an Oriental journey of which he gave an account in his letters, *Viaggi in Turchia, Persia ed India descritti da lui medesimo in 54 lettere famigliari*. Being rather deaf, he misheard the name "k'ahwah," and always speaks of it as "cahne." Writing from Constantinople in February, 1615, he reported: "The Turks consume a black beverage. During the summer they drink it to refresh and cool themselves, whereas in winter they find it warming; yet it is the same drink in both cases, similarly prepared. They take long draughts of it, extremely hot, but not during meal-times, since this would remove their inclination to eat any more. It is consumed after the meal, as a dainty. It also promotes fellowship and conversation, so that there are few assemblies of friends where this beverage is not consumed. They call it 'cahne'; it is the product of a tree which grows in Arabia, in the neighbourhood of Mecca. If we are to believe the Turks, it is good for the stomach and for the digestion and wards off colics and catarrhs. It is also said that, when drunk after supper, it prevents those who consume it from feeling sleepy. For that reason, students who wish to read into the late hours are fond of it." We are told that when della Valle returned to Italy twelve years later, accompanied by a number of Orientals, he showed coffee-beans to the astonished Romans.

Sir Thomas Herbert, a member of a distinguished English family, visited Persia in 1626, when he was twenty years of age, in the suite of Sir Dodmore Cotton, ambassador to the shah. Herbert reports: "There is nothing of which the Persians are fonder than 'coho' or 'copha,' which the Turks call 'caphe.' This beverage is so black and bitter that one might suppose it to have come from the River Styx. It is prepared from rounded beans which resemble the beans of the laurel. Drunk very hot, it is said to be healthy, dispelling melancholy, drying tears, allaying anger, and producing cheerfulness. Still, the Persians would not prize it so greatly as they do, did not tradition inform them that it was brought to earth by the Angel Gabriel in order to revive the flagging energies of Mohammed the Prophet. Mohammed himself declared that when he had drunk this magic potion he felt strong enough to unhorse forty men and to possess forty women."

These are perhaps the most admiring words which any Occidental has ever written about coffee, but their defect is their inaccuracy. No one but Sir Thomas Herbert—and he throws the responsibility on the Prophet—has ever been inclined to describe coffee as an aphrodisiac. Many, indeed, speak of it as having the opposite effect.

Coming back to Kolshitsky, when that worthy opened the first Viennese coffee-house in the Domgasse, where the shadow of St. Stephen's tower falls at noon, cultured circles of the Austrian capital were unquestionably acquainted with coffee by repute. But they had never drunk it. When they now made trials of the beverage, their first impression of the "Turkish muck" was unfavourable—no matter whether they were masters of art, doctors, clerics, or merchants.

The Viennese were wine-bibbers. True, the lovely green-and-gold vines which, since the days of the Roman occupation, had flourished on the western outskirts of Vienna were now destroyed beyond repair. They had been fired together with the suburbs. The tough vine-stems had been cut to make palisades; the acrid urine of thousands of camels, asses, and oxen rendered the soil wellnigh as barren as the steppes of Central Asia. For years to come, the Viennese would not be able to get wine from their own vine-stocks, but would have to import what they needed at great cost. Still, even though deprived of the customary joys of Bacchus, they felt little inclination for the beverage of the Black Apollo.

Yet the vast stores of coffee-beans that Franz Georg Kolshitsky had obtained as booty from the Turkish camp were a disadvantage to him by their very magnitude. Unless he were to make a bonfire of the lot, or commit suicide by having the coffee piled on him until he was suffocated, he must manage to sell his wares. "Well and good," he said to himself, "if my customers don't like Turkish coffee, we must make a Viennese coffee that they will favour!" He used a strainer to rid the beverage of the grounds which made the Viennese choke. The clear liquid thus obtained would have been regarded with scorn by the Turks, the Serbs, and all the inhabitants of the Balkan Peninsula, who were firmly convinced that the virtue of coffee resided in the sediment. Little did Kolshitsky care, however. He was highly satisfied with the clarified decoction. Then he added a sufficiency of well-matured honey, and softened the taste by diluting the black coffee with milk.

The imam of Shehodet Monastery would probably have had a fit at any such notion. What better could you expect from "giaours and dogs" than that they should thus misuse the gift to Mohammed that they had secured as plunder from the Turkish camp outside Vienna? It was rank folly, so the Turkish true believers would have thought, to sweeten coffee and to dilute it with milk!

What did that matter to Kolshitsky? He had found something that was agreeable to Western palates, a beverage that all the European world has gladly drunk ever since. Now there were guests in plenty at the new coffee-house. There were two further attractive innovations. He arranged with Peter Wendler, a neighbouring baker, to supply him with an abundance of light, crescent-shaped rolls. The Viennese burghers, when day after day they ate these crescents, were agreeably reminded, drinking their coffee to wash them down, of the recent defeat of the followers of the Crescent who had come so near to taking Vienna by storm. The other novelty was *Krapfen*, toothsome spherical doughnuts filled with syrup, supplied to Kolshitsky by a baker-woman named Cecilia or Veronica Krapf.

Thus, built upon coffee, milk, crescents, and doughnuts, was established the first Viennese coffee-house—the mother of huge dynasties, offshoots, and crossings.

BOOK TWO

Health of the Nations

6

Venetian Commerce

B Y the then usual channels of world trade, large supplies of coffee
were continually being brought to Vienna, entering the southeastern portal of the empire. For a long time, however, no effect
upon Germany was noticeable.

The soldiers of the allied contingents that had saved the imperial capital from destruction did not take any coffee with them on their return
home. If, for instance, coffee had at that time been brought to Dresden,
we should learn of the fact from Hasche, historian to that town, who
records that three days after the defeat of the Turkish army that had invested Vienna—on September 16, 1683, that is to say—a thanksgiving fes-
tival was held in Dresden. On October 1, behind the Dresden arsenal, a
public exhibition of the war-booty was held. "There were shown five
Turkish tents of multicoloured cotton, tied by cotton ribbons, very
costly articles; also six heavy guns. There was likewise an elephant,
which, however, caught a chill, and soon died; numerous camels, as
well, to which the climate was unsuitable, so that they did not live long.
In addition to many rare manuscripts, there was an ancient copy of the
Koran, the sacred book of the Arabs, beautifully inscribed upon silk paper and illuminated." Had there been any coffee, we cannot doubt that
Hasche would have mentioned the fact. The returning Saxon soldiers
had not brought any.

Thus, to begin with, it could not be said that the opening of Kolshitsky's coffee-house had an effect in Germany, though, no doubt, there
was general talk along the Danube about the way in which the Viennese
had taken to drinking coffee. Still, since even the Viennese were slow to
adopt the new beverage, we cannot be surprised that the South German
States proved tardy in the matter. The use spread up the Danube, for,

three years later, in 1686, the first coffee-house was opened in Ratisbon. Then a jump was made northward, to Nürnberg. Here a halt was called, and it was a long time before coffee made any further advance.

Like every other commodity, coffee is subject to the law of supply and demand. Was there, at that date, an effective supply of coffee? The original Viennese stock was a prize of war, and not for a long time did it occur to anyone to import fresh quantities through the devastated lands of Hungary, Serbia, and Bulgaria. Apart from the fact that, after the Battle of Vienna, the Turkish war continued (for the emperor's armies invaded the Balkans, and had repeated brushes with those of the sultan), land transport of Oriental goods would—the distances being so great—have made them too expensive for German consumption. As far as High Germany and Central Germany were concerned, only marine transport by way of Venice was possible. The position of Venice as against Turkey was peculiar. When the Turks occupied the territories of southeastern Europe, they came everywhere in conflict with the Venetians, who traded along the coasts of Greece and in the Archipelago. Commerce was the only sort of life for Venice. In that city there was no land where grain could be grown or beasts pastured. The citizens of the republic lived in their crowded houses amid the lagoons and canals or on ships that spent most of the time at sea. Nevertheless, though war between the Venetians and Turks went on for hundreds of years, this conflict never completely interrupted trade between them. At a time when the land routes between East and West, between Vienna and Constantinople, were closed by war or the imminence of war, maritime commerce still went on between the Queen of the Adriatic and Morea, Asia Minor, and Egypt. It continued because, religious and political enmity notwithstanding, it was of vital importance both to the Crescent and the Cross.

True, it was the Venetians who engaged in the fiercest sea-fights with the Turks. On the other hand, it was likely enough that, shortly before, one adversary had supplied the other with the timber out of which the ships had been built! The spirit of Mars and the spirit of Mercury were perpetually intermingled. The supple diplomatist was the offspring of the embraces of warrior and merchant.

Thus Venice drew profit continually from the Southeast. But the

King John Sobieski, leader of the Polish-German army at the relief of Vienna, 1683

Leopold I, Holy Roman Emperor

Franz Georg Kolshitsky

receiving the dispatches

as a spy in Turkish dress

Cartoon of a Parisian coffee-seller at the time of Damame's monopoly (1695)

Woman coffee-seller (about 1730)

Allegorical cartoon of Tea and Coffee (about 1720)

Anti-Bacchic Parisian engraving (about 1720)

Venetians, seafaring folk, had little or no inclination to carry on their trade by land routes northward and westward into Europe.

It was strange that the city republic, which morning after morning stared undazzled at the sun as it rose in the East, that the city republic, whose fleet sailed towards all quarters of the compass, shunned the mountains. For the Venetians, the Alps were a psychological barrier, and they shrank from any attempt to scale the heights. It would have been easy enough, otherwise, for them to send their traders by land to Villach, Klagenfurt, over the Tauern, to Salzburg and into Bavaria. Instead of this, they left commerce by land to the Germans, though the latter were, in most respects, far less enterprising. Like the Spanish, the Portuguese, the Dutch, and the British, they were seafarers; and without a thought of carrying their goods by foot over the passes of the Alps, as time went on, they sent them boldly in Venetian bottoms as far as Flanders.

It was not that trade by land routes through Germany ran any special risk. No doubt pillage and blackmail occurred from time to time in Germany, but on the whole the trade routes of the empire were carefully policed. Still, after the Thirty Years War, a sort of public cheating had become widespread in Germany. There was prevalent a "fraud without shedding of blood," of which Guidobaldus, bishop of Ratisbon, complained when, in 1668, he wrote: "It was common for traders fraudulently to dispose of the goods with which they had been entrusted." The bishop charged the estates of the realm to search out these fraudulent traders and inflict condign punishment.

Thus it happened that few Italian traders journeyed into Germany, whereas plenty of German merchants visited Italy. From the Carinthian Alps their wagons rattled down the green valley of the Tagliamento to reach Venice. They passed through Gemona and Portogruaro. Where the Ponte di Rialto spanned the Grand Canal, in the middle of the City of the Lagoons, was the Fondaco dei Tedeschi, the great German warehouse. Here the men from the North found what they needed. The word "fondaco" is derived from the Arabic "funduk." The Arabs, in their turn, had borrowed it from the Greek "pandokos," meaning all-receiving, common to all. Everywhere along the Mediterranean shores the Venetians had erected many-storied buildings that were part inn, part store, part counting-house, and part fortress—like the "factories" of

African and Indian trade at a much later date. In the Fondaco dei Tedeschi, beside the Rialto Bridge, merchants from Nürnberg, Ratisbon, Augsburg, and Ulm rubbed shoulders; men who had come for the spices of the East, and to have them conveyed across the frontier by German wagoners.

Here, far away from home, they slept in clean beds, though the house was an unfamiliar one, built on pillars, in the city of Venice amid the waters which, nevertheless, had a land-beast, a lion, in its coat of arms. And hither, to the Fondaco dei Tedeschi, there came day after day the representatives of the Venetian sea-merchants, to dispose of their wares.

The Germans, however, were not allowed to make their bargains without an official imprimatur. Venice appointed brokers to watch over the contracts, keep records of them, and impose taxes. In the history of painting we learn that no less a man than Titian was one of these brokers. At any rate he was styled a broker, and received a salary therefor. He does not seem to have taken his duties very seriously, and certainly it would not have suited him to install his studio overlooking the packing-yard with its noise of porters and beasts of burden. Had he done so, he might have painted like one of the Dutch or Flemish School!

From this packing-yard, the precious commodities of the Levant started on their long overland journey to Germany: perfumes, spices, silks, and dyes, pearls and pepper, incense and ginger. On the southward journey the wagons had been laden with Syrian ores and Low German textiles, which were to be shipped to Egypt. Most of what was carried northward was included under the name of "groceries and spices." The total quantity was not large. What in those days crossed the passes of the Alps in wagons in a year's time could today be carried through the St. Gotthard tunnel in a couple of freight trains.

Was coffee among these goods? Yes, but in very small quantities. Before the days when Venice began to amuse herself at masked balls where coffee was served, there was little demand for this commodity in Ratisbon and Nürnberg. Beyond Nürnberg, there was no demand at all. For in Central Germany and North Germany coffee had to wrestle with a titan whose powers were enormously greater than those of Bacchus.

This titan was the lord of Northern Europe. His name was Beer.

7

King Beer

I N North Germany at that date the dominion of beer was still comparatively recent, dating from not more than two and a half centuries back. If we were to speak of an exclusive dominion, the
period would be shorter still.

No doubt the early Teutons, like other barbarians such as the Thra-
cians and the Scythians, drank beer; but they did not deify it, did not
make of it a central feature of their lives, as the Hellenes and the Romans
had done with wine. Still, beer in those early days played a fairly important role. This "beverage brewed from malted barley or wheat," concerning which Tacitus disparagingly declared, "it somewhat resembles
wine of an extremely bad quality," moved the Roman historian, who
was not usually critical, to remark of its use by the Teutons, "if we were
to encourage them in their drunkenness, and to give them as much beer
as they are inclined to swill, it would be easier, thanks to this vice of
theirs, to overthrow them than it is to do so by force of arms." But the
beer drunk by the ancient Teutons must have been different from the
beer known to us today, inasmuch as no hops were grown in Germany
before the eighth century A.D., and the flowers of the hop-plant were
not used as an ingredient of beer earlier than the year 1070. The early
Scandinavians speak more of mead or metheglin (made from honey dissolved in water and fermented) than of beer.

Beer-drinking, however, steadily decreased among the Germans, along
their frontiers, as they came into closer contact with Roman civilization.
Where Roman legionaries, Roman traders, and Roman lawyers dwelt,
beer was out of fashion. Bacchus quickly put an end to brewing in Spain
and in Gaul—that is to say, on Roman territory. Pliny tells us that beer

was in those days called "cerevisia," that is to say, the "force of Ceres." But Bacchus was stronger than Ceres, wine was stronger than beer. This was so even in the western and southern parts of Germany. Where the Romans colonized effectively, John Barleycorn has never become a supreme monarch even down to our own day.

The folk-migrations, bringing the Germans to the shores of the Mediterranean, convinced them of the superiority of wine over beer. Throughout the rise of German civilization during the Middle Ages, beer played a very small part. At the princely courts on the Danube, among the minnesingers of Zurich, on the Lake of Constance, on the Neckar, and on the Main, no one, in those days, drank beer. King Beer, as a great industrial power, did not extend his rule into South Germany until the close of the Middle Ages, his realm spreading from the north. He first ascended the throne in that proud city which, for five centuries, had flourished among the mists of the North Sea.

Beer was one of the main sources of wealth in Hamburg. About a century before, setting out from Mecca, coffee began the subjugation of the Ottoman Empire; beer, on the other hand, set forth from Hamburg upon its invasion of Holland and Jutland, Sweden and Russia. Through the Skagerrak and the Kattegat, by the waters of the Sound and the Belt, sailed the freighters of the Hamburgers. They were deeply laden with beer, and with tubs of another commodity, which goes so well with beer and increases the thirst for it, pickled herrings. Wherever these vessels came to port, there were promoted orgies of beer-drinking and herring-eating. Salted gullets had to be slaked with Hamburg beer. On the Zuider Zee and among the Frisian islands, in Bergen and Helsingborg, in Danzig and Riga and Königsberg, beer flowed abundantly, a yellow sea capped with white froth. At the masthead of the freighters fluttered the flag of the Hanseatic League.

There are documents to show that throughout the fourteenth century the cargo of the vessels that set sail from Rostock, another of the Hansa ports, was chiefly beer. Their usual destination was Bruges; but the thievish Danes often plundered them in the Sound, and carried off the beer-casks in triumph to Copenhagen. Shakespeare recorded the Danish fondness for beer in immortal verse. They drank deep at the court of King Claudius, Hamlet's uncle, and when the monarch raised his tankard, cannon were fired:

This heavy-headed revel east and west
Makes us traduced and tax'd of other nations;
They clepe us drunkards, and with swinish phrase
Soil our addition; and indeed it takes
From our achievements, though perform'd at height,
The pith and marrow of our attribute.

Hamlet would be greatly astonished, could he be resurrected today
and read in the reports of the Brazilian Coffee Institute for the year 1932
that little Denmark had become the greatest coffee-importing country
in the world—eleven and a half pounds per head of population!

In those days, drunkenness was prevalent throughout Northern Europe. A reeling giant, armed with battle-ax and sword, Beer sailed the
seas. In their voyages through ice-encumbered waters, the Vikings kept
themselves warm with copious potations. Their sails were sprayed with
beer as well as with water. The smell of malted liquor accompanied them
wherever they went; their beards were stained with it; and to replenish
their tankards, the heady potion flowed freely out of the spigot.

The whole of the Northwest, the whole of the Northeast, became
gigantic beer depositories. The eyes, the blood-vessels, the senses of the
men of those days were soused in beer. It choked their livers, their voices,
and their hearts. They thought, they felt, they reckoned in beer. In the
budget of the war carried on by Hamburg against Denmark, payments
for beer constituted the main item of expenditure. Two-thirds of Stral-
sund's provision for its troops and sea-fighters was devoted to beer; of
2640 marks spent by Lübeck upon a naval campaign, 1140 marks were
assigned to beer. We find it recorded in the Hansa account-books that
twenty sailors consumed on an average per diem no less than fifty-seven
gallons of beer. In a list of occupations in the town of Hamburg dating
from the year 1400 and dealing with 1200 persons, we find mention of
460 brewers and more than 100 coopers, so that forty-five per cent of
occupied persons were engaged in the beer industry.

The brewers were traders and monopolists as well. They did all they
could to promote the sale of beer in Holland and Friesland, until at
length, shortly before 1400, for the protection of the brewers of Haar-
lem, the import of beer from North Germany was prohibited. By now
Flanders, too, had taken to brewing its own beer. Indeed, according to a
local myth, Flanders and not Germany was the original homeland of

beer. The name of "Gambrinus," the deity who presides as a wooden image in many modern beer-halls, is said to be derived from Jan primus, or Jan I, Duke of Brabant in the thirteenth century. Jan may have been real enough, but Gambrinus is supposed to have been the Flemish inventor of beer. This worthy finds mention as a contemporary of Charlemagne. When, many centuries later, King Philip of Spain, a wine consuming land, occupied the Low Countries, Spanish vintages encountered the stubborn resistance of beer in street and market-place and guild-house.

At the close of the Middle Ages and the opening of the modern era, a new type of beauty began to be depicted in northern European art—the type of the man whose bones are thoroughly well covered. Gothic artistry knew nothing of this type. Neither in the stone statues of Naumburg cathedral, nor yet at Strasbourg, Bamberg, or Magdeburg, nor in the countless recumbent figures on the tombs of knights and dignitaries of the Church, do we see persons with a "corporation." Since sculptors in the hey-day of cathedral building took nature as their model, and, despite an occasional inclination to carve grotesques, generally depicted what they saw around them, and since many of the figures on the tombs were indubitably portraits, we are justified in the inference that in northern Europe of those days obesity must have been extremely rare. The obese were exceptions; they were subjects for caricatures, like Sancho Panza in Spain; they were not typical. Such a type as John Bull, supposed to be a characteristic English country squire, was inconceivable in the Middle Ages.

At the opening of the humanist epoch, there was a sudden change of bodily type in northwestern and northeastern Europe. The Scots, the English, the Dutch, the Danes, the Norwegians, the Swedes, the Finns, and, above all, the Low Germans, began to put on flesh. Especially the leaders—princes, artists, men of learning, generals, priests, persons of taste or of musical genius—were fat folk. An amazing transformation! Never, since the world had been turning on its axis and since human beings had dwelt on its surface, was the belief prevalent that obesity was practically synonymous with health, power, genius, and dignity. Yet from 1400 to 1700 this belief, inconspicuously, gained predominance throughout northern Europe.

A large number of notables during that period were exceedingly stout: Gustavus Adolphus and Henry VIII, Georg von Frundsberg and Martin Luther, Pirckheimer and Johann von Staupitz, Peter Vischer and Hans Sachs, Handel, Johann Sebastian Bach, Christian IV of Denmark, and countless others, were amazingly corpulent.

To us, these worthies look unpleasantly fat. They themselves regarded their pot-bellies as so natural that they would be puzzled to learn that we find it necessary, for æsthetic reasons, to tone down their outlines. No sculptor today, modelling a memorial statue of Gustavus Adolphus, the Protestant hero who fell at Lützen, would dream of giving his image the huge belly which the king really possessed. To the sentiment of their day, they seemed all that could be desired. Leanness was then looked upon as morbid. It is true that Erasmus of Rotterdam, Prince Eugene, and Frederick the Great were by no means healthy persons, but of the morbidly asthenic type. Nevertheless, if we were to meet them today in a dinner-jacket or a lounge suit, we should regard them, precisely because of their leanness, as much healthier persons than, say Philipp Emanuel Bach or George Frederick Handel.

But it was only in northern Europe that this "monstrous regiment" of the fat prevailed. Southern Europe clung to its lean and sinewy type. The men of the wine-drinking countries, the Spanish, the dwellers in central and southern France, the Italians and the Greeks, the Hungarians and Danubian vintners, did not share, or shared very little, in the inflation of bodily type. For the inflation was the outcome of a new mode of nutrition, the outcome of beer-swilling.

Whereas wine is mainly a beverage that washes out the intestines and the tissues, and that (except for the heavier wines) exerts its magical influence almost exclusively upon the central nervous system, beer is a food. In addition to alcohol and water, it contains albumin, dextrin, nutritive salts, and sugar. A litre of good beer contains five grammes (one part in two hundred) of albumin, and fifty grammes (one part in twenty) of carbohydrates. The fact that these nutritive substances are introduced into the organism in a fluid and readily assimilable form, accompanied by effervescent carbonic acid, probably accounts for the revolution in the aspect of the human figure that had never been observed before beer became a popular beverage.

At the time when the consumption of beer reached its climax, which was in the fifteenth, sixteenth, and seventeenth centuries, this beverage was not, as most commonly today, drunk in public-houses or saloons. It was drunk at home; and therein lay the danger, for it was brewed where it was drunk. Whoever was granted the freedom of the city had the right to brew what beer he needed for his own use. The authorities had no objection, since every beverage was taxable. The consumption was recorded, but a tax edict promulgated by Elector John George in 1661 shows that in the countryside illicit brewing was common. This edict expressly forbade that home-brewed beer should "on any account be sold or publicly provided." Still, no one bothered about the edict. All got their beer wherever they pleased.

The vital importance of any comestible can best be realized from the shadow it casts upon legal life. Julius Bernhard von Rohr, who, in 1719, made a compendium of the laws relating to the necessary and useful supplies of a German household, in a work of one thousand pages devoted more than twenty to "matters that concern the brewing of beer." This gives plain proof how great a part beer had come to play in the economic and domestic life of the Germans. Beer-drinking likewise left many traces among German family names. In the fifteenth century began the lines of Biermer, Biermann, Bierschwale, Bierhals, Bierfreund. Bierwagen, Biertümpel, Biersack—waggish names to begin with, conferred upon persons whose potations of beer were especially copious.

The citizen's day began and ended with beer. A good draught to wet your whistle at the start. At the noonday meal there was a beer soup; and at supper, of course, there must be egg-flip made with beer. Raisin-beer and sugar-beer, fish and sausages boiled in beer, beer in all conceivable forms, to say nothing of abundant draughts of plain beer when paying visits, talking business, at baptisms, and at funerals. Thus the body was deluged with carbohydrates, which were transmogrified into fat as already described. When we remember that the main purpose of the process of respiration is to rid our blood of carbonic acid, we can see that the unceasing supersaturation of the human organism with H_2CO_3 cannot fail to have remarkable effects both on the individual and on the community. Whereas wine makes people bold and lively, beer makes them maudlin and bad-tempered.

In twentieth-century Scandinavia there has been a very effective temperance movement, and the Nordic slimness and persistent youthfulness of the inhabitants of the peninsula bear witness to the fact. Goethe longed for a similar movement among the Germans. Of all the enemies of excessive beer-drinking, no one had keener insight than he. Writing to Knebel, tutor to the princes at the court of Weimar, he said that beer dulled the nerves and thickened the blood. "If our people go on swilling beer and smoking as they now do for another three generations, woe to Germany! The effect will first become noticeable in the stupidity and poverty of our literature, and our descendants will declare themselves greatly astonished thereat!"

But how was coffee to wage war successfully against this titan? The combat was too unequal. Especially so at a time when beer was routing wine, so that in certain parts of Germany viticulture was coming to an end.

Prior to the victory of beer, the vine had gained a strong footing in Germany. During the Middle Ages, vineyards were successfully established in the northern and eastern parts of the country. If they have now disappeared, the ignorant are likely to suppose that the disappearance is due to a change of climate. There are, however, no reasons for such an assumption. It is far more probable that the Germans, fatigued by the wars of religion, were prone to abandon the more difficult culture of the vine and the more delicate processes of preparing wine for the much easier preparation of beer.

German viticulture receded southward and westward, into the valleys of the Rhine, the Main, and the Danube. Everywhere else, King Beer was victorious. This took place, more especially, after Gambrinus, at a comparatively late date and helped by the invasion of master-brewers from Brunswick, had occupied the Munich plateau. How could coffee be expected to advance from Vienna and Ratisbon into this beer country? No one felt the need for a beverage that was looked upon as un-German.

Liselotte of the Palatinate, wife of Philip Duke of Orléans, and therefore obliged to live in Paris, is a signal example of this trend. In her letters, she is perpetually railing against coffee. Thus, in 1712, at Christmas, she writes: "I cannot endure coffee, tea, or chocolate, nor am I able to understand why anyone likes to drink them. Give me a beer-soup; that is what I should like best. But you can't get it here, for French beer is no good." On October 22, 1714: "I am always amazed that people here are so fond of coffee, tea, and chocolate. To my way of thinking sauerkraut and smoked sausages make a meal fit for a king . . . I like cabbage-soup with bacon in it better than all the dainties people prize so much in Paris." On February 26, 1716: "I seldom take any breakfast; and when I do, it is only a roll and butter. I loathe all these foreign spices. I never drink either coffee, tea, or chocolate, for I detest them. I have remained thoroughly German in my tastes, and like to eat and drink what my forefathers used to."

This conservatism in national habits certainly has its seamy side. If coffee made its way more slowly in central Europe than in the West, so that it did not become a popular beverage in High Germany until eighty years after it had been generally esteemed in England and France, the upshot was that in Central Europe the drinking of heavy liquors continued far longer than elsewhere. As I have said, at the beginning of the modern age the Germans were heavy drinkers, and during the Thirty Years War all classes were intemperate. Excessive consumption of brandy and beer, and of wine likewise where this was not too expensive, seemed to be the only way in which, throughout those terrible decades, people could drown their sorrows. Whereas the English, who, as we shall see, were also heavy drinkers, had begun to detoxicate themselves at this period, the Germans, in general, had no knowledge of anti-Bacchic beverages.

In Germany, during those times, alcohol became a part of life. It was used not merely to satisfy thirst, but to create more thirst, so that drinkers positively wallowed in their potations. Princes, sovereigns, handicraftsmen, men of learning, peasants, soldiers, and the nobility drank to excess. The effects of such universal drunkenness were worse than would have been those of a second Thirty Years War.

At some of the courts "unchristian and bestial drinking" was prohibited, but few bothered about these prohibitions. In a fit of self-criticism, the Elector of Saxony hung upon the wall of his dining-room a picture showing swine and dogs engaged in deep potations.

Sophia Charlotte of Hanover relates that on one occasion the Duke of Holstein drank from so mighty a tankard that his stomach rejected its contents, whereon he drank his vomit once more. "Et il l'avala une seconde fois pour marquer la passion, qu'il avait pour moy." Only in those parts where wine-growing was still in fashion, on the Italian border, in Tyrol, and in Styria, were the courts better behaved. At the

Kaiserhof in Vienna, where Burgundian and Spanish manners prevailed, such swinish drunkenness was, of course, out of the question—at least in theory, for there were exceptions!

This was the strange epoch when Jacob Balde, a Jesuit father and a famous preacher, founded the "Congregatio Macilentorum," the Society of the Lean. For in 1638, a slim and upright German figure had become a rarity among the well-to-do; one and all of them were pot-bellied. Somewhat prematurely, G. W. Leibniz, returning in 1690 from his Italian tour, wrote that people were no longer so "crazy and full of beer" in the north. That is was premature was shown by the fact that he went on to write, concerning the vice of drunkenness: "If our forefathers could come back to life and rub shoulders with us, we should regard them as impoverished peasants." We gather from this that the men of the seventeenth century were much harder drinkers than their ancestors had been!

On the forty-eighth birthday of King Augustus the Strong of Saxony and Poland, Countess Dönhoff gave a banquet. It was in the year 1718. We are told that the Elbgarten was illuminated, and that the ladies were dressed as shepherdesses. There were parrots, monkeys, and blackamoors on show—every conceivable ornament suitable to a wealthy court of the Baroque era. Now there happened something which could never have taken place at a contemporary Italian court. "People drank deep where the king was," relates Johann Michael von Loen, "and of a sudden there were issued strict orders that no one was to leave the garden. The Saxon courtiers had resolved to drink their Warsaw guests under the table, to show that they had stronger heads than the Polish magnates who, although there was a personal union of the crowns of Saxony and Poland, were regarded as rivals. The Poles, unused to such deep potations, were already pale as death, their heads waggling on their shoulders, their gait unsteady, so that they reeled as they walked before the king."

The underlings naturally followed the bad example set by their "betters." The general idea, in other countries, therefore, was that a German must be an obese beer-swiller. When the Saxon Count Dohna, a man of culture and of refined aspect, went abroad, he aroused widespread astonishment. King Henry IV, presenting this Count Dohna to Marie de' Medici said: "Le voilà! Le prendriez-vous bien pour un Allemand?"

At that date civilization and morals in central Europe were indeed mightily debased. Armin Vambery (1832–1913), the Hungarian traveller and orientalist, inquired in all seriousness whether the Turks, though they appeared at the gates of Vienna as invaders and devastators, were not, at that time, a more highly civilized people than the Germans.

Of course there were German courts at which the rulers would not allow such excesses. Frederick William of Brandenburg was a monarch of this order, so that early in these licentious times Berlin acquired a good reputation.

This Frederick William, styled the Great Elector, had many of the best characteristics of a Western sovereign. At his accession, the Thirty Years War was still in progress, and his dominions had been greatly wasted thereby. Contemplating his neighbours with an outlet on the Atlantic, he saw that, while Germany was squandering its energies in fratricidal strife, they were expanding across the seas. Holland, too, was winning a colonial empire and prospering. During the Pomeranian war between Brandenburg and Sweden, Raulé, a Dutchman, equipped a navy for Frederick William. When the war was over, the Elector retained the little armada, and sent it to the Guinea coast to found a colony on African soil. Von der Groeben, the navigator, established the Gross-Friedrichsburg port, and hoisted the Brandenburg flag upon the Gold Coast. A deputation of Negro chiefs came to Berlin to pay honour to the Elector of Brandenburg. In Senegal, likewise, a settlement was established, and was held for a few decades until the jealousy of Amsterdam nipped this early German colonial empire in the bud.

What had induced Frederick William, a petty territorial prince, to found these distant settlements? Not merely the will-to-power, but in addition the belief that, in days when ships laden with spices were returning across the seas, he would be able to secure supplies for his own country without paying tariffs. West Africa furnished gold and sugar, timber, palm-oil and other fats, ground-nuts, ostrich feathers, and ivory.

The Great Elector was by no means satisfied with the limited produce of his own narrow territories. Remarkable to tell, at his court in Berlin, though only in restricted circles, coffee was being drunk in the sixteen seventies. Supplies for the Elector and his lady came from Holland. There can be little or no doubt that the Elector, a man eager for new knowledge, was made acquainted with coffee by his Dutch physician-in-ordinary, Cornelius Buntekuh. This scientist, who would have attained wide celebrity had he not died prematurely, aimed at the reformation of dietetics. His real name was Cornelius Decker. In Alkmar, where he was born, his father kept an inn, at the sign of the "Bunte Kuh," the mottled cow. His fellow-citizens therefore nicknamed him "Bontekoe." This pseudonym was used by Cornelius as signature to his scientic publications. Having studied the writings of Descartes, he went to Amsterdam and then to Hamburg; wrote a book containing new chemical outlooks upon the nature of acids and bases; and was ultimately appointed by Frederick William as professor at the University of Frankfurt-on-the-Oder.

René Descartes came to regard human thought as a mode of motion, summing up his views in the pithy phrase, "Cogito, ergo sum." The most noteworthy physiological analogy to this psychological notion was provided by William Harvey, in 1619, when he announced the discovery of the circulation of the blood. Decker was never weary of telling his students that Harvey's discovery of the circulation had been the greatest discovery, not only of the century, but of many centuries. No one before Harvey had been able to establish the fact of this perpetual flow of the blood through all the organs of the body, irrigating them and nourishing them as the Nile irrigates and nourishes the soil of Egypt. One of the most marvellous features of the process was the elliptical course of the circulation, akin to the elliptical orbits of the planets, which begin and end their movements at the same spot. The blood pumped by the left ventricle into the aortic arch, returns into the heart through the right auricle twenty-three seconds later. One who has acquired a vivid impression of this unceasing circulation of the blood, gains thereby a new outlook upon the nature of man—so much more active and mobile than the nature of any plant; be-pinioned, as it were. One of the cravings of the period was connected with this discovery of the circulation of the blood: the craving to circumnavigate the globe. All parts of the earth were to be interconnected and fertilized by an ellipse of traffic. It was only to be expected that the bold outlook of his physician should encourage a sovereign to engage in navigation and foreign trade. From the macrocosm, however, Buntekuh came back to the microcosm; since he knew that blood was not healthy and useful unless it was in lively motion, he was inclined to think well of anything that could accelerate the circulation.

Above all he recognized that tea and coffee were able to overcome the inertia of the blood. They could stimulate the working of the vital machine (Descartes' view was that men and the lower animals were vital machines) by promoting the circulation of the blood. Coffee released the wheel-work from the brakes.

Buntekuh went too far in his recommendation of the use of tea. In his *Medizinischen Elementarlehre*, he writes: "We advise tea for the whole nation and for every nation. We advise men and women to drink tea daily; hour by hour if possible; beginning with ten cups a day, and increasing the dose to the utmost quantity the stomach can contain and the kidneys eliminate." Since he informs us that he prescribed for his patients as many as fifty cups per diem, it can hardly be doubted that, at the court of Berlin, Buntekuh helped a good many sick people out of the world. All the same, an epoch in which notables were, as a rule, hurried to an early death by carbonic acid, alcohol, and apoplexy, could find admirable use for such a man as Buntekuh.

He himself was only thirty-eight when he died. He was not a very satisfactory advertisement for his treatise on the prolongation of life by the use of tea, coffee, and chocolate (*Traktat von het excellentie kruyt thee, coffi, schokolate*). Still, it would be wrong to leave the reader under the impression that Buntekuh died through taking too much of his own medicine. He perished by an accident. On January 10, 1685, he was carrying books downstairs for the Elector. The staircase was dark, he stumbled, and broke his neck.

Thus, the internal ellipse of his circulation was brought to a standstill, and there was ended all too soon a life that might have taught much more to his contemporaries. With the death of Buntekuh, caffeine disappeared for the time from Berlin.

This was only two years after Kolshitsky had discovered the beverage for Vienna and the Viennese.

8

Doctorial Discussions in Marseille

A MONG all who envied the republic of Venice its trade with the Levant, there were no more remarkable people than the inhabitants of Marseille. Their existence was not so strange and adventurous a one as that of the Venetians, who lived in houses built on piles amid lagoons; but nonetheless the origin of the Marseille folk had been peculiar.

The settlement of Massalia or Massilia was founded about 600 B.C. in Gallia Viennensis by persons of Greek stock, merchant adventurers from Phocaea in Asia Minor. These Hellenes took to themselves Gallic wives. A few centuries later, when the expansion of the Roman dominion was in progress, Roman settlers came and married the descendants of the Helleno-Celts. To mix the blood yet further, Hannibal, with Spanish and African troops, marched through Provence from the Iberian Peninsula on his way to invade Northern Italy. In the days of Marius, the Cimbri and the Teutoni, barbarians of different stocks, crossed the mouths of the Rhone on their way to and from Spain. Much later still, the blond Goths came down from the north and added to the mixture of colours on the palette of the north Mediterranean coast.

The Rhone, joined at Lyons by the Saône, and swelled by the turbulent waters of the Durance, the Gard and numerous other tributaries, becomes a mighty river which booms its way down to the sea. Accompanied by the murmur of the centuries—sometimes increased to a roar by burning towns and villages, sometimes reduced to a whisper of wind in the olive groves—Marseille waxed merrily, grew strong, loquacious, and huge. Made glorious by the Greek strain, virile through the Roman heritage, amorous from Gallic descent, inclined to trade and profit-making as had been the Carthaginians of old, the Marseillais were also heavy drinkers. They did not, like most dwellers in the South, drink merely to slake their thirst. The Nordic blood in them made them crave for the jingle that wine could produce. Their names were as various as their descent. Some had a Greek patronymic, such as Panurge or Thèopomp; others were called after Franconian knights, such as Lenthéric, Alberich, Walther, or Audibert; and Marius was one of the favourite baptismal names, given in memory of the Roman general who had crushed the Cimbri and the Teutoni.

They were merry fellows, their eyes lit up with wine. Open-air folk: oil-millers, vintners, carpenters, stone-masons, longshoremen, sail-makers, oystermen. A Marseillais could turn his hand to almost any job. One thing alone went against the grain: the thought of becoming a Frenchman! They laughed when they heard that the country north of Lyons, dissensions notwithstanding, was uniting to form France. Ere long, however, their hilarity changed to anxiety. They heard talk of that city called Paris, a petty place, far away from the sea, and on a river of no great importance. But the soothsayers declared that Paris was destined to outdo Marseille. Who could take such babble seriously? The revellers of Marseille would say to one another o' nights, as they lurched along the Cannebière, the street lined with taverns: "Si Paris eût une Cannebière, ça serait peut-être un petit Marseille."

But mocking laughter could not avert the peril. The power of the kings of France extended farther and farther south into the gay land of Provence. France had reached the Mediterranean coast. Still, the rulers of France left Marseille on their eastern border. New Mediterranean ports, French ports, began to flourish. The town council of the republic of Marseille looked askance. There was that infernal settlement of Aigues-Mortes, a French seacoast town, trying to rival Venice and Genoa!

The Marseillais, however, found an ally, and no city in the world has ever had a stranger one. The kings of France were but men, anointed yet mortal. Marseille's ally was a river, or, better, a river-god. The Rhone, Rhodanus; a self-willed old fellow, equipped with immense power. He did not reach the sea by way of Marseille, his course from the Swiss Alps entering the Mediterranean many miles westward of Massilia. He had a strange habit of silting up whatever his waters touched. At a day's march from the Mediterranean, he expanded into a delta. The land between and on either side of his many mouths was marshy plain. Nothing grew there but the weedy vegetation of salt marshes. Father Rhone had a way of thrusting the marsh land between what had been a seaport and the sea. Aigues-Mortes itself, which had carried on a brisk trade with Syria, flourished only for a century, to find itself in the end left high and dry amid the reedy lagoons.

All the better for Marseille, which, by a wise dispensation, had not been established on one of the mouths of the Rhone. It was the only first-class harbour adjoining Italy on the southern coast of Gaul. The kings of France found this undeniable, and wanted to come to terms with arrogant Marseille.

King Francis I, a thoroughgoing patriot, studied the map assiduously. He could not see any good reason why the products of his country should be shipped to the Levant from Venice, Pisa, or Genoa. He was proud to know that Turkey could not get on without French produce. The textiles made by the weavers of Languedoc and Catalonia were in demand in the bazaars of Constantinople and Alexandria. Nay more, camels bore them to Mecca, and thence to India. King Francis would hardly have believed this had he not, with his own eyes, seen accounts and bills of lading in the Italian tongue that confirmed the supposition. They taught him that in Mohammedan Egypt the pagan women loved to dress in linen from Rheims. Why should not Rheims textiles be shipped to the Levant in French bottoms?

Why not, indeed? In the year of grace 1535, no intelligent Frenchman doubted the possibility.

A century later, in 1634, a vessel engaged in the Levantine trade lay in Marseille roads. There disembarked from it a Monsieur de la Roque, a wealthy man who had just returned from Constantinople. He had a fine countryhouse in the environs of Marseille, commanding a view of the sea and of vineyards. Here, when he unpacked the baggage he had brought with him from the Levant, his astonished friends saw, among other things, a metal pot and some beans which were now roasted till they were black. From them a beverage was prepared which, in its effects, proved no less amazing to the Marseillais friends of Monsieur de la Roque.

The stock the traveller had brought with him was soon exhausted, and it was more than ten years before pack-mules laden with bags of coffee were frequently to be seen making their way from the harbour to the villas of the well-to-do. At length, in 1660, a big ship, freighted only with coffee, arrived from Egypt. Where were the bales to be consigned? To the proper place—to the drug-stores. For it was a general belief that the strange substance that could keep people awake all night was not an ordinary beverage, but a drug.

Not for long, however, did this belief prevail. In 1664 was published a widely circulated book, Jean de Thévenot's *Relation d'un voyage fait au Levant*. Like all who have leisure and enjoy the beauties of life, the well-to-do of Marseille were great readers of history. Naturally, therefore, they read to themselves, or read aloud to one another, the chapter on coffee in Monsieur de Thévenot's book, which showed clearly that this beverage was, in the land of its origin, an article of daily consumption, and not a mere drug.

"The Turks," wrote de Thévenot, "have a drink that they are accustomed to consume at all hours. This drink, known as 'cavé,' is prepared from a black bean. They roast the bean over the fire in a metal pan; when it has been roasted, they pound it into a fine powder. To prepare the beverage, they take a metal pot which they call 'ibrik,' fill it with water, and raise the water to boiling-point; then they throw into the pot a large spoonful of the powdered grain. Very soon after this they withdraw the kettle or pot from the fire, for otherwise the fluid would boil over. Then they put it back again on the fire until it begins to bubble once more, repeating this process ten or twelve times. Thereafter they decant the black drink into porcelain cups, which are handed round upon a painted tray. This beverage must be consumed exceedingly hot, but only in sips, for if taken at a draught the taste is not fully savoured.

"The drink must be bitter and black, and must have a burnt taste. Another reason for consuming it in little sips is that otherwise, being very hot, it might scald the mouth. In a 'cavéhane,' as they call the houses where coffee is prepared and sold, the sound of sipping is continuous. The drink prevents the ordinary vapours of satiety rising from the stomach into the head; it also hinders sleep. When our French merchants have many letters to write and wish to work through the night, they would find it advantageous to drink one or two cups of cavé at about ten in the evening. As regards the taste of this beverage, although it is disagreeable the first time, the second time one drinks it one already begins to find it agreeable. It fortifies the stomach and helps digestion. The Turks also believe that it cures a number of maladies and promotes longevity. In Turkey it is drunk both by the poor and by the rich; it is one of those things which a husband is universally expected to provide for his wife.

"There are public coffee-houses, where the drink is prepared in very big pots for the numerous guests. At these places guests mingle without distinction of rank or creed; nor does anyone think it amiss to enter such places, where people go to pass their leisure time. In front of the coffee-houses are benches with small mats, where those sit who would rather remain in the fresh air and amuse themselves by watching the passers-by. Sometimes the coffee-house keeper engages flute-players and violin-players, and also singers, to entertain his guests. If anyone is sitting in the 'cavéhane' and sees a friend enter, it is good form for him to nod to the proprietor, signifying that the newcomer is to be served free of charge, to be 'treated.' The first comer receives the other as his guest. This is expressed by a word to the coffee-house proprietor. The word is 'jaba,' which means 'gratis.' "

The foregoing quotation shows clearly enough that, in the Levant, people did not get their coffee from the drug-stores. There were as many coffee-houses as there were drinking-saloons in the West. Soon after the publication of de Thévenot's book, the first coffee-house was opened in Marseille, partly for residents and partly for sailors.

The first coffee-house keeper found imitators, but two classes of people began to complain. To begin with, the vintners. Bacchus inspired them to wrath. Had not these disciples of Mohammed uprooted the vine along the southern coast of the Mediterranean? Now coffee had come to the northern shore—coffee, which had derived advantage from the rout of Bacchus—the Black Apollo of the barbarians had sailed hither on shipboard, into the Christian wine-bibbing city of Marseille! He was going to continue his work of destruction there. He would convert the Marseillais into disdainers of wine.

Those were strange times, times when people ran to extremes. Every passion had an absolute ring. It was exclusive and jealous. No one dreamed that coffee could join forces with wine, and that a good coffee-drinker could also be a good wine-drinker. This experience, so familiar to ourselves, had not then been tasted.

Thus Dionysus inflamed the wrath of vine-dressers and wine-dealers alike. They were vigorously supported by the doctors. These children of Æsculapius were enraged that coffee had escaped the restraints of their prescriptions. For several years, like other rarities, it had been consumed only by doctors' orders. Before anyone could get coffee, he had to consult his physician, and then go to the apothecary's shop. Now the Marseillais declared themselves independent in this matter, much to the annoyance of the faculty. The line taken by the physicians was a singular one. They declared that coffee was a poison. Amid the many onslaughts that had been made upon coffee during the centuries since its use had first begun, this was a novelty. Religious zealots and state authorities had persecuted it, but never before had a doctor declared coffee to be harmful. On the contrary, the Arab, Persian, and Turkish physicians had extolled its health-giving virtues, maintaining that it dispelled fatigue and melancholy, refreshing the body. The doctors of Marseille were now singing another tune. Maybe they were also moved by worthier reasons than the thought of their prescription fee. It is possible that these doctors were the first to have an inkling of the biological differences between individual human beings and particular races. Coffee might be good for Arabs living in a tropical or sub-tropical climate; it might be even better, because of its warming qualities, for the inhabitants of northern climes; and yet it might be altogether superfluous for those who dwell in a land of the golden mean. It might be superfluous or even harmful in Marseille, where the weather is neither very hot as in Mecca nor very raw and damp as in London.

Messieurs Castillon and Fouqué, doctors of the faculty of Aix, invited Monsieur Colomb, at a public reception by the members of the Marseille faculty, to read a thesis upon the question "whether the use of coffee is harmful to the inhabitants of Marseille."

Monsieur Colomb understood what was expected of him. In Marseille town-hall, which had been lent for the purpose, clad in his academic robes, he mounted the rostrum and addressed a large assembly. He emphasized the fact that wherever coffee had made good its standing it had speedily shown itself to be a tyrant. It aroused such a passion for its use that warnings and even persecution were of no avail against it.

Amid murmurs of applause, the young physician continued: "We note with horror that this beverage, thanks to the qualities that have been incautiously ascribed to it, has tended almost completely to disaccustom people from the enjoyment of wine—although any candid observer must admit that neither in respect of taste or smell, nor yet of colour, nor yet of any of its essential characteristics, is it worthy to be named in the same breath with fermented liquor, with wine!" Loud was the acclamation as these words echoed through the town-hall of Marseille. Monsieur Colomb felt himself in good vein, and, his black gown rustling as he spoke, he went on to say that certain physicians had not hesitated, at the outset, to extol coffee. "And why? Because the Arabs had described it as excellent. They had done so because it was one of their own national products, and also because its use had been disclosed to men by goats, by camels, or God knows what beasts!" These were poor reasons to influence a receptive mind. In the neighbourhood of Marseille there was plenty of fodder for goats, and no one in this part of the world had as yet thought of rearing camels. Unquestionably coffee was not a proper drink for human beings in that quarter of the earth.

"Some assure us that coffee is a cooling drink, and for this reason they recommend us to drink it very hot. . . . But the actual truth is that coffee, in its nature, is a hot and very dry substance. I say this not only following such authorities as Avicenna and Prosper Albanus, but also because these effects are obvious to me. The burned particles, which it contains in large quantities, have so violent an energy that, when they enter the blood, they attract the lymph and dry the kidneys. Furthermore, they are dangerous to the brain, for, after having dried up the cerebro-spinal fluid and the convolutions, they open the pores of the body, with the result that the somniferous animal forces are overcome. In this way the ashes contained in coffee produce such obstinate wakefulness that the nervous juices are dried up; . . . the upshot being general exhaustion, paralysis, and impotence. Through the acidification of the blood, which has already assumed the condition of a river-bed at midsummer, all the parts of the body are deprived of their juices, and the whole frame becomes excessively lean.

"These evils are especially noticeable in persons who are by nature of a bilious temperament, who from birth onwards have suffered from a hot liver and a hot brain; in persons whose intelligence is extremely subtle, and whose blood is already superheated. For these reasons we have to infer that the drinking and the use of coffee would be injurious to the inhabitants of Marseille."

Did the Marseillais thereupon abandon the use of coffee? They had, by this time, been Frenchmen far too long not to scent the ludicrous in such dithyrambs. They knew what doctors were like with their hair-splitting dissertations. In dozens of contemporary plays, physicians were represented as objects of ridicule, as would-be-learned ignoramuses. People "with no sense of humour," for instance the English, the Germans, and the Dutch, might be imposed upon by medical bombast; but among the cheery Provençals, among the sceptics of Marseille, such froth could only arouse a spirit of contradiction.

All the same, the adverse judgment of the Marseille doctors did a good deal of harm to coffee. Although the masses were uninfluenced by it, it made way among the learned. The great majority of French physicians at the close of the seventeenth century, influenced by Colomb's dissertation, were opponents of coffee-drinking. They held that the fruit of this Arabian plant was only a drug, and must not be used to prepare a beverage for daily use. Various rumours were disseminated about coffee-poisoning, and found credence, though they were manifestly absurd. When Jean Baptiste Colbert died in 1683, at the age of sixty-four, seemingly from over-fatigue, it was bruited abroad that he had burned out his stomach with coffee. Liselotte of the Palatinate wrote in one of her letters that the Princess of Hanau-Birkenfeld had died of coffee-drinking. At the post-mortem examination it was disclosed that this poisonous drink had produced hundreds of ulcers in the unfortunate woman's stomach, and that all of them were filled with black coffee-grounds! (One gathers that the princess succumbed to multiple cancer of the stomach. As we learn from the famous report of the autopsy of Napoleon, cancerous tissue looks very like coffee-grounds.)

Other physicians, however, raised their voices to refute so preposterous a calumny. One of the most meritorious was Sylvestre Dufour, who hit upon the idea of making a chemical analysis of coffee, with the aid of two Lyons doctors. Collaborating with these, Spon and Cassaigne, in the year 1685, he penned the first quasi-modern description of the constituents of coffee, and showed what, thanks to its chemical constitution, were the effects of coffee on human beings. Coffee, said Dufour, counteracted drunkenness and nausea, and was helpful in disorders of menstruation. It promoted the flow of urine, strengthened the heart, relieved dropsy, gravel, and gout. It cured hypochondria and scurvy. It strengthened the air-passages and the voice, reduced fever and relieved migraine. Dufour must obviously have made numerous experiments on human beings. He came across some of those rare specimens of mankind who can drink coffee at bedtime and nevertheless sleep soundly—which seemed to him wonderful. He said that they must be persons who were so highly nervous that the coffee "relieved their disquiet, and removed their feeling of anxiety," thus enabling them to sleep.

Notwithstanding these experimental investigations, it proved very hard to eradicate from the French mind the notion that coffee had a "dessicative influence." Dr. Duncan of Montpellier, a man of Scottish extraction, pointed out, rightly, that coffee was good for persons "whose blood circulates sluggishly, who are of a damp and cold nature." It might have seemed an obvious inference from this that coffee would be especially useful for Dutchmen, Englishmen, and Germans; but Duncan did not draw this conclusion. Starting from the premise that the circulation of the blood of Frenchmen did not need to be accelerated, he became one of the adversaries of coffee. Well on in the eighteenth century, when coffee had already passed into general use, Dr. Tissot took the same view in his *Von der Gesundheit der Gelehrten*, published at Leipzig in 1769. Tissot held that Cornelius Buntekuh, the Great Elector's physician-in-ordinary, had "corrupted the whole of northern Europe." The mistaken belief that a sick person could usefully be given "a hundred cups of tea" had incurred the most disastrous consequences. Buntekuh's theory concerning coffee was crazy; the quickening of the circulation was only of apparent value. "It is a foolish belief of many sick persons that their ailments are due to an excessive thickness of the blood. Owing to this fallacy, they drink the harmful beverage coffee. The coffee-pots and teapots that I find upon their tables remind me of Pandora's box, out of which all evils came!"

Like his predecessors, Tissot was willing to allow coffee "a place in the pharmacopœia"; but the daily use of the beverage was harmful and to be condemned. "The repeated stimulation of the fibres of the stomach weakens them in the end; the tough mucus which normally clings to the inner coats of the organ is washed away; the nerves are stimulated, and become unduly sensitive; the energies are dissipated; the patient suffers from a slow fever, and from other troubles whose cause often remains obscure; and these troubles affect, not only the fluid parts, but also the blood-vessels." Of the worldwide struggle coffee was waging against the evils of alcoholism, Dr. Tissot had no idea. On the other hand, he was obliged to admit that "if coffee be drunk now and again only, it clarifies the ideas and certainly sharpens the understanding, for which reason men of letters make much use of it." Still, he adds emphatically, "we have to ask ourselves whether Homer, Thucydides, Plato, Lucretius, Virgil, Ovid, and Horace, whose works will be a joy for all time, ever drank coffee."

These disputations were left to the learned, among whom they continued for decades; but the worthy citizens of Marseille took no heed of them. Since the Marseillais were great topers, it came easy to them to gulp down a huge draught of coffee as if it were wine. But now there was noised abroad a calumny—in print first, then whispered, then shouted from the housetops—that did more harm to coffee than either Bacchus or Æsculapius could do. It was a charge brought against the beverage by Venus.

Few German books were then read in southern France. One German work, however, became well known, thanks to a French translation. The original was entitled *Reise Adam Oelschlägers zu Moskowitern, Tataren, und Persern*—the translation by Wicquefort, *Relation du voyage d'Adam Olearius en Moscovie, Tartarie et Perse*, having been published at Paris in the year 1666. This traveller's tale—the journey had been undertaken with Paul Fleming, the German poet, as companion, at the instance of the Duke of Holstein—was, for the most part, true. Unfortunately, however, the author recorded a legend concerning the king of Persia, Mahomet Kosvin, who, as Oelschläger puts it, "had become so habituated to the use of coffee that he took a dislike for women. When one day the queen, looking out of the window, saw that a stallion was being emasculated, she asked why so well-bred a beast was thus shamefully handled. The men engaged in the operation told her that the stallion was too spirited and therefore troublesome, and that they were gelding it to tame it. The queen answered that they were wasting their pains, for coffee had the same influence. If they gave the stallion a sufficiency of coffee, within a few days it would become as cold as the king of Persia was towards herself, his wife."

This tale had the effect in Marseille of alienating many who had hitherto been the friends of coffee. Not a few of its adherents fell away. Those whose forefathers had been Greeks, Romans, Phœnicians, Goths, and Franks wanted their town to remain populous and immortal. With a mischievous smile they left the rediscovery of coffee to their rivals, the Parisians.

9

Suleiman Aga and the Parisians

I N the middle of the seventeenth century it seemed as if the sun
were shining continuously on France, and especially upon the
gardens of Versailles. King Louis XIV, the "Roi Soleil," was growing to manhood. He had a taste for brilliant court festivals and imposing
architecture. Where the king was, were warmth and sunshine and fruitfulness. Thanks to him, Paris and Versailles became the centre of the
world. Anyone near to him was happy, whereas those removed from
the sunlight of his countenance were cold and miserable.

The princes and peoples of the world directed eager glances towards
Paris, towards the sunlit court of Louis XIV. They were dazzled by the
spectacle. The servants and the satellites of the Roi Soleil shone by
reflected radiance. Colbert, who was making all Frenchmen rich, was
the Mercury of industry; Vauban, who built fortresses throughout the
realm, was a French Hephæstus; Turenne was a new Mars; Boileau, a
legislative Apollo; and there were several Venuses.

To this richly equipped court there came in 1669 tidings that the
sultan was about to send an ambassador. Weighty news this, for was
not Turkey the natural ally of the Roi Soleil against Germany? How
could the Bourbons continue to hold Strasbourg and the left bank of the
Rhine unless the fighting forces of the Holy Roman Emperor were kept
occupied in the East? On the other hand, there was something scandalous about the idea of an alliance with Turkey, for was not the king
of France the "Most Christian King"? Of course young Louis (now
thirty-one years of age) had never hesitated to stir up Hungary against
the emperor. But to join forces with the Turks, with Mohammedans,
was another story. He could not venture to do so openly. Even in that
age of absolutist rule, there was a public opinion which imposed moral

restrictions upon the activities of a monarch whose motto was "L'Etat, c'est moi."

It might have been wiser to receive the ambassador privately. But His Majesty King Louis liked to be in the limelight. All his doings must be open to the gaze of the world. Louis XIV, therefore, ordered a new suit of clothes in which to receive Suleiman Aga. It was sparkling with diamonds, looking as if woven out of stars. A contemporary informs us that the king's coat, which was worn only once, cost fourteen million livres. The courtiers, likewise, were glittering with gold and jewels. The French ruler's throne was placed upon a broad gallery, hung with silks and Burgundian tapestries. In front of it was a table made of solid silver.

The ambassador arrived. He came alone, leaving his servants on the doormat. Clad in simple woollen robes, he approached with slow and stately steps. He seemed quite unimpressed by the brilliant attire of the French monarch and the courtiers. Showing neither astonishment nor reverence, he stepped up to the seated king, did not prostrate himself as had been expected, but merely bowed his head a little and laid his hand upon his breast. Having stood thus for a few seconds, he held out the letter which the sultan had written to his "brother in the West." King Louis did not take the letter, but nodded towards the left, where one of his marshals was standing. This official opened the letter and held it in front of the king. Louis spoke in a whisper—such subdued tones contrasting strangely with the big aquiline nose and the immense wig—saying that the sultan's letter looked rather long, and he would read it later, at leisure.

To Suleiman Aga it seemed monstrous that what came from the hands of the Grand Turk should be so unceremoniously treated, that the West should apparently disdain the East, so he instantly made a dignified protest. Likewise speaking in low tones, the ambassador asked His Majesty why His Majesty had not risen to his feet on perceiving the name of the sultan at the foot of the document. While the shocked courtiers stared at this unheard-of impertinence, His Majesty replied that the king of France was a law unto himself, and accountable to no one for his actions. Thereupon the Turkish ambassador was dismissed, in high dudgeon.

He and his servants were driven back to Paris in one of the royal chariots. He rented a stately palace, and, whereas all had been astonished at his appearing before King Louis in a simple woollen robe, he now blinded the eyes of the Parisians with a glorious display. The word ran that within the palace an artificial climate was maintained; that Persian fountains played in the rooms; and that the rose-leaf odours of Constantinople had been charmed into the dwelling of Suleiman Aga. These were exaggerations; still, when the inquisitive French nobles secured an entry to the palace, what they saw was wonderful enough.

The rooms were dimly lighted. The furniture was made of scented wood; the walls were covered with glazed tiles, and in them were recesses from the tops of which hung stalactites. The ceilings were multicoloured domes. There were no chairs! This seemed uncomfortable at first, but the guests soon found great ease in sitting or half-reclining upon cushions. It was a relaxation to the muscles. Quite a different sort of sociability from the tense and intriguing sociability of the West, but a sociability of a new kind. After all, it was not so difficult to squat Turkish fashion. The men were offered voluminous dressing-gowns, and were encouraged to loll as they pleased and to lean on their elbows. At first, however, few men came; they preferred to send their wives. The marquises and duchesses, sumptuously clad, swam rather than walked into Suleiman Aga's wonder-palace. They were so gracious as to sink into his cushions. Dark-skinned slaves, clad in flowing Turkish robes, presented gifts of damask serviettes with gold tassels. They also served a beverage, boiling hot and with a detestable taste. Most of the ladies would have liked to spit it out again, but they recognized that this would have been bad manners. The privilege of visiting Suleiman Aga's house had to be paid for by drinking coffee. Would their host be annoyed if they sweetened the drink? A viscountess pretended that she was about to tempt the ambassador's singing birds with a lump of sugar, but, on the sly, dropped it into the bitter black beverage. Their host's solemn face showed the glimmer of a smile. He made no remark, but next day sugar was served to the ladies with their coffee.

Through their visits to the Turkish ambassador, although he was out of favour with the Roi Soleil, the former was kept informed as to what was going on at court, was told about French armaments, French manufactures, officers' commissions, regiments, and what not. He learned about alliances, about new schemes that were forming themselves in

His Majesty's brain—and he was told these things by persons who never realized that they were giving away important secrets. He wove the threads together, as if weaving a Bukharan carpet. Soon he became aware that he must not take King Louis seriously. France needed the Turks

A VIZIER DRINKING COFFEE
(Middle of the seventeenth century)

only in order to round off her own frontiers, by using the prospect of a Turkish alliance as a bogy to frighten the Germans. If the sultan were to dispatch another army to besiege Vienna, King Louis would not send so much as an auxiliary corps down the Swabian Danube!

It was with the aid of coffee that Suleiman Aga enticed this gossip out of his distinguished lady visitors. Thrown off their guard by the unaccustomed stimulant, they prattled away without knowing what they were saying. They wanted to draw out Suleiman Aga, and to extract information about Turkish manners and customs. Above all, they wanted to know more about this strange beverage whose aroma filled the air of the room.

Their host, sitting on a cushion among them, was ready enough to tell them anything they wanted to know. His black eyes, inscrutable as the black drink, lit up when he was talking about the national beverage.

He told them how, centuries ago, two Arabian monks had discovered the coffee-tree. Prayers to their memory were still offered up. One of them had been named Al Shadhili, the other Abd Al Aidrus. The inhabitants of Algiers, it was true, did not agree that the pious Al Shadhili had been an Arab. They claimed him as one of their own people, and for that reason in Algeria coffee was also known as "shadilye."

Distant and almost fabulous lands loomed before the eyes of the ladies when Suleiman Aga was thus speaking. As he stroked his black beard, he admitted that he himself did not believe the legend. It was doubtful whether Al Shadhili and Abd Al Aidrus had really been the discoverers of coffee. Certainly the latter had known very little about the preparation of the beverage, for he had thrown away the grounds, which were the best part of it. It had taken a long time to discover the most satisfactory way of preparing coffee. In many parts of the Turkish empire, people added ginger and spices. This was wrong and almost sinful. Just as there was but one Koran, so there was but one coffee.

He said this with an emphasis that inspired belief. While violet foam, tinged with orange and every other colour of the rainbow, formed on the surface of the fluid that was boiling in the metal pot, Suleiman went on extolling the virtues of coffee. He had himself visited plantations in southwestern Arabia, a countryside favoured by sunshine and moisture. To protect the precious coffee-trees from locusts, they were surrounded by hedges of tamarisk, and by tall spreading carob trees. Many old men in Araby had such a fondness for coffee that they made a paste of ground coffee and butter, and swallowed it. Although that might seem foolish, it must not be forgotten that religion, bodily strength, and good morals were buttressed upon coffee. A pious teacher, Achmet Ben Jadab, had declared: "He who dies with coffee in his body will not suffer the fires of hell." Coffee was a stimulus to goodness, and favoured works of piety.

The word "k'ahwah" denoted "energy," and, by drinking coffee, the Moslems could enjoy the delights of Paradise before death.

Thus did the ambassador talk to his lady visitors, and, when he let his memory dwell upon the coffee-growing regions of the land of Yemen, he was too ready to forget the business for which he had come to this far western land, was too ready to forget politics and Paris. He had moved towards the other pole of Moslem nature, towards the contemplativeness of a sufi. A few years later, the Turks were defeated near Vienna without Louis XIV having moved a soldier across the Rhine to assist them—or to repel their onslaught, as might have been expected of the Most Christian King. Ranke opined that the reason the French monarch did not take up arms against the Turks on this occasion was that he hoped they would advance as far as the Rhine and capture Strasbourg. Then he would have hurled his forces against the Mohammedans, and, as the saviour of Christendom and Germany, have been able to assume the crown of the Holy Roman Empire. However that may be, the Osmanlis returned to the Balkans. But coffee, "the wine of Islam," had by that time conquered Vienna and Paris.

Conquered? Hardly yet. It was still too dear for widespread consumption. Coffee-beans were to be bought only in Marseille, where they cost eighty francs a pound, so that none but the wealthiest of the wealthy could have supplies sent to them from Provence. Only they could spend such vast sums on behalf of their "Turkomania."

The greatest satirist of the day was Molière. When, in 1670, he wrote *Le bourgeois gentilhomme*—a satire which he had to tone down before it was produced at court—he depicted Turkomania as the climax of absurdity. Suleiman Aga, the ambassador, had spent at least a year in Paris, and was still the rage among persons of quality. Molière, therefore, staged a crowd of urchins decked out as Turks, who danced round Monsieur Jourdain, declaring they would make a Turkish prince of the foolish burgher:

> Voler far un mamamouchi
> di Giordina, di Giordina.

This skit must have opened the eyes of many of the Parisians, must have made them recognize that the "Oriental fashion" was more than a little ridiculous. It must have made them recognize, at any rate, that they were silly to think themselves Turks because they dressed up in turbans and pseudo-Oriental robes.

Thus coffee fell into disrepute among persons who were critical of the follies of the mode in the French baroque epoch. Those who made a cult of its use were somewhat ludicrous. A level-headed woman, Madame de Sévigné, was moved to protest. In May 1676, she congratulated her daughter for having given up drinking coffee. "Mademoiselle de Méry, too, has expelled it from her house in disgrace; after two such mishaps, it will not easily come into favour again!" The mother went on to say she was convinced that all heating beverages must have undesirable effects as compared with those which refreshed the blood. She held that the constitution of the lymph was closely dependent upon the heat of the intestines. Internal ablutions with Vichy water, in conjunction with a fruit diet, were much more wholesome than coffee.

The writer was speaking from experience. Her enmity to coffee was not that of a woman at war with fashion, but that of an anxious mother. She wrote, perhaps, the most affectionate words ever penned by a mother to a daughter: "On my knees, dear, I implore you with tears, by the affection you have for me, not again to write me so long a letter as the last one. If I had to regard myself as the cause of your sense of weakness and exhaustion, then, my child, I should feel partly responsible for your illness and perhaps for your death!" The Countess of Grignan had then long outgrown her childhood, but her delicate health was a perpetual anxiety to her mother. Thus, on Wednesday, November 8, 1679, Madame de Sévigné wrote: "I recently met Dr. Duchêne. He is sincerely attached to you, and I regard him as more conscientious than other doctors. He is greatly distressed to learn how much you have been losing weight. . . . He recommends that instead of milk, you should take plenty of porridge and of chicken broth, for, unless the condition of your blood improves, the consequences may be serious. Duchêne is also of opinion that coffee heats the blood and makes it circulate too quickly—that it is a beverage to be recommended only to persons who suffer from catarrh or consumption. He says he would never recommend it in anyone of so thin a habit of body as yourself. Do not be too slow to realize, my dear daughter, that the strength that coffee appears to give you is fallacious. It comes only from the quicken-

At the St.-Germain Fair (set for a play)

London coffee-house in the eighteenth century

The "Bourse" in Lloyd's Coffee-house (about 1798)

ing of the circulation, which ought not to be quickened, but rather the reverse. Do not forget, my daughter, that Dr. Duchêne gave me all this advice for you in the friendliest way possible." We see that coffee was still regarded as a medicine rather than a beverage.

In the days of Suleiman Aga, when the French nobility were taking sides for and against coffee, the bourgeoisie had no chance of drinking it. It was consumed only occasionally in the houses of distinguished persons, whose family economy was self-contained. Members of good society in Paris did not then visit houses of public entertainment.

The first attempt to convert the general public into consumers of coffee was made by a man whose only resemblance to Suleiman Aga was his Oriental origin. This was an Armenian named Pascal, who, in 1672, opened the first French coffee-house in the market-place of Saint-Germain. Even then it was not a genuine coffee-house, being no more than the dependency of a fair.

At that time, in Saint-Germain market-place, there was held every September a huge fair, which was an exhibition as well as a pleasure-resort. The booths of the fair were erected in nine streets, and in one hundred and forty of the booths, the products of industry were exhibited. The Parisians flocked thither, thus reinforcing the local patrons. In the brightly lit Luna Park, which was an annex to the fair, one could see dwarfs and fat women, dromedaries and camels. Amid this noisy jumble of exhibitions and side-shows, Pascal the Armenian established his "Maison de Caova" as an interrogation-mark to the French, asking them whether they would like coffee. His café was a replica of a Constantinople coffee-house with which Pascal had been acquainted, and, by its Turkish style, attracted the petty-bourgeois crowd. The most amazing thing was that they could afford to pay for their coffee. It was sold at no more than three sous a cup. Pascal, having a good head for business, realized that coffee could not become a popular beverage unless it was sold as cheaply as wine. With this end in view, the shrewd Armenian cut out the middleman, and imported his coffee direct from the Levant.

All the same, Pascal had miscalculated. What he had believed to be a genuine interest in the beverage he sold had been nothing more than a desire to participate in "all the fun of the fair." When he removed his establishment to the Quai de l'Ecole in Paris, he soon went bankrupt. The very same persons who, as excursionists to Saint-Germain, had been ready enough to fork out their three sous, turned their backs contemptuously upon the Parisian café. A further trouble was that supplies languished, and, in the endeavour to keep down the price of the beverage, Pascal had to adulterate his coffee with dogberries and acorns. Since he was a connoisseur, this probably went much against the grain. In the end, he fled by moonlight to London.

Within five years, however, another Armenian, heedless of Pascal's failure, made a fresh trial, opening a small Turkish coffee-house in the Rue Férou. That he might not be wholly dependent upon the purveying of coffee, he sold tobacco as well. His name was Maliban. After a time, he migrated to Holland, and a Christianized Persian named Gregor, who had been his assistant, took over the Paris business.

Gregor remembered that in his own country there was an intimate connexion between coffee and literature. Why not in Paris, too? There must be a spirit hidden away in the coffee-bean akin to artistic inspiration. Would it not be a good move to transplant the coffee-house to the Rue Mazarin, close to the Comédie Française? That theatre was then the centre of the fashionable world—far more so than the very exclusive court of the Roi Soleil at Versailles. Theatre-goers were great talkers; they talked about plays, actors, first nights; they gossiped and put on airs; they liked a "salon." It was a bright thought of Gregor's to establish himself so near the Comédie Française, and he gave a genial welcome to the gossips who looked in during the entr'acte and when the performance was over. Although Gregor's "refreshment-room" was not directly connected with the theatre, it was sufficiently linked to follow the Comédie Française when that institution moved to new quarters. Now, therefore, in 1689, was founded the first theatre café.

Since Gregor did not go bankrupt, imitators were encouraged. The original coffee-house that the Persian had taken over from Maliban had been transferred to a fellow-countryman named Makar. In Persian, "makar" means "happy," or "fortunate." Makar the coffee-house keeper, however, won so little good fortune from the sale of coffee that, suffering from nostalgia, he quitted Paris and France for ever. He lacked the felicity and adroitness of the smooth-tongued Gregor, who could hold his own among the popes of literature as if to the manner born, could

COFFEE-POT WITH SPIRIT LAMP AND EXTINGUISHER
(*Louis XIV*)

converse with the disciples of Boileau about "unity of place," and could chatter with the respective admirers of Racine and Corneille while serving them with coffee. Even had Makar been able to hold his own among such customers, he could not attract them to his out-of-the-way establishment. When he left, his successor was a Fleming known as the "Man of Ghent."

Prior to the year 1700, very few Parisians by birth had become coffee-house keepers. The occupation had still an alien flavour. An acquaint-anceship with literature, the friendship between the Black Apollo and the "periwigs," did not suffice, as yet, to give a café the necessary smack of the French soil. That could not happen until—as was not far off—the whole great nation became a literary one, and until coffee had become the chief nutriment of French brains.

About the year 1690, a little man with a limp came to settle in Paris. He was a Greek from Crete, which was then under Turkish rule, and he became generally known as "the Candiot." Lacking funds to open a coffee-house, he made a virtue of necessity, inventing a new trade, hawking hot coffee from door to door. He wore a clean white apron, which set off the brown of his face and hands. On one arm he carried a little brazier surmounted by a coffee-pot, and as he walked he sang, in his native tongue, a song which, translated, may have run much as follows:

> O drink that I love,
> Rule by right divine!
> Wean the drinker from the grape;
> Far better, thou, than wine!

Having knocked at a customer's door, for two sous he would fill three cups. Then he limped on as quickly as he could to the next customer. Thus the aromatic odour of the black beverage was introduced into the houses of the multitude.

"The Candiot" found imitators, one of whom was Joseph "the Levantine." Still, this hawking of coffee from door to door in the morning like new bread did not catch on. It soon became apparent that the immediate future of the beverage did not belong to family life, not to the home, not to the four walls of the citizens; it required a more public setting.

For, at the turn of the century, public life in France was assuming a new form, characterized by a fondness for conversation and criticism which had not been known in the baroque epoch. The Teutonic, the Franconian, characteristics of the Parisians were disappearing. These Parisians, like the other inhabitants of the Latin countries—like the Milanese, the Neapolitans, and the Marseillais—were acquiring a taste for street life on other occasions than the annual fairs. The exercise of this new taste was becoming a daily custom, and coffee played its part in breaking down the walls of the home. The talk of the streets, although it was still far from exerting a marked influence upon politics or upon business, was found, as in the South, to be enheartening. There had dawned the century at whose close civic freedom would be discovered like a new continent. In the year 1702, as a mark of changing times, the first really modern great café was opened in Paris. The founder of this "Café Procope" was Procopio di Coltello, a gentleman from Palermo who, like all the dwellers in Mediterranean ports, had made acquaintance with coffee far earlier than had the Parisians and the Viennese. Though a man of family, having fallen on evil days he made his way to Paris, and, at the age of twenty-two, became a waiter in the coffee-house of Pascal the Armenian. Three years later he married a Parisian woman named Marguerite Crouin, and by her had, as was the custom in those days, a large family: eight children. When his first wife died in 1669, Coltello married a Frenchwoman of family, and by her had four more children.

After he had so lustily done his duty to the populating of France, and had, incidentally, given the lie to the Marseille calumnies concerning the anaphrodisiac effects of coffee, it seemed to him time to disguise his foreign origin, so he called himself Couteau instead of Coltello. Soon he added to the new name the designation "maître distillateur," and in 1702 he bought a roomy building that faced the Théâtre Français.

This Café Procope was the prototype of all the Parisian coffee-houses of the eighteenth century. Coltello-Couteau owed his success to his having broken away from the fashionable or sometime fashionable craze of Turkish decoration. His motto was "Paris for the Parisians." He now provided comforts which previously his customers were forced to imagine, although Paris abounded in them; he installed mirrors, candelabras, and marble-topped tables. He reinforced coffee with chocolate, liqueurs and ice, sherbet, and dainties. His establishment thus somewhat resembled the modern confectioner's shop, a type from which, however, the café was destined to depart. Anyhow, the Café Procope was the first distinctively European coffeehouse. Starting from this focus, all France became, as the Abbé Galiani has told us, "le café de l'Europe."

Brother Coffee

WHEN William Harvey (1578–1657) was nearing his end, he summoned a solicitor and showed the man of law a coffee-bean. Thrusting his finger-nail caressingly into the groove of the bean, he said with a smile: "This little fruit is the source of happiness and wit!" In his will, he bequeathed to the London College of Physicians the greatest treasure in his laboratory, fifty-six pounds of coffee, directing that his colleagues, so long as the supply lasted, should assemble, month by month, to commemorate the day of his death by drinking coffee together. Only fifty-six pounds of coffee! This indicates that coffee was then consumed in very small quantities, being regarded as hardly less precious a beverage than the vinegar in which Cleopatra is fabled to have dissolved a pearl. Above all, it was looked upon as a medicine, which indeed it is.

Harvey never dreamed that twenty years after his death London would be full of coffee-houses; or that coffee, of which he had procured a sack from Venice at great cost, would by then be brought to England in shiploads, to fill the warehouses at the docks.

Yet nowadays we do not find it easy to associate the idea of the English with that of coffee-houses and coffee. Tea has become the typically British beverage. A reddish-gold infusion served in wide cups of egg-shell porcelain—a "dish of tea." Just as wine was the national beverage of Hellas, coffee that of the Arabs and subsequently of the French, so has tea become the national beverage of the English. Yet from 1680 to 1730, for half a century, London consumed more coffee than any other city in the world. The day of tea was to come later.

In the year 1650, the body of the English nation was in a morbid state which, it would seem, could only be cured by strong doses of trimethyldioxypurin. The vice of drunkenness, the malady of alcoholism, prevailed among all classes. The prolonged bloodshed of the Civil War had made people wish to drown their sorrows in drink. There were taverns at every turn, not only in London but in provincial towns and villages. The populace needed dope—not knowing whether, from day to day, a new dictator might rise to power, or whether—the memories of the burnings at Smithfield a century before being still vivid—the Catholics might not again win the upper hand over the Protestants. In the seaports, sailors wished to forget the miseries of long and tedious voyages, to forget the brutality of life at sea. There were taverns waiting for them directly they set foot ashore. Inland, too, drink was everywhere on sale. Violence was universal, bottles and tankards being often used as weapons.

No writer at the close of the sixteenth century and the opening years of the seventeenth has given such lively pictures of drunkenness as those that have come down to us from Shakespeare's hand. Shakespeare described what he had seen. He lived among men whose muscles were made out of beef, and whose breath reeked of alcohol. Not only in the case of Falstaff, but also in that of many of the playwright's other characters, we look on with alarm, wondering whether these bloated creatures will not perish from spontaneous combustion, consumed in a blue flame of rum and gin and brandy. Besides distilled liquors, they swallowed vast quantities of heavy wines—malmsey, Canary, Madeira, sherris-sack, port, and what not. Those that could afford to buy such luxuries, of course! The young men of family who drank in the Mitre, the Falcon, or the Mermaid, could pay for the best; but the numerous poor devils whom Shakespeare likewise knew, the prototypes of Bardolph and Pistol, consumed other drinks. "Never before and never afterwards," writes Brandes, "were there so many different kinds of strong drink in England. Malt liquors galore, called indifferently ale and beer, ranging down to small beer [recall the words of the drinking song, an expansion of some lines by Fletcher, the Elizabethan dramatist: 'He who drinks small beer, and goes to bed sober, falls as the leaves do fall, and dies in rank October; but he who drinks strong beer, and goes to bed mellow, lives as he ought to live, and dies an honest fellow']; three sorts of mead, prepared by fermenting a solution of honey; and each beverage was flavoured with some particular plant. White mead, for instance, contained rosemary, thyme, wild rose, mint, cress, fever-few, maidenhair, petunia, eyebright, campanula, holly-root, wormwood, tamarisk, and saxifrage." The alcohol flavoured with this multifarious flora ran riot in the system. Every brain and every belly became an aquarium of craziness. These drinks were comparatively cheap, consumed mainly by common folk. For persons with a palate, who could afford to indulge it, there were fifty-six kinds of French wines and thirty-six kinds of Spanish, with Portuguese and Italian wines as well. People did not usually get drunk on these beverages in the lands of their origin. Only when they had been shipped to England did they make the consumers' heads spin.

It was natural enough, therefore, that Iago should say of his drinking song: "I learned it in England, where, indeed, they are most potent in potting: your Dane, your German, and your swag-bellied Hollander . . . are nothing to your English." When Cassio demurs, Iago pushes the point home, asseverating: "Why, he drinks you, with facility, your Dane dead-drunk; he sweats not to overthrow your Almain; he gives your Hollander a vomit ere the next pottle can be filled."

Such was the world into which coffee was now introduced, at first as a medicament. For some time after its introduction it was an officinal preparation, kept in a drawer whose front was adorned with a scroll and to which was affixed a white porcelain label bearing the legend "*Coff. arab.*" At length a physician of note discovered its main quality. Walter Rumsey, who had been a pupil of Francis Bacon as well as of William Harvey, declared that coffee was able "to cure drunkards." The chapter in which he makes this statement is characteristically entitled "Experiments of Cophee." Every draught of coffee was then experimental. Now whereas in the France of Molière the medical profession was almost universally derided, in England at the same date physicians were held in high repute; and it was the faith of Englishmen belonging to the best circles in the dicta of physicians that gave coffee a good start in that country. The doctors declared that the new beverage was needed to cope with the frightful prevalence of drunkenness; and this appeal to the Puritan ideals that slumbered in every Briton made people pay heed to medical advice in the matter.

Apart from the recommendation of coffee as an anti-Bacchic, Edward Pococke, Dr. Sloane, and above all the famous Radcliffe, went so far as to describe coffee as a panacea. Taken fasting, the first thing in the morning, it was of the utmost value in consumption, ophthalmia, and dropsy. Nay, it could cure gout and scurvy, even smallpox. But these polyhistors, comically ignorant despite the wealth of their knowledge, issued solemn warnings against the dilution of coffee with milk. That, they said, would involve a risk of becoming affected with leprosy. Presumably the pundits did not mean true leprosy, but only the skin disease more commonly known as psoriasis. In modern London they were as superstitious, and as much a prey to the doctrine of similars, as had been the Arabs of old. I have explained that the legend of the discovery of coffee by goats probably originated from the resemblance of coffee-beans to goats' dung; so, now, the skin that formed on the top of coffee with milk reminded the physicians of an eruption!

Still, that was the way in which "Brother Coffee" came to London, a very different introduction from that to Paris. The French were already hot-blooded enough, and their doctors were afraid they would become superheated. The English were cold, and their blood circulated sluggishly. Hitherto the only way of warming them up had been to dose them with alcohol. But there was another way of instilling fire into their veins. Many of them were melancholic and many of them irascible. Often wrath and gloom were combined. Now coffee came and sat down at table with them for half a century. Though it was a popular beverage, it appeared on the scene as a black-clad Puritan, wearing a Dutch broad-brimmed hat, a ruff, and white sleeves. Often the guest was smoking a short clay pipe; and, while in France Brother Coffee made people who were already sleepless more sleepless than ever, and increased the frivolousness of those who were already inclined to be frivolous, in London, when coffee came into fashion, it introduced an atmosphere of sobriety—just as if a clergyman had entered the room. "Don't forget that you are good Christians!" . . . "Be sure and go regularly to church, and to be quite sober when you go!" . . . "Above all, behave like gentlemen, remembering that the proper place for your knife is beside your plate, and not between your neighbour's ribs!"

When Pascal, the Armenian who had gone bankrupt in Paris, fled by moonlight to London, he found, strangely enough, a competitor of the same name already established in the English capital. This was the Greek, Pascal Rosea; really a Greco-Venetian, for he came from Ragusa, upon which the lion of St. Mark had fixed its claws during the Middle Ages. Daniel Edwards, a London merchant, had voyaged to Smyrna, and, during the return journey, when his ship touched at Ragusa on a fine summer morning, he landed, to encounter the coffee-man Rosea, who was wearing a Greek cap. Although in Smyrna the traveller took it as a matter of course that everyone there, as throughout Asia Minor, knew how to make coffee, it was strange to meet a coffee-man when well on his way back to England. That was why Edwards thought it would be a good thing to pick up this fellow Pascal Rosea from the outskirts of the Greco-Levantine world, and take him back to London. Pascal became the Englishman's servant, and made coffee for his master every morning. "This entirely new practice brought so many friends to visit Edwards," writes Anderson in his *History of Commerce*, "that by the time afternoon came Edwards had found it necessary to satisfy the curiosity of all these inquisitives." Then, as ever, coffee affected those who made its acquaintance for the first time with "loquacitate quadam," with a marked garrulousness. Since Daniel Edwards had other work to do than to satisfy his friends' curiosity and to provide them with coffee, he established Pascal Rosea in an open booth outside the house, where coffee was provided without any trouble to the master. The "potus niger et garrulus"—the "black and tongue-loosening drink"— migrated under supervision of Pascal Rosea from this booth into a shop. The first English coffee-house was thus opened in Cornhill, opposite St. Michael's church, and therefore in the odour of sanctity. "The virtue of coffee-drink first publiquely made and sold in England by Pasqua Rosee" was worthy of its reputation.

But Daniel Edwards' protégé failed to reckon with a mighty enemy. Beer, the titan, the ruler of all northern realms, assembled his forces. Brewers and publicans were not inclined to allow liquor prepared from malt and hops to be driven off the field by the decoction from the little coffee-bean. They therefore denounced the Levantine to the Lord Mayor as being "no freeman." Since when had there been warrant for allowing a foreigner to interfere with domestic trade? The Lord Mayor admitted that this was a nice point, and therefore installed his coachman, Bowman by name, as Pascal Rosea's partner. The brewers, still dissatisfied, demanded that the new trade should be highly taxed. Pascal Rosea, therefore, paid an impost of one thousand sixpences per annum.

Even this did not suffice the beer trade, and Bowman—the Greek by this time having been squeezed out of the business—was compelled to sell beer in his coffee-house as well as coffee. Nevertheless, the success of coffee was so striking that a Fleet Street barber, James Farr by name, also took to providing coffee for his customers. Thereupon the whole force of the trade (it is significant that in England "the trade" without qualification means the trade in alcoholic liquor) was marshalled against Farr. They took out a summons against him. "We hereby accuse James Farr, a barber by occupation, with boiling and selling a beverage he calls coffee; with, thereby, causing a nuisance to his neighbours by the evil stench of his brew; furthermore, that in order to prepare the drink, he keeps a fire constantly going, not only by day, but most of the night as well, which causes great danger and unnameable terrors to the whole neighbourhood."

In spite of this base denunciation, Farr's Coffee-House escaped the Great Fire of London in 1666, which destroyed the major part of the ancient city. Farr's Coffee-House still stands.

In the theatrical quarter, round Covent Garden, numerous coffee-houses were now opened, Button's, Garraway's, Will's, and Tom's becoming famous. Here persons of distinction, well-to-do merchants, lawyers, doctors, and parliamentarians, assembled to enjoy the new stimulant. Here, wearing a great periwig with ringlets reaching to the shoulders, appeared the spirit of the nation to sip shrewdness and sobriety from the bowl of the Black Apollo.

Gambrinus, the rough god of beer, had to put up with his defeat. Now, however, Juno intervened in the quarrel—for there has always been a quarrel wherever coffee has first shown its face. Perturbed by the defeat which another goddess, Venus, had recently sustained in Marseille, she incited the women of London to a Homeric resistance against the black beverage. As early as 1674, wives who found themselves left too much alone in the evenings made a fierce protest. They complained "that coffee makes a man as barren as the desert out of which this unlucky berry has been imported; that since its coming the offspring of our mighty forefathers are on the way to disappear as if they were monkeys and swine."

The husbands replied to their wives' invective in a pamphlet defending their behaviour and preaching the virtues of coffee, repudiating the scandalous calumnies that had been circulated against the new beverage.

The men were victorious. The intemperate way in which the London wives had railed against coffee alienated public sympathy.

Even though Juno had thus been defeated, the plaint against coffee reappeared again and again, in the form of references to disordered domesticity and interference with business. It was said that the frequenting of coffee-houses made men idle—this being no more than a variant of the ancient invectives against taverns. "The coffee-houses," we read in a leaflet, "have become great enemies of industry. Many a promising gentleman and merchant, who had previously been a trustworthy person, has found this to his cost. To converse with his friends, he will spend three or four hours in a coffee-house. These friends bring other friends, and thus many a worthy man is kept away from his occupation for six or even eight hours."

That can certainly be said with far more justice of tavern-frequenters. Nevertheless, the god Gambrinus, who was suffering from the competition of coffee, and who was being robbed of his congregations, occasionally raised his voice in opposition. Now he did so as a political economist. "The growth of coffee-houses has greatly hindered the sale of oats, malt, wheat, and other home products. Our farmers are being ruined because they cannot sell their grain; and with them the landowners, because they can no longer collect their rents."

These diatribes notwithstanding, the spread of the use of coffee was manifestly increasing the sobriety of the nation. Not until coffee came into conflict with Jupiter himself, with the political order, was a halt called. In the mythology of coffee, there is a perpetual recurrence of the similar; and just as viceroy Khair Bey, in Mecca, had persecuted coffee-drinkers because their beverage made them inclined to meddle in politics, so in London were coffee-houses miscalled for the same reason, being described as, in reality, political clubs. In a petition through the lines of which we seem to read that it must have been inspired by neglected wives, we are told: "What a curse it is that ordinary working-men should sit the whole day in coffee-houses simply to chatter about politics, while their unhappy children are wailing at home for lack of bread! Sometimes, too, an artisan's business goes to ruin because he has been flung into jail or pressed into the army!"

These were not baseless calumnies. The coffee-houses were, in very

truth, focuses of political conspiracy. Party politicians among the frequenters of coffee-houses ultimately elbowed out the unorganized and
indifferent consumers of the beverage. The democrats, the whigs,
patronized St. James' or the Smyrna Coffee-House. The tories, the
members of the aristocracy—whom today no one would look for in a
coffee-house—and their supporters likewise had their favourite haunts.
Despite partisan differences, the parliamentarians were agreed with
Pope, who wrote in *The Rape of the Lock:*

> Coffee, which makes the politican wise,
> And see thro' all things with his half-shut eyes.

The government, weary of the uncontrollable, undesirable dynamo that
was continually supercharging the coffee-houses, closed them by proc-
lamation. Forty-eight hours before New Year's Day in 1676 there was
posted on the boardings the order of William Jones, attorney-general,
closing the coffee-houses in London "because in them harm has been
done to the King's Majesty and to the realm by the spreading of malicious and shameful reports."

What now ensued showed the power of a sobered nation. All parties
combined "against the unnatural and illegal decree." The coffee-houses
had become the headquarters of the parliamentary parties, and, at the
same time, their recruiting-halls. How could politicians get on without
them? Excitement in London was immense, so that Macaulay tells us
"there was a universal outcry."

Within a few days, the Crown was forced to give way. The coffee-
houses were reopened, their proprietors having given a pledge that
books, pamphlets, and leaflets should not be sold in them, nor demagogic
orators be allowed to make speeches. Thenceforward anyone who
pleased could drink coffee peacefully in a place of public resort.

Today in England, when tea has become the universal beverage, it is
hard to imagine what an influence coffee and coffee-houses had on English literature round about the year 1700. The English style of the
Restoration epoch was still completely lacking in dialectics, in the easy-
going and pungent argumentativeness of the literature of Latin countries.
Upon one page a French author would discuss more pros and cons than
an English author would upon thirty. But coffee introduced a taste for

brisk conversation, which is so foreign to the English national character. Previously, the tendency of English writers had been towards a sluggish river of unending monologue. They had lacked the stylistic taste for interludes that have the effect of rapids. So marked was the disconnected prolixity of the prevailing style that, as Harold Routh writes in the *Cambridge History*, official protests were uttered against it. But, as Routh goes on to say, such protests would have been of no avail but for the influence of the coffee-houses.

These prolix writers were, as a rule, unsociably silent when they found themselves in company. In his *Notes sur l'Angleterre*, published in 1872, Hippolyte Taine speaks of highly cultured persons "who fancied themselves good conversationalists. Really, however, conversation was disagreeable to them. They would receive guests, would watch the liveliest conversations and discussions, without themselves saying a single word. Not that they were inattentive, bored, or even distrait; they listened, and that sufficed them. If they were asked a question point-blank, they would civilly relate their experiences in a single sentence. Having thus discharged their obligations, they would relapse into silence, and no one was surprised thereat. Of such persons we are wont to say: 'He is a man of few words.' "

The reader may imagine that coffee had a remarkable effect upon those of such a temperament. The Englishman, chary of words so far as conversation was concerned, sought compensation in his solitude by abundant reading. Coffee put an end to his solitude, and, on the other hand, it deflated the monomania of self-centred oracular talk. "Conversation," says Harold Routh, "has a strange effect upon nascent ideas. He who has trained his mind by an exchange of thoughts in conversation, becomes more subtle and pliable than when he has nourished his spirit exclusively by reading. He speaks in more pithy sentences, because the ear cannot, so easily as the eye, follow long periods. . . . Thus the middle classes began to complete their education. Coffee-houses provided them with a place for the interchange of ideas, and for the formation of public opinion. They were (although those who frequented them were not fully conscious of the fact) brotherhoods for the diffusion of a new humanism—and only at these foci could an author come into contact with the thought of his generation."

Thus, the most prominent representatives of English literature round about the year 1700 were coffee-drinkers and frequenters of coffee-houses. Dryden, Congreve, Addison, Swift, Steele, Pope, John Philips, Pepys, and Arbuthnot spent most of their time in coffee-houses. Dryden wrote his letters in one; he felt so much at home at Will's that he invited his business friends and his publisher to meet him there. "Come to me at the coffee-house this afternoon," he would say. Samuel Johnson writes of the poet's life at Will's: "Dryden's armchair, which in winter was close to the fire, migrated in summer to the veranda; the poet, who loved his ease, speaking of these as his winter and summer quarters respectively. From this coign of vantage he expressed his views upon men and books, surrounded by an admiring crowd who said ay to all his remarks."

"Dryden," we learn from Edward Robinson, "spent evening after evening in Will's Coffee-House, expounding his views on poetry and kindred topics. He presided there, just as seventy years earlier Ben Jonson had presided in the Mitre Tavern." But what a difference there was in the products of the two periods! Beer, and heavy Canary wine, beaten up with eggs and spiced with nutmeg and cinnamon, provided a very different soil for the culture of verses than did the beverage of the ironists, the subtle and sceptical coffee. Shakspere's troup of centaurs no longer rode through the forest of poesy. The Gallic phase of English literature had begun. Instead of a flux of tedious words, keen dialectic and finished elegance were dominant. Literary and political adversaries were no longer drowned, like maudlin Clarence, in a malmsey butt, but in coffee.

Dryden classified the intellectual world with inimitable dexterity, separating the sheep from the goats. All the continent (meaning France, of which England happened to be a mere outpost) was discussed and criticized. Racine's latest tragedy, the dicta of Boileau, the question whether Perrault was right in his approval of modern literature—upon all these matters, Dryden passed judgment. "His disciples listened timidly," Walter Besant tells us, "wondering whether they could venture to speak; if one of them was bold enough to give an opinion, he congratulated himself should it secure Dryden's commendation." We see from this, and smile as we see, that coffee did not succeed in promoting equality in England. Englishmen remained Englishmen, with a strong sense of

Nürnberg coffee-drinker Girl with coffee-mill

The Abbé's morning coffee (about 1740)

Richter's coffee-house in Leipzig (about 1750)

The Coffee Tax of Frederick the Great (1784)

precedence; dignified and ceremonious, despite the relaxation produced by the drug.

Nor was man's primitive roughness dispelled by coffee. In France and in Italy, outraged "honour" was often avenged at the sword's point, in the duel. Our plainspoken Dryden, however, was not challenged to a duel. The Earl of Rochester's serving-men seized him one night as he was on his way home from the coffee-house, and gave him a drubbing. Dryden considered the earl to be a mediocre poet, and had said so often enough. That was why John Wilmot, Earl of Rochester, courtier and poet, had his successful rival cudgelled by masked serving-men rigged out as bandits.

The London coffee-houses of that day had a very different aspect from those with which we are now familiar. The Turkish, the French, and the Austrian types have persisted down to our own times. All over the world you will find Oriental cafés, Parisian cafés and Viennese cafés, with other varieties; but the London type of Dryden's day has vanished. Why is this? The furnishing of those coffee-houses, with its unique mingling of comfort and disorder, was so English, that the un-English element, the coffee, could not maintain itself permanently in such an atmosphere. We have an amusing description of one of the old coffee-houses penned by Edward Ward: "Come with me, said my friend, and I will show you my favourite coffee-house. Since you are a stranger in the town, it will amuse you. . . . As he was speaking, he reached the door of the coffee-house in question. The entry was dark, so that we were hard put to it not to stumble. Mounting a few steps, we made our way into a big room which was equipped in an old-fashioned way. There was a rabble going hither and thither, reminding me of a swarm of rats in a ruinous cheese-store. Some came, others went; some were scribbling, others were talking; some were drinking, some smoking, and some arguing; the whole place stank of tobacco like the cabin of a barge. On the corner of a long table, close by the armchair, was lying a Bible. . . . Beside it were earthenware pitchers, long clay pipes, a little fire on the hearth, and over it the huge coffee-pot. Beneath a small book-shelf, on which were bottles, cups, and an advertisement of a beautifier to improve the complexion, was hanging a parliamentary ordinance against drinking and the use of bad language. The walls were decorated with gilt frames, much as a smithy is decorated with horse-shoes. In the frames were rarities: phials of a yellowish elixir, favourite pills and hair-tonics, packets of snuff, toothpowder made of coffee-grounds, caramels, and cough lozenges—all vaunted as infallible. These medicaments were supposed to be panaceas. Had not my friend told me that he had taken me into a coffee-house, I should have regarded the place as the big booth of a cheap-jack. . . . When I had sat there for a while, and taken in my surroundings, I myself felt inclined for a cup of coffee."

We feel instantly that there is an uncongenial element in the room, and that this uncongenial element is coffee. Ale and porter would have been better suited to such surroundings. Of course the description is satirical, and there were more commodious and better furnished coffee-houses than this one. Still, the coffee of which they were the shrines remained estranged from them. Even though for half a century the English, especially in London, were frequenters of coffee-houses, many of them because they had acquired the habit, and others out of mere imitativeness, the day came when the fashion was dead. In the year 1730, the English "caffeomania" vanished as suddenly as it had begun.

Alcohol, however, did not succeed to the inheritance of Brother Coffee. The heir was a distant cousin, another member of the magical family trimethyldioxypurin—the wonderful Chinese tea.

We must not forget that coffee made its appearance as an antidote, when individuals and the nation were given to gross excess in the consumption of alcoholic liquors. But in England it remained a foreigner. It had cultivated an excitability and an acuteness which were not, in the long run, accordant with the English character. "A man's house is his castle." Coffee ran counter to this family isolation of the Briton. It was not a family beverage; it made people talkative and disputatious, even though in a sublime fashion. It made them critical and analytical. It could work wonders, but it could not produce comfort. It did not promote sitting in a circle round the hearth, while the burning logs crackled and were gradually reduced to ashes.

One can become addicted to sobriety as one can become addicted to intoxication. Coffee promoted neither the one nor the other. Coffee was anti-Bacchic, true enough, but in a stormy fashion. Tea promotes quietude, Buddhist self-absorption. It is a beverage for taciturn people, and is therefore better suited than coffee to the English.

Long before the nineteenth century had discovered the chemical identity of theine and caffeine, the active principles of tea and coffee respectively, legend had drawn attention to the fact. The saga of tea, like that of coffee, opens with the story of the wakefulness that ensues when people consume trimethyldioxypurin in the form of tea.

Dharma, the son of an Indian monarch and a Buddhist apostle, voyaged to China as a missionary. He led the life of an ascetic under the open sky. His food consisted exclusively of leaves. In search of perfection, he vowed never to sleep, and, even when the stars had replaced the sun in the sky, to remain wide awake for perpetual communion with God. But his body was stronger than his will, and, while engaged in pious contemplation, he was overcome with sleep.

On awakening, Dharma was intensely contrite at his failure. He was so much enraged at his eyelids, which, by closing, had made him unfaithful to his vow of perpetual devotion, that he tore them off, hoping in this way to prevent himself from again falling asleep. When, next day, he revisited the place of his affliction, he saw that the pale skin of the eyelids he had flung upon the ground had struck roots in the soil. From these roots, the tea-plant sprouted. Dharma praised God for His goodness. He laid leaves of this plant upon his eyes, and lo, there grew two new lids. Then he chewed some of the leaves, and immediately felt enhanced liveliness, which passed into tranquil cheerfulness and firm determination. Frequently, thereafter, he drank an infusion of these tea-leaves, and inculcated the practice upon his disciples, that they might be able, without fatigue and without slumbering, to devote themselves to the contemplation of God.

Since then, in the Far East, tea has been "as light and wakeful as the eyelids of Dharma." A wonderful legend, this! Tea produces wakefulness, and does so easily. Coffee is a heavier drink, and more difficult to prepare. Tea is as unexacting as was Buddha himself, whereas coffee aspires to world dominion, as did Mohammed. The distinction between the two doctrines, the profound difference between farther and nearer Asia, is symbolized by the favourite beverages of the two regions. But there is no favourite beverage to which any nation gives itself up uninterruptedly without an inner compulsion. People cling to that which uplifts them. The Arab drank coffee because it made him more of an Arab; the Chinese and the Indians drank tea because it promoted self-realization. Tea has encouraged a peculiarly vigorous tranquillity, leanness, and wakefulness in the inhabitants of farther Asia.

Coffee is as black as meteoric iron, and produces little impression upon the eye. Tea, on the other hand, is glistening and transparent like a precious stone, and by its mere aspect promotes cheerfulness. The wakefulness that radiates from the aroma of coffee invites to spiritual adventures; the aroma of tea encourages a distinguished relaxation. In the mouths of men and of nations, each of these two beverages plays its own peculiar symphony. There is no notation for gustatory experiences, or we could read the respective tastes from a score.

Trimethyldioxypurin, no matter whether it be imbibed in the form of coffee or in the form of tea, has like effects upon the central nervous system, the brain, and the blood-vessels. But there are obvious differences in the intellectual consequences. The Japanese writer Okakura, who enjoys "the sweet reserve of Confucius and the Path of Lao-tze" in the "fluid amber of tea," sees a vision of an extensive landscape when he looks into a teacup. For him "the aromatic tea-leaves hang like a cloud in the serene skies, or float like water-lilies upon the gentle emerald-green stream." Amiability, politeness, and kindliness invade the body of the drinker; the fourth cup produces a gentle perspiration, and all the evils and injustices of life are extruded through the pores of his skin. With the fifth cup, the purification is complete. The sixth cup summons him to ultra-mundane regions; and, with the seventh cup, a wind from that remote land bellies in his sleeves . . . No one could write in that way of coffee.

The natural modesty of tea has won the heart of all the nations with which it has come into close contact during recent centuries: the Chinese, the Russians, the British. Is not tea the most faithful of companions? Is it not like a watch-dog on the steppes of cold and heat? For the Tibetans, tea is the fundamental energy of motion. They use a cup of tea as a measure of time and space. Sir Francis Younghusband, in the Central Asiatic highlands, asked a peasant lad how far it was to the next village. "Three cups of tea," replied the youngster. This meant five miles. And just as in those regions tea has become a measure of distance and time, so among the nomads it is currency, in place of silver. Indispensable, divine, and precious.

The English have long been closely allied with this trustworthy companion. For two hundred years, now, tea has been the cornerstone of their mental life and of their empire. There were economic reasons why tea drove out coffee towards the year 1730. The conquest of India was beginning, and the British were becoming the owners of a tea-growing country. Hindustan belonged to Britain, and tea bore the same sort of relation to Greater Britain that hops bore to London.

Coffee was in a very different position. Since the English did not own Arabia, nor had the monopoly of the Levantine trade, coffee was not a British Empire commodity like tea.

In part, similar reasons explain why the French remained true to coffee when the English were being unfaithful to it. The more the French had to yield ground before the English in Farther Asia, the less fondness they had for tea. In the year 1766, the Chinese export of tea to England amounted to six million pounds, but in France only to two million. Since then, Paris and France have worshipped the gift of Araby, whereas London has become devoted to the gentle, yellow, Chinese god.

Planters, Traders, and Kings

11

The Island Realm of the Dutch

THE modern age begins, not only with Columbus, but also with Vasco da Gama.

In 1492 Columbus set sail westward to find the sea-route to the Indies, and by chance discovered America. In 1498, Vasco da Gama set sail to the south, circumnavigated Africa, and actually discovered the eastern sea-route to the Indies.

India! Throughout the Middle Ages, Europeans had been content to trade with Persia and Hindustan by means of Arab caravans. The Venetians, and subsequently the French, carried the Mediterranean part of the traffic. Then came the Turks, who thrust a huge barrier between Europe and the East. Thereupon trade with the Levant became more perilous and was greatly reduced. "How can we circumvent this obstacle imposed by the Turks?" grumbled the people of the West. "How can we get, as we used to do, spices and gold from the distant East without the Turks seizing them on the way?" That was the motive of the expedition from Spain, commanded by Columbus, the Genoese. Vasco da Gama, the Portuguese, set forth on the same quest six years later, and this time the venture was successful. Round the huge continent of Africa, tawny and arid as a lion's skin, round the mountains, the deserts, and the forests, he made his way into the ocean which lies southward from Araby.

The miracle had been performed. Christians in European vessels, men of the Cross, thus got behind the men of the Crescent. If the world was less amazed than it might have been at Vasco da Gama's exploit, this was because people's minds were fully occupied with the American miracle of Columbus.

To the Mohammedans, who had overthrown the eastern empire half a century before and had installed themselves at Constantinople, it came as a thunderclap that Portugal, lying so far off in the West, had sent an armada to the East. Great was the alarm in Mecca. Jidda, the port of the Holy City, was hastily fortified by a sea-wall. But the Christians made no attack upon the metropolis of Islam. They left Arabia well to their left, landed on the coast of Hindustan, took tribute, and sailed yet farther east. At length they reached an archipelago, a medley of islands like scattered fragments of a world jutting out of the lukewarm sea. They discovered Sumatra, Java, the Celebes, surrounded by a swarm of smaller islands, atolls, reefs, and rocklets. This was an India of Indias, a garden of fruit, a paradise. The Portuguese cast anchor. Here they would stay, the God-sent masters of the Malay Archipelago.

The adventurous spirit of the Portuguese carried the name of Lisbon to the margin of the habitable earth, at the same time that the Spaniards were extending their dominion over the new continent in the West. But the earth had no margin, for it was a globe. It seemed as if the Spaniards and the Portuguese, the former sailing steadily westward, and the latter steadily eastward, would come into conflict one with the other. There would be jealousy and enmity between two Christian nations.

Both applied to the Holy Father as arbiter. Alexander VI divided up the earth. This was in 1493, when the American continent was still unknown (for Columbus landed only in the West Indian islands), and years before Vasco da Gama sailed around the Cape of Good Hope. By the papal bull of May 4, 1493, a meridian was drawn "one hundred leagues west of the Azores and the Cape Verde Islands," giving to Spain the right of conquest to the west of it, and to Portugal the same right to the east. Portugal protested this as unfair, and next year, on June 7, 1494, was signed the Convention of Tordesillas between Spain and Portugal, by which "the line" was shifted two hundred and seventy leagues farther west, so that it lay along the fiftieth degree, west longitude. Thus, when the South American continent swam into their ken, Brazil, from the mouth of the Amazon to Punto Alegre, lay to the east of the Tordesillas meridian and was clearly in the area assigned to Portugal, but was ignored by that power until 1532, during the reign of John III. Meanwhile, under Cortez and under Pizarro, the Spaniards made extensive conquests in the Americas, the northern and the southern continents respectively. Eventually they also seized the Philippines, which were clearly within the domain assigned to the Spanish by the Pope. The Portuguese, on the other hand, never established themselves effectively in the Malay Archipelago, and in time their East Indian empire became a dream, commemorated in *The Lusiads* of Camoens.

Portuguese ships and navigators were not the first to reach the Malay Archipelago. The primitives of Sumatra, Java, and the lesser islands had already endured several foreign dominions. As early as the third century A.D., the Hindus had arrived from the Ganges, and among the Malayan islands had founded two empires for the Indian gods, Madyapahit and Crividyaya. They introduced Hindu architecture, poetry, and music. The natives, who were little more than children in intelligence, were taught how to cultivate rice and which were the best seasons for field-work. Planting should begin when the constellation of the Plough rose at sunset, that is to say, on December 15. As long as the Seven Stars were ploughing in the heavens, the tropical earth was in fit condition for its tillers. But the Hindus brought the Malays and the Javanese other arts, even more wonderful. They taught barter so that goods could be exchanged for other goods, voluntarily and without deception. A new art of dyeing was disclosed. Melted wax was poured on white linen; the wax was skilfully removed here and there, so that when a dye was applied it stained all parts except those that were still covered with wax. These "colour-prints" are still known in that part of the world by the Malay name of batik. Such ingenuities pleased the simple-minded folk, but they laughed awry when the Indian princes imposed a heavy poll-tax. They could offer no resistance. First of all, their weapons were much less effective than those of their conquerors; secondly the Hindus had gods of wonderful power, Ganesa, the elephant-god, for instance. As a rule he was sculptured in a seated position, lord of reflection and cunning, with his trunk peacefully rolled to one side; but if Ganesa were to stand up, were to raise his trunk and to trumpet, probably Java and Sumatra would sink beneath the level of the sea.

Yet, after a thousand years, the dominion of the Hindu god collapsed. A much mightier god appeared on the scene. He made his way into the country with the Arab traders, and was far more terrible than the other gods because he was invisible. Allah! This Allah was invisible, he could be everywhere at once. Attacking from the topmost heaven and from the depths of the earth, from the forest and the jungle, he destroyed the elephant-god and the temples of the Brahmans. The fires of religious war ravaged Java and Sumatra. New Mohammedan realms were formed, to carry on war against the old established kingdoms. Again and again pirate raiders came, as the rumour of the wealth of the Malay Archipelago spread. To the men from the Indian Ocean, the Arabian Sea, and the Persian Gulf it seemed like a fabled paradise. The Chinese came, too, and were astonished. When the north wind blew steadily, they voyaged southward for weeks on junks with dragons as figure-heads. They landed upon these islands which, with their towns and their mountains, were at once so homelike and so uncanny. In this volcanic region, the ocean channels varied from spring to spring. Many islands had vanished after a year's absence, and new ones had appeared.

One bright morning in the year 1510, a little Chinese fleet encountered some Arab traders or pirates who were taking a consignment of cloves from the clamorous natives. After a long dispute, the three parties drew their knives to settle the question of ownership. Then, of a sudden the yellow men from the North, the light-brown Arabs, and the dark-brown natives lowered their weapons. Something fearful had happened. Big vessels with white sails, vessels like huge sea-birds, were coming on amain from the West. Majestically they advanced. It was the Portuguese fleet.

These first Europeans to visit the Malay Archipelago stole more than cloves. Their nostrils dilated with covetousness as they inhaled the aromatic odours; and just as the Spaniards had sailed westward to the "isles of gold," so had the Portuguese sailed eastward to the "spice islands." Gold and spices amounted to much the same thing. Pepper could be converted into gold; so could nutmegs, which, in the Moluccas (still known as the Spice Islands), could be bought for one-twentieth of the price they commanded elsewhere. The Arab traders, whose business had in any case been interfered with by the spread of the empire of the Turks, who in 1517 conquered almost the whole of Arabia, now found their enterprises threatened from another quarter. They had formidable rivals in the transport of goods to the Mediterranean coast, where the Venetians took over the freight. The Portuguese conveyed the wares of eastern Asia to Europe by the cheaper sea route round the Cape of Good Hope.

The local sovereigns, who were at war with one another, appealed severally for aid to these mighty strangers. With their heavy guns, the Portuguese established order and founded trading-stations of their own. Everywhere forts were erected. By 1522, they had not only secured a monopoly of the spice trade, but on the island of Timor, for instance, the handling of sandal-wood was in their control. They were told that the Chinese used this odorous wood for religious purposes, and so they carried shiploads of it northward. In the very decade when Martin Luther renounced allegiance to the Pope and founded the great Protestant schism in Germany, the Catholic faith won over millions of Malays in the East. High on the poop of the Portuguese galleon, above the account-book and above the musket, stood the Cross.

One day, however, the colonists who were fighting for trade and dominion in this far country heard tidings of grave confusion in their homeland. The greatness of Portugal had passed its zenith. To the conquistadores, the news came like the rumble of a distant earthquake; the power of Lisbon, for which the national heroes Vasco da Gama, Antonio d'Abreu, and d'Albuquerque had fought, was on the wane. The energy of the Portuguese nation, squandered in distant seas, was exhausted. Within a few decades, among the Malay islands where the power of the Portuguese had loomed so large, the war-fleets of another land were sailing. A new marine empire was spreading over the bulge of the southern ocean—the empire of the Dutch.

One needed only to look at the Dutch in order to be convinced that they were likely to stay wherever they set their feet. They possessed far more patience than the livelier Portuguese; though they thought more slowly, they thought with more fixity and concentration. They were men of Teutonic stock, living in the delta of the Rhine, and beside the lower waters of the Schelde and the Meuse. One day, to their own astonishment, they found themselves a nation, and immediately brushed back their blond hair from their foreheads and began to launch ships. Broad of girth, solidly built in mind as well as in body, the Hollanders were untroubled by doubts, and within a few decades they had become unrivalled navigators and sea-fighters. The noise of the shipwrights' hammers was unceasing in Rotterdam. Vessel after vessel glided down the soaped wooden slipways into the sea. When Christian

Europe was trembling before the Turks, the Dutch, had they wished, might well have made short work of the sultan. Anyhow, with their navy, which was the mightiest on earth, they could have attacked him by way of the Red Sea.

For while impoverished Germany was finding it a great effort to relieve the siege of Vienna, the power and the wealth of Europe had flowed away to the northwest, to the Dutch capital and seaport of Amsterdam. In 1683, the year when Vienna was invested by the Turks, the three chief western powers, Holland, England, and France, had, in all, a mercantile marine comprising of twenty thousand ships. Of these, the Dutch had sixteen thousand, England thirty-five hundred, and France no more than five hundred. If the Hollanders had cared, by attacking Islam from the east they could have made the onslaught of the Ottomans against Central Europe an anachronism. But they did not care. Their vessels were sailing round the Cape of Good Hope to the Persian Gulf and the Indies. Not with the object of seizing Arabia, or of shaking the power of the Crescent. Their goals were Hindustan, Malacca, and Java. They wanted to dispossess the Portuguese. The Dutch flag soon replaced that of Portugal above the forts in the Malay Archipelago.

When the Hollanders landed in Sumatra, Celebes, and the Moluccas, they felt, as the Portuguese had felt before them, that they were entering a new world. These great islands were a warm garden, a polychrome intermingling of land and water. The mellow horizon was never without a landfall. Here conical islands projected; there mountain chains loomed over the sea, all thickly grown, the slopes slipping down into red, green, and golden waters. Those who were approaching land could smell its aromatic and effervescent waters miles upon miles away. The primeval forests were full of strange mammals, reptiles, and birds.

On many of the hitherto undiscovered islands, the life of the natives was still pleasant enough. As in the legendary Garden of Eden, the earth brought forth its fruits without any need for human labour. The gods of the air had planted the trees. There they stood, enormous in height, surrounded by a vigorous undergrowth, and the winds saw to the dissemination of their seed. Mango-trees flourished, grapefruits in plenty, palms abounded, among them the bountiful breadfruit tree. Then there was the durian, a huge spiny fruit with an offensive odour but a taste that is ambrosial to those who have acquired a liking for it. Coco-nut palms in profusion. In Sumatra, the natives had trained monkeys to climb the trees and throw down the huge nuts. Dates, bananas, pomegranates, and many other fruits grew without the trouble of cultivating them. The Javanese, as aforesaid, had long since been made acquainted the art of rice-growing. The damp, hot-house lands of the Malay Archipelago were not pestilent marshes like those of Africa. The Javanese climate was one of eternal summer, though troubled by daily rain-storms and frequent thunder. The countless island peaks gathered the vapours that the Indian Ocean gave off from its glowing mirror. Frequently the clouds discharged their waters, and the murmuring rain moistened the humus of the forests and washed down fertilizing mineral salts from the sides of the volcanoes. The foot-hills were terraced, and the waters were distributed to the terraces by canals and sluices. In this brown and variegated landscape, across which the heavy, grey clouds of the monsoon blew, rice prospered abundantly. In the "nursery," before it was planted out, the young rice-plant made emerald-green plots, contrasting strongly with the violet background of the hills so that the Hollanders were startled thereby. But for the prevailing heat, which made them sweat unceasingly, they might have believed themselves, at the river-mouths, to be among the green polders of their fertile native country.

Still there was a spirit of evil and of death abroad among the islands. Amid the tree-ferns, he displayed the symbols of his destructive supremacy, blocks of vitreous black obsidian. Or a crater which for hundreds of years had been quiescent exhaled whitish-yellow clouds of sulphurous vapour. This volcanic deity, who had created the whole region, could destroy it when the fancy seized him; and often he agitated it with earthquakes.

In Java he produced lakes of warm liquid mud. A porridge-like pale-blue milky substance boiled in great mountain cauldrons. Birds that winged their way amid the vapours rising from these cauldrons fell dead into the seething mass. "The volcano swallows birds," said the natives with a shudder, as they stood bare-footed, painfully enduring the heat emanating from the adjoining rocks. But the Dutch were not frightened. They had thick soles to their leather boots, so that their feet were not scorched. Their eyes were blue and steadfast, and were not to be intimidated by any sight of horror.

The Dutch were anything but dreamers, being distinguished in that from all other peoples. Distinguished from the Spaniards, the French, and the Germans, and especially from the Portuguese, who, when engaged in the most concrete activities, are accustomed to mingle in their undertakings the energy of dreams. The Dutch did not dream of fame or of world dominion; they did not dream the mystical dream of extending the realm of Christ. All they wanted was to pursue a profitable trade.

They were a calculating race, these men who had grown up under the damp and heavy skies of Amsterdam; black-clad Mynheers, such as Rembrandt has depicted for us. The noises of the seaport did not intrude into their council-chamber, where the long and empty table symbolized the greatness of the world. Outside, the seasons seemed to be perpetual autumn, and harsh winds blew falling leaves into the canals. There they sat smoking long clay pipes—"churchwardens," the English call them—while billet after billet of wood was consumed in the big tiled stove. Here the merchants reckoned up the capital that would be needed for the long voyage to the East Indies, for which the Portuguese had broken trail. Here shipping companies were founded, to run joint-stock enterprises. Weapons were shipped as well as merchandise. The captains insisted that their sailors must be armed. To begin with, of course, no one thought of war. But when the men in possession, the Portuguese owners of the archipelago, received the Dutchmen with cannon-fire, the merchants gave them a Roland for their Oliver. Then, just as the Dutch had learned in Brabant that Spaniards could be killed, so did they learn in the East Indies that the cousins of the Spaniards, the Portuguese, were likewise mortal men.

Business throve, and an increasing number of mercantile competitors equipped new fleets. Then, in 1602, the State took a hand in the game. It united the private competitors into an "imperialist" joint-stock company, giving these organized merchant-adventurers not only legal protection, but also sovereignty in the lands they were trading with and settling. On March 20, 1602, the Dutch East India Company was formed. It was not the first of its kind, for the English had been beforehand in the field, founding the English East India Company incorporated by Queen Elizabeth on December 31, 1600, under the title of

Pro-coffee engraving (about 1730)

The Townswoman's breakfast (1780)

Frau Kaffeeschwester and Herr Bierwanst (about 1790)

State coffee-pot of Augustus the Strong
(1701)

English coffee-pot (1681)

Coffee-mills, pot, and sugar bowls and tongs (Louis-Quinze)

"The Governors and Company of Merchants of London trading with the East Indies."

The relation of the Dutch East India Company to the homeland was that of a private trading association which had bought the monopoly of carrying on commerce eastward of the Cape of Good Hope. But on the great islands on either side of the Strait of Sunda, it ruled as a sultan who does not buy the produce of his subjects, but demands its surrender without compensation. The suzerainty of the rulers of Holland did not extend into these island realms. It was met half-way by the home-flowing current of gold, and, as long as this current continued, the Dutch government was glad to renew the rights of the company. Every twenty-one years a fresh charter was granted.

The Javanese had welcomed the coming of the Hollanders with songs and dances, but their joy was short-lived. The Dutch were ruthless exploiters, until, at length, the gentle Javanese were stimulated into showing their discontent. One morning the new rulers found that the palisades of a fort they had just built had been destroyed. The natives thought there were more than enough strongholds in the archipelago. Inquiry, trial, and judgment followed. The rebellious Javanese, it seemed, had been stirred up by English agents—and there can be no doubt that English ships, expectant, were anchored in the neighbourhood.

But before a rising could occur, the Dutch took measures to retain their grip on the islands. No chance of freedom was left for the natives. Soon there were no more Malays or Javanese who were not compelled to serve their European overlords.

The policy of the planters was determined by the directors of the Dutch East India Company in Amsterdam. The guiding motives were not the development of the crops in the archipelago, not an increase or diminution in this product or that, but the conditions that prevailed in the home exchanges. The amount of land put under cultivation was determined by the prices that ruled in Amsterdam. The Javanese could not understand this. For them it was too subtle a distinction that one year they must slave to produce a bumper crop, and next year must burn their harvest as useless. They knew nothing of the old rule in accordance with which "civilized" men strove to produce now a glut and now a deficit, now to increase supplies and now reduce them. The natives could not possibly understand this, and regarded as mere caprice what was the outcome of careful calculation.

Out of what did the Mynheers make their money? First of all from the clove-tree, a crop that the Javanese watered with their sweat; a laurel-like shrub of the myrtle family with red, fleshy calyces. The flowers were picked, and were then roasted over a slow fire. The heat developed the aromatic oil. Nothing could be more agreeable to the palate, the pharynx, the stomach. Vast quantities of the half-dried cloves were shipped to the colder climes of Europe. In those days people were much more hearty eaters than are their descendants. Oil of cloves promoted appetite and digestion.

Then there was pepper. Who would have thought that *Piper nigrum*, with its inconspicuous reddish berries, had golden roots? Man is a strange animal. Pepper burns his tongue; and yet, this substance, which works upon the taste-buds as if the sunlight had been concentrated on them by a burning-glass, is highly prized, and, being rare at that time, and, moreover, widely used as a preservative, commanded good prices.

But the Dutch found their main source of wealth in coffee. Before the arrival of the men from the Low Countries, hardly anyone in the Sunda Isles knew anything about coffee. At most, the Arab traders had brought supplies with them for their own daily use. No one had hitherto dreamed of planting it in the Malay Archipelago. It was to the Dutchman, Willem van Outborn, that the idea first occurred to start coffee-plantations in Java and Sumatra. The natives of those parts had hitherto drunk tea as a sobering drink, having learned its use from the Indians; as intoxicants they used arrack and palm-wine.

Certain Dutch sailors, anchoring off the coast of Arabia, had, in 1690, cut a few shoots from coffee-shrubs. At first they were brought to Amsterdam as curiosities, and planted in hot-houses, where, to the delight of botanical specialists, they flourished. Then arose the idea of conveying shoots to a country with a tropical climate. Thus it was that living plants were shipped from Arabia to Batavia. They took root in the hot soil, which was always damp and porous. As if the Sunda archipelago had only been waiting for this immigrant, the coffee-shrubs soon multiplied a hundredfold in Java. They grew abundantly, swiftly, and showed increasing fruitfulness.

Here was an unexpected revolution in natural processes. The Arabian plant, from which an aromatic drink could be made, was added to all the other spice-plants of the "spice islands." There was a revolution, too, in the market, when supplies began to arrive from new sources. As early as 1696, the Paris *Mercure galant* had spoken of the coffee-trade with the Arabs of the Levant as if it were a fixture for all time. "Coffee is harvested in the neighbourhood of Mecca. Thence it is conveyed to the port of Jidda. Thence it is shipped to Suez, and transported by camels to Alexandria. There, in the Egyptian warehouses, French and Venetian merchants buy the stock of coffee-beans they require for their respective homelands."

A few years later, Arabia occupied a second place in the production of coffee. This commodity was no longer shipped by way of Suez, but took the long sea-route round the Cape of Good Hope. It was carried in Dutch bottoms, not being touched by any other hands than those of the Hollanders from the time it was shipped in Batavia to the time of being landed at Rotterdam. From 1700 onwards, for many, many years, the Dutch East Indies controlled the price of coffee in the world market.

The Dutch Indies became a stable concern. What the Teutons of the folk-migrations had failed to achieve (the occupation of any tropical or sub-tropical land: for instance, the permanent settlement of the northern coast of Africa), was now achieved in the Malay Archipelago by the northwestern Teutons. True, the Netherlanders who dwelt under equatorial skies were compelled to abandon their industrious habits. They could not go on working as they had been used to work at home. For persons of their build, this would have been fatal in so hot a climate.

The lean Malays and Javanese, acclimatized to the tropics, worked for the Dutch. Their masters built themselves habitations that recalled those of the homeland, yet met the special demands of a tropical clime. They were constructed of stone, with a wide veranda, and set upon mushroom-shaped stone "stilts," so that the air circulated freely between the floor of the house and the earth, while serpents and other venomous beasts were kept at a distance. The house proper consisted exclusively of dwelling quarters. Whatever might pollute the air—kitchens, bathrooms, and store-rooms—stood apart in out-houses. During the frequent, heavy rains, access to these out-houses could be gained by paved and covered ways. There were no ornaments on the

ROASTING COFFEE IN AN OPEN PAN
(*Dutch East Indies*)

walls, no pictures, nor anything else that could break the surface, for in the shadow of such objects poisonous spiders would make their nests, and mosquitoes would lurk.

The white lords of the islands stirred for only a few hours every day. They spent most of their time in reclining chairs, with hardwood frames, rattan seats and backs, and prolonged arms on which they rested their outspread legs. Although they ate, and continue to eat, more heartily than is wholesome for white men in the tropics, they could not indulge their appetites as freely as they had been wont to do at home. As for drowsiness, they had a means for keeping that at bay. Mohammed had extolled it long ago! For the lords of the isles were not merely traders in coffee; they had learned to consume the beverage themselves. These heavy-footed children of the mouths of the Rhine and of the Schelde drank it gladly in their homeland, and even more gladly in the tropics; for the beverage was a magic potion which, in the north, warmed their bodies, and in the tropics relieved them from the

lethargy the climate is likely to induce in whites. Of course they drank
a good deal else besides coffee, being blond and vigorous Nordics with
a confirmed taste for beer. The fleets of coffee-freighters, sailing southward and westward to the Cape of Good Hope and then northward
to the Netherlands, often spoke outward-bound ships laden with beer.
Not ordinary beer of the Low Countries, which would have gone sour
beneath the tropical sun. It was Brunswick beer, specially prepared for
use in hot climes by the nearest neighbours and kin of the wealthy
Hollanders. Who had discovered it? A German chemist, in the same
year that Columbus discovered America, a chemist who had been moved
by the desire to brew a beer that would withstand the heat of the
tropics. Christian Mumme was his name; and the beverage is still known
as "*Mumme*," or in English as "mum"—a thick and sugary malt-beer,
which, stored in tin-lined cases, can be safely shipped across the Line.

For the first time in the history of coffee, its free-born aroma was
mingled with the heavy scent of the sweat of slave labour. The Arabian
peasants had been freemen, who, three thousand feet above sea-level,
cultivated the "fruit of eternal wakefulness." "O coffee!" said Abd el
Kader, apostrophizing the sacred beverage, "you, friend of Allah, dis-
peller of sorrow! You provide health, wisdom, and truth, and you resemble gold because wherever you are obtainable the best of men
will be found!"

Coffee now resembled gold in another fashion. It was increasing
slavery on earth.

Hitherto the Malays had done forced labour for their native princes
alone. Now they underwent a harder lot. The Hollanders compelled
princes to let their arable land on lease; the inhabitants, bound to the
soil, went with the land, and became bond-slaves under harsher masters.

Often enough the native princes as well as the lords of the Dutch East
India Company gained much money. At the beginning of the eighteenth
century, throughout western Europe, literature and custom made the
demand for coffee exceed the supply. Under the stimulus of rising
prices, the Dutch and the Mohammedan princes who were their de-
pendents greatly extended the cultivation of coffee in the Dutch Indies. But as soon as the European market began to be sated, the old
fears of falling prices and over-production made the Dutch planters

destroy the coffee-crop. The natives were incapable of grasping fine distinctions. Imagining that their masters' wrath was directed against the plants as such, they were not content to cut down the shrubs before the berries ripened, but uprooted them as if to drive out demons. Thereupon the poor wretches were executed as malefactors, and thus new terrors were the fruit of the silent coffee-shrub. Blacker and bitterer than ever became the beverage!

Then, as the Dutch had come like a tidal wave sweeping away the Portuguese, so rumours of a new tidal wave came across the seas to the ears of the mighty Dutch. The ocean had given birth to a Triton. The North Sea had been in labour, and Britain, the future lord of the seas (and of many lands), began to take a leading place among the nations of the north. The young marine giant was quick to challenge the naval supremacy of Holland. The young leviathan had founded an East India Company two years before the Lowlanders, and now challenged the Dutch. The Navigation Act of 1651 was tightened up. "No foreign product shall be conveyed to an English harbour in a foreign ship!"

This was a blow directed, not against the produce of the Dutch colonies, but against the shipping trade of Amsterdam. Under the ægis of the Navigation Act, British shipbuilding was greatly intensified; nor was it long before these "peaceful traders" began to carry artillery. Along the distant ocean routes between London and Amsterdam on the one hand, and on the other, the Cape of Good Hope and thence across the Indian Ocean to the Malay Archipelago, sea-fights were fought. Huge piles of coffee lay in the Javanese store-houses, coffee that could no longer be conveyed to Amsterdam across waters that had become unsafe. Still, wars do not last for ever, and a swift frigate was dispatched from Rotterdam to Batavia conveying orders to destroy the accumulated stores, lest, when peace was signed, a glut in the European market should force down the price. This decision had been made in the board-room of the Dutch East India Company; but the planters, who lived in the sunshine, amid tropical vegetation, did not believe in the wisdom of the European exchanges. Often enough, before, they had obeyed the commands of their directors; this time they proved unruly. Perhaps they were afraid of arousing a revolt among the natives by ordering a fresh destruction of the crops; perhaps, for once, they had come to consider that wealth consisted of goods and not of a variable medium of exchange. Anyhow, they refused to obey. Immediately peace had been signed, they shipped enormous quantities of coffee to the Amsterdam market. Prices came down with a rush, and the brokers were ruined. Never had coffee been so cheap in Holland as it was in the year 1782.

12

Coffee and Absolutism

URING the first decade after its introduction into western Europe, coffee was no more than an article of fancy; it had not yet come to play an important part in economic life. Not until consumption and production had simultaneously increased to an enormous extent, did this "fancy" compel the state to take it into account. Coffee had become an important commodity; it stimulated the interest of States and potentates who were able, and upon whom it was incumbent, to protect goods and trade.

The attitude of the states might vary, but obviously they had to assume one attitude or another. No matter whether these states were republics, parliamentary monarchies, or absolute monarchies after the model dear to Hobbes, they were forced to canalize and regulate the influx of goods from lands many of which were new to history.

The most interesting (I do not say the most successful) directions were those taken by such regulations in France, the earliest of truly modern States. French absolutism, though it went bankrupt in the end, was the first form of government to attempt the planning of a nationalist economy.

The economic director of France in the age of Louis XIV was Colbert.

Philosophers and reformers, especially in the political domain, are not guided exclusively by the intention of reaching some particular goal. Unquestionably they are moved also by the longing to avoid certain things regarded as undesirable. The vigorous industrial France that Colbert wished to create was, in a measure, to be the antithesis of Spain and the counterpart of the Netherlands. By the discovery of America and the extensive import of the precious metals, Spain had become the richest country in Europe, and had acquired hegemony over half the globe. But within a few decades it became plain that gold and silver were not bearing fruit in Spain. The Spanish grandees, whose eyes were not directed towards worldly aims and whose bodies were lean and ascetic, despised that arduous toil without which gold and silver remain barren dross. No doubt there were Spanish merchants, able and successful ones; but they were few. The Spaniards produced a far greater number of avaricious conquistadores, high-handed robbers; for people are always more ready to rob those with whom they have no intimate relationships. The horticultural metaphor of the "frutti di arte monetaria" could have occurred only to an Italian. The Spaniard was temperamentally unable to devote himself affectionately and laboriously to an occupation that seemed to him degrading, to the laborious cultivation of money and wealth. Wealth had come from the Americas in plenty, thanks to the (perhaps?) undesirable discoveries of Christopher Columbus, and promptly the nation in which every beggar was an aristocrat began to doubt the value of this wealth. Must not its possession be stabilized by labour and by wearisome toil? But the offspring of the Goths and the Iberians refused to toil. They were willing to fight or to beg; to live by plunder, and if no plunder were to be had, they would draw their belts tight.

The Spanish example taught Colbert the valuelessness of wealth that is not rooted in labour. Turning his eyes northward, Colbert saw the desirable counterpart, the happiness of the diligent Netherlands. This good fortune of theirs was not due merely to the winning of a war and to the control of the mouths of certain great rivers; these were merely the preconditions of the rise of the Dutch to wealth and power. The merit and the good fortune of the Dutch were that they were also, and simultaneously, manufacturers and traders.

The basis of the French national character seemed to Colbert just as good as that of the Dutch. Frenchmen (who are diligent enough, though not diligent to excess—and only inclined to work so long as work pleases them) were sufficiently skilled. No more cunning fingers than theirs could be found for any kind of handicraft. These fingers might be usefully employed at work ranging from silk-spinning and silk-weaving to the making of steel. Colbert, therefore, began to invest money in industry. Manufacturing was not only to provide wares for

export, but also to relieve the cancer of unemployment in France—
the chief cause of the prevailing poverty. The establishment of factories in barren lands would be "un moyen assuré de retirer ceux qui
s'y appliqueroient de l'oisiveté honteuse, dans laquelle ils estoient
plongés"; and, at the same time, these factories would be instruments for
providing universal plenty.

Colbert's disastrous error was his belief that he could promote popular welfare in a land where "national production" was able to advantage
only the absolute monarchy; but, most unfortunately, most tragically,
he was too short-sighted to see as much. His attitude towards the monarch, like that of all his contemporaries, was one of Oriental adulation.
Louis XIV's insistence that he himself was the state did not seem to
Colbert hyperbolical, but tantamount to the expression of a natural
law. To his way of thinking, there could perfectly well exist a human
being to whose sublime intelligence the state might turn in every
emergency—so that this man would not merely symbolize the French
state, but would in very truth be the state. The Roi Soleil was such a
semi-divine being, such a Pharaoh. Colbert was not moved by a servile
spirit of flattery, but by genuine conviction, when he wrote to King
Louis: "Il faut, Sire, se taire, admirer, remercier Dieu tous les jours de
nous avoir fait naistre sous le règne d'un roy tel que vostre Majesté qui
n'aura d'autres bornes de sa puissance que sa volonté."

Thus a fruitful commercial policy would mean increase of exports
in conjunction with the greatest possible restriction of imports. The
result would be a steady influx of money. To facilitate the circulation
of goods in the homeland, internal customs dues, which had hitherto
been imposed at the gates of every town and at the crossings of every
river, were reduced. On the other hand, the tariffs payable at the
frontiers of the country were greatly increased.

Nothing must be imported into France which France could herself
produce—no Italian or Flemish manufactured wares, for instance. Or,
if their importation were not absolutely prohibited, high duties would
have to be paid. But articles which could not be produced on French
soil were also taxed at the frontier. Tropical spices had to pay customs. So had coffee.

In the outlook of the mercantilists, the world consisted of countless items of goods. Only to outward semblance did mercantilism lean towards the notion of national autarchy, which is far from "thinking in commodities" because, from the start, the autarchists refuse to look upon a national economy as a part of the world economy, a part which has to come into relationship with the world economy through foreign trade. Colbert, therefore, was not an autarchist, but a mercantilist. If he put a high import duty upon coffee, this was only as a means of revenue. He had no inclination whatever towards such national-pedagogic opinions as those that were later to be uttered by J. G. Fichte. Nor had Louis XIV's minister for finance anything to do with the campaign of the doctors against the daily use of coffee as a beverage. On the contrary, when a governmental edict of that period made any reference to coffee, the drink was described as wholesome. A monarchy had no reason for declaring a commodity poisonous when its sale proved an abundant source of revenue.

The absolutism of the baroque period, whose aim in all political matters was to centralize as far as possible, toyed, in the economy of the country as well, with the idea of monopoly. Monopoly could control prices. One who controlled prices, could also, if there should be no falling-off in consumption, count upon a fixed revenue. Yet there seemed to be excellent reasons why the state should not itself control such a monopoly, but sell it to an entrepreneur.

The sale of monopolies to farmers-general became almost indispensable when the mercantilist state was in urgent need of ready money owing to reverses on the field of battle. In the year 1692, France was in such a position. During the naval encounter of La Hogue, the French fleet under de Tourville was defeated and dispersed by the combined British and Dutch fleets under Admirals Russell and van Allemonde; two days later Admiral Rooke destroyed thirteen of the French men-of-war and some transports. The armies of the Grand Alliance—Britain, Holland, Austria, Spain, and Saxony—were taking vengeance for the devastation wrought in the Palatinate by the troops of General Mélac. Louis was in dire need of fresh funds for the carrying on of the war. Colbert had died ten years before, a disappointed man. Perhaps had he still lived, some better financial scheme might have been excogitated than the one which was now adopted by the French monarchy in its scarcity of funds. A monopoly of coffee was announced, and was farmed out to a wealthy citizen of Paris, reputedly a banker, François Damame by name.

This first coffee monopoly ceded by the state to a private individual is of interest to the history of civilization. From its text, that of the *edit du Roy*, "portant règlement pour la vente et la distribution du café," or, rather, from the preamble to the document, we learn in so many words that the king intended "d'en tirer quelque secours dans l'occurrence de la présente guerre."

"His Majesty, [the document declared] after listening to the advice of the Council of State, has granted to Maître François Damame the exclusive privilege, for three years from January 1, 1692, of selling coffee, tea, chocolate, and the materials out of which they are made; likewise cocoa and vanilla; in all the provinces, towns, and domains of the realm of France.

"From the aforesaid day onward, the Sieur Damame has the right of enjoying all the fruits of this traffic, of seeing to it that his privilege shall be sustained and administered; of granting commissions and appointing employees according to his own will and pleasure.

"His Most Christian Majesty consequently forbids everyone to participate in the provision or in the sale by wholesale or retail of the aforesaid commodities without a special permit from the lessee Damame.

"His Most Christian Majesty ordains that all merchants and shopkeepers who have coffee whether in beans or powdered, or tea or chocolate, in store, shall immediately make a return of the amount of the same. In Monsieur Damame's offices, thereupon, the aforesaid wares will be weighed, investigated, marked, labelled, and sealed. Then the aforesaid wares will be stored in safe warehouses. Anyone who evades this edict concerning the notification of coffee, tea, etc., whether it be the owner or his assistants, will be liable to a fine of 1500 livres. The unnotified stores and the fines will accrue to the lessee Damame; with the exception that the informer will receive a third.

"His Majesty prohibits the import of coffee, tea, and chocolate by any other ports than Marseille and Rouen—except in the case of such quantities as may be seized as prizes of war, and which it may be expedient to land at the nearest possible harbour. His Majesty, however, warns any possible offenders against the smuggling of the aforesaid wares into the kingdom to the detriment of the lessee Damame.

"His Majesty forbids the lessees and owners of coaches, wagons, or boats, and also forbids porters, to move any of the aforesaid substances from place to place without having received a permit from the lessee Damame. As to any who may act in default of such a permit, not only will the goods be impounded, but their horses, harness, carriages, wagons, and boats will likewise be forfeited. All merchants, shopkeepers, and purveyors must write bills of lading on which the commodities they are sending are specified.

"Furthermore, His Majesty grants to the lessee François Damame the right to appoint as many salaried employees as he thinks fit in all towns of the realm, at fairs and markets, camps and barracks, with the army on active service, and also at court and in the household of his Royal Majesty. These employees will be concerned with the sale and provision of the aforesaid beverages, and will enjoy identical privileges with those granted by His Majesty to the employees of other lessees of royal privileges.

"The coffee that is sold may not be mixed with oats, peas or beans, or any other adulterant. The same applies to tea, cocoa, and chocolate, which must be sold pure. Anyone who adulterates them becomes liable to flogging and to a fine of 1500 livres.

"His Most Christian Majesty issues strict instructions to Lieutenant-General de la Reynie, governor of Paris, as well as to the local governors throughout the realm, to see to it that this edict shall everywhere be read aloud, published, and posted, and that action shall be taken accordingly."

Colbert, as financial adviser to King Louis, had put a very considerable duty on coffee, but he had seen to it that this duty was not so high as to check consumption. François Damame, the coffee monopolist, was an amateur in financial matters, and was already insolvent when the king granted him the monopoly. Besides, the concession was deprived of all value because, by an edict simultaneously issued, the price of a pound of coffee was fixed at the dizzy height of four livres. Six months later, Damame came to the king wringing his hands, and begging that the gap should be bridged between the old price, 28 sous the pound, and the new. "There has been a terrible falling-off in consumption; most of the former drinkers of coffee have abandoned its use. Unless a change is made, coffee will no longer be drunk." His Majesty would do well to think of the setback to his own revenue; for the declining demand that would be the ruin of Monsieur Damame would affect the royal budget as well. The amateur financiers at court could not fail to see that they had made a blunder. The price of coffee was now fixed at fifty sous the pound.

But it was too late! Exactly a year and a half after the monopoly had been granted, François Damame had to retire as lessee of the royal privilege. The excessive price had ruined the monopoly; the unhappy monopolist, by helping to finance the king's war, had lost his own campaign. He begged of Louis XIV the favour to be released from his privilege. "We have recognized," runs the unctuous wording of His Majesty's revocation, "that the heavy expenses that Monsieur Damame has incurred in order to make use of his privilege have deprived him of the advantages which might otherwise have accrued to him. We have, further, examined the offers made to us by other dealers; it has been suggested to us that we should fix the import duty at any height we please, and that we should agree to liberate the trade in coffee from the tribute that was payable to Monsieur Damame." The merchants might very well recommend free competition, even if there was to be a high import duty and a high price, for they had not to pay the cost of supervising a monopoly.

The import duty on coffee was now, therefore, increased by ten sous the pound. But at the same time the monopoly was abolished, and free trade in coffee was allowed within the realm, as the traders had wished. By the year 1700 there was such an increase in consumption that the crown regretted having done away with the monopoly!

A quarter of a century later, a second monopoly was established. Louis XIV was dead. The condition of national finances was so deplorable that in a present-day state it would have led to public bankruptcy. Still, the absolute monarchy was able to hide the disastrous situation for another fifty years. Louis XV conceded the tobacco monopoly to the French West India Company, which colonized the French settlements on the American mainland and in the West Indies. When the affairs of the company were in a bad way, he tried to help it out of its difficulties by granting to it, in addition, a coffee monopoly that was even more comprehensive than the one which had been conceded to Monsieur Damame.

Lest the new monopoly should instantly become unpopular, the top price of coffee was fixed at five livres per pound. Smuggling was made punishable by flogging, branding, fines, and banishment. The French West India Company was given unlimited powers of espionage on French soil. "The agents and inspectors of the West India Company will be henceforward allowed to search all stores, shops, villas, and houses, even the residences and palaces of the king, as well as the domiciles of the nobles, monasteries, guild-buildings, in a word every place that has hitherto been regarded as privileged. . . . We therefore command the administrators of the aforesaid domiciles, including those of the royal palaces, the venerable priors of the monasteries, and the masters of all guild-buildings whatsoever to open their doors to the aforesaid inspectors whenever these may demand entry. . . . In case of resistance, the inspectors are hereby allowed to open the doors with the aid of locksmiths they may bring with them."

But even this monopoly, with its grievous invasion of civic freedom, was useless to the concessionnaires. Like Damame, the chiefs of the West India Company found that the costs of supervising the coffee trade exceeded the profits. Within a few years it was necessary to return to a regime of freedom.

One who studies the influence that, towards the year 1700, French coffee-houses had on the social life of the country, will be inclined to envy the coffee-house keepers. Had they not an abundance of guests and consumers every hour of the day? In fact, however, their lot was by no means a happy one. The monarchy hovered like a vulture over every means of livelihood. The predatory policy that had been characteristic of Louis XIV in world commerce, was exercised by this monarch on the small scale likewise. If in Paris or in the provinces an industry collapsed, one could generally guess that the royal tax-gatherers had been busily at work.

The coffee-house keepers of Paris belonged to a guild of persons who called themselves "maîtres-distillateurs," or, in more modern paraphrase, "refreshment-providers." Refreshing drinks already existed in great numbers, ranging from lemonade to the stronger sorts of alcoholic liquors.

Anyone who wanted to belong to this guild, must take out a licence. The licences were already drafted when it occurred to King Louis that the Society of the Lemonade-Sellers had no fixed rules, or was in need of new rules. For the official sanctioning of this change of rules, His Majesty demanded three hundred livres. Naturally the lemonade-sellers did not pay; whereupon King Louis waxed angry and sent a sheriff's officer to the guild-house. This official announced that next day he would unceremoniously confiscate all the maîtres-distillateurs' supplies unless he were immediately paid one hundred and fifty livres. The lemonade-sellers gave way.

Yet the maîtres-distillateurs had good reason for resisting the new ordinance. The change of rules promulgated by His Majesty opened vast opportunities for humbug. Henceforward anyone who paid a sufficient sum to the state treasury could call himself a distillateur. He need not show any proof of capacity, any certificate of apprenticeship. The king needed money, and the money of the unskilled was worth just as much in the king's treasury as the money of the skilled.

A certain Audiger, a "cook and confectioner by God's grace" like many more that existed by the same title in France, writes with much bitterness: "Two hundred ignoramuses were yesterday granted the right to style themselves masters of the craft, at a fee of fifty crowns per head, though they were drawn from the dregs of the people. Had my advice been asked, I could have drafted rules for an excellent Parisian guild to which all respectable persons in the trade would wish to belong. I should have appointed one hundred masters of the art, worthy practitioners of our profession; I should have amalgamated the guild of the lemonade-sellers with the guild of the sugar-bakers. That would have brought His Majesty a sum of 100,000 francs. Now he has received much less than this, while the town has been flooded with humbugs."

Two hundred new "distillateurs" had been added to the fifty already in existence. These two hundred and fifty had had to buy from the king a licence to practise their occupation. This licence gave them a measure of protection, for no one who was not a member of the guild could sell lemonade, liqueurs, or coffee.

"The Coffee Tree," Leipzig. The relief above the door was commissioned by Augustus the Strong

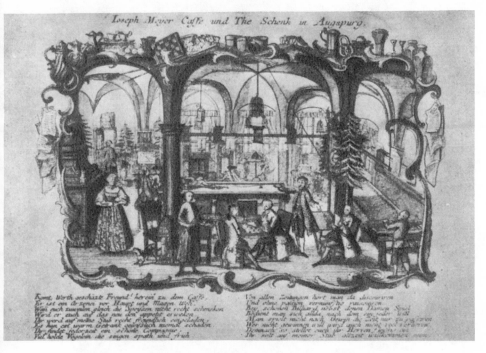

Plan for Augsburg coffee-house in the Viennese style

Coffee and the military gentlemen

Coffee out of doors (about 1850)

While most refreshing beverages showed a seasonal consumption, the consumption of coffee went on increasing throughout the year to such an extent that His Majesty's attention was drawn to the matter. In the year 1704 Louis XIV was once more short of funds. He looked round uneasily for a chance of raising the wind. He regretted having, a few years before, granted the lemonade-sellers a licence at fifty crowns per head. He made up his mind that every one of them should now pay him a more adequate sum, and, from the height of absolutism whence he radiated his beams, he decreed without more ado the closing down of the guild. With this thunder-clap, of course, the rights of its individual members were extinguished. The previous licensees got together, not to resist openly, since they could do nothing against the halberds and harquebuses of His Majesty. They only assembled to implore the king that he would allow them once more to buy the privileges they had previously enjoyed.

His Majesty played the ungracious. One of the rascally intendants who acted in his name declared that the crown intended to restrict the number of lemonade-sellers. This was a proposal not necessarily disagreeable to the trade, as a whole, though it might be undesirable to those who would be crowded out! For this proof of double-edged grace, which was warranted to restrict competition, the treasury must be promptly indemnified with the sum of two hundred thousand livres. The percentages payable to the intendants were not counted in. The lemonade-sellers agreed to the exaction, having no stomach for a fight. How lucrative must have been their business—especially the sale of coffee—since they could afford to put up such a sum!

The elderly tyrant's appetite for money was only stimulated by his easy victory. In July 1705 he repealed the edict of 1704, and demanded from the guild payment for a third charter. To mask his rapacity, he conceded to the lemonade-sellers certain new privileges: they might sell gin, might supply cocoa and vanilla, might offer chocolate in cups. The members of the guild agreed, but they were deceived in their calculations. By the year 1706 they still owed the king as much as forty thousand livres. There were fresh reprisals and visits from sheriff's officers. But the amount needed was not forthcoming. Then His Majesty again broke his royal word, and proceeded to issue a new type of licence, making the occupation hereditary. Well, it would have been only decent to pay back to the lemonade-sellers the one hundred and sixty thousand livres he had already had from them. He looked round for an intermediary, who could get a share of the profits from the new licences if he would put up the money that was immediately needed. His Majesty had in mind to issue five hundred licences. But the fish were shy. It had been bruited abroad that the monarch intended to suppress the trade; those who were engaged in it sought other occupations; and, instead of the expected five hundred lemonade-sellers, only one hundred and forty were to be found. The guild no longer existed, and the new licences were unsaleable. Anyone to whom the guild had been indebted now dunned individual members. Things went ill with those from whom the sunshine of the king's favour had been so manifestly withdrawn. At length, around Christmas 1713, a royal edict re-established the old position, and the guild was once more put upon a legal footing.

This story of the lemonade-sellers (they were mainly, though not exclusively, coffee-house keepers) was dug up from the archives by Alfred Franklin, who gathered such a wealth of information concerning old-time Paris. It gives us an instructive cross-section view of the position of the bourgeoisie. We see in it one of the thousand causes of the French Revolution—not the principal cause, of course, but a typical and significant one.

The Literary Century

THE eighteenth century may be described as the literary century.

In this epoch it happened for the first time that the domain of literature ceased to be restricted to the world of books, extending its realm unresisted through every sphere of life.

During the eighteenth century the conquest of literature in all departments of existence was effected with the suddenness and violence of a volcanic eruption. Every love-letter was penned in a literary style; every scientific discovery was presented in a literary form. The physician, while taking his patient's pulse at the bed-side, conversed in the tongue of letters. Religion became literature. The revolution that was approaching heralded its coming not only in the field of social transformation but also, and above all, as literature.

Hence the significance of coffee for the eighteenth century. People living in this unmystical period (in contradistinction to those of the baroque era) were prone to self-mockery, frequently drawing attention to the fact. Coffee, declared the cynics, equips with intelligence vast numbers of persons who would otherwise have never committed their thoughts to paper:

> To those of little wit
> Coffee is a brightener.
> The most barren of authors
> Is thereby made fertile.
> It has in it a virtue
> Strengthening the memory,
> So that a pedant can talk,
> Without rhyme or reason,
> Spouting fable and history.

Coffee works a miracle,
Sharpening the brains of the stupid.
No author refreshed thereby
Need languish in silence.
Coffee's strength and virtue
Double the memory.
Every drop empowers us
To gabble without pause,
And, discarding the crutches of rhyme,
To spout fable as history.

In his *Lettres persanes*, Montesquieu writes sarcastically: "Great is the vogue of coffee in Paris. In the houses where it is supplied, the proprietors know how to prepare it in such a way that it gives wit to those who drink it. At any rate, when they depart, all of them believe themselves to be at least four times as brainy as when they entered the doors."

The aspect of the eighteenth century is summarized for us in the word "rococo." It is a basic fact of the literary century that all those who lived in it were under the spell of the rococo. With them it had become a primary article of faith that a thing did not begin to exist until it existed in the reason, and until it could be expressed in black upon white. Could there have been two persons more obviously different than Louis XV and Voltaire? What a contrast there was, once more, between a cocotte who picked up her customers at a coffee-house and the Marquise de Pompadour. Yet the four of them had this much in common, that restrained expression (of which the book is but a symbol) was dominant in every gesture of their lives. Just as in earlier epochs religion had been supreme, its sap rising into the finest ramifications of daily life, so in this century of the rococo did the aroma of literature overpower all others. Historians declare that members of the French nobility must have been extraordinarily foolish not to take warning when they watched a performance of Beaumarchais' *Le mariage de Figaro*. But the historians are wrong. Notwithstanding the severance of the classes that this drama pointed out, all members of Beaumarchais' audience were united in the recognition that they were contemplating the performance of an extremely witty play, a fine piece of literature!

The rococo created an outlook on life that unified even those who were greatly at odds as regards their several views on politics or philosophy. The Encyclopædists, though they were looking forward to the coming of a generation of rationalists and were trying to guide their contemporaries into new paths, were likewise men of the rococo, wearing knee-breeches, pigtails, and swords. Love of God and atheism, monarchical loyalty and republicanism, wore the same clothes and rubbed shoulders amicably one with another. Expression, conversation, and amenity were for all. The magical fumes emanating from the kitchen of the Black Apollo mitigated the clash of conflicting opinion, and thus wrought the aforesaid miracle. All the sayings of the period had the strange aromatic flavour of coffee:

> This gentle vapour that rises in clouds
> Will develop for us, la, la,
> Our imagination, tum, tum,
> To produce a fine work.

The sense of literary self-appreciation was equally strong in all these persons, whether they had espoused the cause of reaction, or the cause of progress. It has been usual to describe the eighteenth century as non-moral, although our most important social and progressive ideas have come down to us from it. Perhaps the reproach is justified. One reproach, however, is not justified. We have no right to decry the eighteenth century as an age of weaklings. People are apt to regard the rococo epoch as effeminate, because in its frills and furbelows, in its hooped petticoats and gallantries, it showed greater extravagance than had ever been known before. Nevertheless a gallant period is always virile—virile to excess, for gallantry is an arduous sport.

The eighteenth century excelled all previous centuries in its capacity for enjoyment. Now enjoyment is active and virile, is anything but passive. The enjoyments of those days made great demands upon body, soul, and spirit. One who regards the men of the rococo period as slothful is suffering from an illusion which is the outcome of the social consciousness of our own time. We, avowedly, can neither understand nor approve the trend of eighteenth-century activities. Gallantry was a test of patience. The eighteenth-century gallant had to key himself up to his amusements, and can no more be described as indolent than can one who, for a wager, plays dominoes for twenty-four hours at a stretch.

All that has been written about the "softness" of the rococo is belied
by the characterization of the period written by the Marquise du
Deffand, towards the close of her long life: "We knew in those days
how to live and to die. We concealed our infirmities. If one had an
attack of gout, one did not hang one's head and proclaim the fact to
the world; one was careful to conceal one's troubles; one accepted ruin
without changing countenance—just as a 'good loser' at the dice shows
no emotion. If one had accepted an invitation to the hunt, one went
thither, even though sick unto death. It was considered better to die
at a dance or in the theatre than in bed. We enjoyed life; and when
the hour of leave-taking struck, we felt it behoved us to say farewell
with a good grace."

These fine phrases reveal to us how much of the heroic there was
behind expression, conversation, and amenity; they tell us what sort of
human beings were those who were mentally and physically invigorated
by the magical vapours from Araby.

The idea of shifting the centre of gravity of social life from the home
to a more public *milieu*, which Coltelli-Couteau, the founder of the
Café Procope, had created, was infectious. By 1720, there were three
hundred and eighty coffee-houses in the town of Paris. In these numerous sluices, reservoirs, chambers of the spirit, life itself became
transformed both in content and in form.

What sort of company foregathered in Parisian coffee-houses? "The
coffee-houses," we read in a pamphlet of the day, "are visited by respectable persons of both sexes. We see among them very various types:
men-about-town, coquettish women, abbés, warriors, country bumpkins, nouvellistes,[1] officers, the parties to a law-suit, drinkers, gamesters,
parasites, adventurers in the field of love or industry, young men of
fortune, elderly lovers, braggarts, spurious heroes, dilettantes, men of
letters—in a word, an unending series of persons." The society that frequented these places was not really a "society," for it lacked the
homogeneity which is the basic principle of such—but this very lack
of homogeneity was a large part of its charm. Never before had the

---

[1] "Nouvellistes" were not writers of "nouvelles," but people who told the latest
news, moved either by vanity or by the desire of gain.

French assembled in such a fashion. A café was a sea of human beings, and to bathe therein was an adventure.

Among the coffee-houses that had this new feature of "being open to persons of all kinds and at any moment," there were, of course, conventicles interspersed—coffee-houses that made special appeal to certain groups of interests. If we are to believe Alfred Franklin's detailed study of old Paris, the Café Bourette was chiefly frequented by men of letters, the Café Anglais by actors and by the lovers of the Comédie Française, while the Café Alexandre was the meeting-place of the devotees of music. The Café des Armes d'Espagne was a favourite haunt of army officers, while the Café des Arts, then close to the Palais Royal, was frequented by opera singers and their friends. Close at hand was the Café des Aveugles, where the music was provided by an orchestra of blind performers. This was a favourite hunting-ground of prostitutes. Prudhomme, in his *Miroir de l'ancien et du nouveau Paris* relates that these wenches were in league with the flower-girls, who could sell the same bouquet eight times over before midnight. Then the partners divided the amount of which the unsuspecting country bumpkins had been cozened. There is nothing new under the sun!

Many of these coffee-houses had a history, as well as a circle of regular customers. This remark applies, for instance, to the Café Bourette, whose proprietress, Charlotte Bourette-Curée, was a literary phenomenon. Under the title *Muse limonadière*, she published two volumes of verses, which contained, not only dedicatory poems, but also the answers to these penned by persons of high station. For example, Madame Bourette-Curée sent an ode to Frederick the Great. "When I was composing it," she wrote, "I was seized by such a frenzy of poetic vigour that I transcended myself. Enthusiasm is the author of these lines, rather than myself. In return for this successful masterpiece I received from the distant north such flowery compliments as are heard more often in the Orient than here." The "flowery compliments" consisted of a gold-brocade handbag sent her by the King of Prussia. Grimm, the Encyclopædist, was a trifle annoyed about the matter. "We have here a cafetière whose head has been turned by a craze for writing verses. She indites poems to all and sundry, but unfortunately they are almost invariably bad. An exception may perhaps be made of her ode to the king of Prussia, which contains some of the best verses she has ever penned. Some of them, indeed, seem so good that one doubts that she herself composed them." When we learn that Fontenelle bestowed upon this Madame Bourette-Curée the complete edition of his works, that the Duke of Sèvres became godfather to her child, and that Voltaire one day presented her with a costly decanter with the accompanying goblets (he had paid sixty livres for it), we cannot but suspect that these gentlemen were trying to purchase immunity from the lady's flattering verses! Voltaire, cynical as usual, said as much in a letter.

Now let us turn to the Café des Boucheries, where the theatrical managers could recruit their casts, for the place was a sort of actors' exchange. "Here one can hire queens, and lovers of both sexes; noble heads of families who believe it to be incumbent upon them to speak the live-long day with tears in their voices and with tremulous hands; here can be found the impudent lackey, with features to fit his part; here, too, can be found the modest confidant, as useless in real life as he is in the bad plays that he makes still worse by his acting. . . ."

The frequenters formed a strange mishmash, if we are to believe Mercier, who has given rather a spiteful account of the history of this café. Mediocrities plumed themselves like peacocks, telling of the salvos of applause "earned last October in an out-of-the-way corner of France where the inhabitants hardly knew how to speak French."

How cordial were the greetings exchanged when old friendships were renewed—though the cordiality often rang false! One had come by diligence from Roubaix, another from Marseille and "was leaving next morning for Strasbourg, where he expected to earn a better salary." Two hours later, gnashing his teeth, he accepted the pitiful offer made him by a manager from Toulouse. "Why the devil," he would ask himself that evening in his hotel, "since my destination was Toulouse, did I come all this way north to Paris?"

The Café Cuisinier was frequented by connoisseurs and persons of taste, who tried various blends. At the Café Defoy, near the Palais Royal, ices were served as well as coffee. The Café Frary, in the rue Montmartre, was famous. The Café Hardy was extolled for its déjeuners. The most celebrated of all the Parisian cafés of this period was the Café Parnasse, run by the Widow Laurent. This café vied with the Café Procope for the honour of having the largest number of poets among its regular guests. "He regards himself as a person of importance because he goes every day to the Procope," said Voltaire maliciously of a nincompoop called Linant.

The Café de la Régence was a favourite haunt of Saint-Foix, Rousseau, Marmontel, Le Sage, and Friedrich Melchior Grimm; it was renowned for its tranquillity and its contemplative atmosphere. "There," writes Le Sage, "in a large mirrored hall, you will find a dozen or so of persons who, with deadly earnest, are playing draughts or chess. They are seated at marble-topped tables, and are surrounded by silent spectators who watch them closely. So profound is the silence that it is broken only by the gentle click of the pieces when they are moved. To my way of thinking such a café might well be called the Café Horus, for the first impression a newcomer gets of the place is that it must be a vast solitude, although, when he looks more closely, he sees there may be as many as sixty persons present."

The gift for cynical but vigorous scrutiny that was characteristic of the rococo always inclined the adepts of the epoch, when matters which they regarded as serious were at stake, to draw upon the treasures of classical mythology. Now for them coffee was a serious matter—one of the few sacred things that were still venerated by the apostles of *L'homme machine*. Le Sage, whose long life extended from the baroque into the rococo, had good reason for comparing coffee to the "Sun of the Underworld," to Horus, the falcon-headed deity of the Egyptians, winging his way with a mirror through the silent realm of thought.

Apollo and Horus may be identified. Limojon de Saint-Didier, who wrote an epic poem in praise of coffee, proclaimed the identity of the god who dwells in coffee and of the god who shines on us from the heavens:

> The god who from his chariot shines in our skies
> Is the same Apollo who reigns in the east.
> When his eyes were looking upon Arabia Felix,
> He saw the birth of this famous plant.
> Quaffing long draughts of the fuming decoction,
> He felt the effect of its conquering power.
> As one sees, of a sudden, the waters from a slight cloud
> Tranquillize the atmosphere and disperse the storm,

The potent virtues of this new nectar
Can raise our spirits when depressed by over-long study,
Drive away the vapours disseminated by impure blood,
Restore calm to the mind, bring joy to the heart.

Whereas the court of Louis XIV shunned coffee, being (altogether
in the spirit of the periwig period) influenced by medical warnings
against it, under Louis XV the beverage established itself in court
circles. Louis XV, indeed, had a passion for coffee, and liked to do
honour to his friends by making coffee for them with his own hands.
Lenormand, head gardener at Versailles, had planted a dozen coffee-
shrubs in the hot-houses of the palace, and from these every year six
pounds of berries could be harvested. Louis XV had the coffee-beans
dried and roasted, and served his guests with coffee of his own making.
Madame du Barry had herself painted as a sultana drinking coffee.

Lazare Duvaux, court jeweller, kept a diary that bears witness to the
king's passion for coffee. In January 1754, Louis ordered "a golden
coffee-pot, chased and polished." Duvaux was to provide it with "a
spirit-lamp, furnished with wick and extinguisher"; and in March of
the same year we read of another "golden coffee-pot, with a spirit-
lamp and a small steel pan, having gilt feet."

These entries show that the coffee was brought to the boil over a
spirit-lamp. In fact, the requisite quantity of water having been added
to the ground coffee, the coffee-pot was brought to the boil a dozen
times in succession, being removed from the flame the instant it began
to bubble. In 1763, L'Aîné, a tinsmith, made a new kind of coffee-pot,
in which the ground coffee was treated like tea, being placed in the
bottom of the utensil and then having freshly boiled water poured
upon it. But this method of preparation did not catch on.

The coffee that Louis XV drank was French coffee, grown on French
soil, though in hot-houses. Rousseau and Diderot, Maupertuis and
d'Alembert, also drank French coffee, though not that which was grown
in His Majesty's forcing-houses. By the middle of the eighteenth century, the French colonies were already supplying the homeland with
all the coffee they needed.

The story of the introduction of coffee into the French Antilles is
one of those touching and heroic vignettes in which the eighteenth
century abounds. Gabriel Mathieu Desclieux, captain of infantry, sta-

tioned in Martinique, a natural hot-house among the West Indian islands, had a good deal of spare time on his hands. He was a great reader, learning from his books, and doubtless from travellers as well, that the Dutch had transferred from Arabia to the East Indies the cultivation of a plant most useful to mankind. Desclieux was aware that the fan-palm with which he had become familiar in the Antilles grew also in the East Indies. There was, therefore, a kinship between the air and soil of the two regions, the warm, salt-laden atmosphere that blew across the East Indies and the West Indies from the tropical seas. Both alike were volcanic, agitated by earthquakes, frequently devastated by eruptions and tidal waves. Surely, then, the coffee-shrub of Arabia and the Dutch Indies must be found in the French Antilles as well? Desclieux explored Martinique in every direction without finding that of which he was in search. Not one of the plants he discovered corresponded to the description of coffee.

Consumed by the desire to grow coffee in Martinique, Desclieux went home to France on furlough. He found that everyone drank coffee; but it was Arabian coffee, or else coffee from the Dutch East Indies brought to Europe round the Cape of Good Hope. True, in 1714, the mayor of Amsterdam had made Louis XIV a present of a coffee-shrub, and Monsieur de Jussieu, a famous botanist, had planted it in one of the royal hot-houses. But Jussieu and his friends had such a craze for rarity that it was years before they were willing to part with a shoot. At length, however, Desclieux explained to the king's physician-in-ordinary that he had sound patriotic reasons for wishing to grow coffee in Martinique, and, behind the backs of the botanists, the doctor secured for him a cutting of the coffee-shrub and permission to export it.

On a fine May morning in the year 1723, Monsieur Desclieux boarded a ship at Nantes for the voyage back to Martinique. Now began that Odyssey, that "peck of troubles," by which fate seemed determined to prevent the transport of coffee to the New World. The captain was conveying his treasure in a glass chest, wherein the precious plant could be kept warm beneath the rays of the sun. This little portable "frame" was brought up on deck day after day. Close by it, watching, sat Desclieux. Soon he became aware that a man unknown to him (who was travelling under a false name) seemed to take a strange interest in his plant. This fellow-passenger spoke French with a Dutch accent. Once, when the ship was off the coast of Spain, Desclieux dozed for a while at his post, and, on awaking, he saw to his horror that this Dutch spy must have opened the little glass frame, for one of the shoots had been bent and broken. Had the plant been mortally injured? In truth, Desclieux's conscience was more seriously wounded than the cutting. He vowed not to be caught napping again so long as the Dutchman was on board. Do we not see how the legend of wakefulness, which ever accompanies coffee in its progress, was at work likewise on this ship?

The Dutchman disembarked at Madeira. A day's voyage farther west, a new danger loomed in the offing. This was one of those pests of the seas, a Barbary corsair. Desclieux' vessel had to keep the pirate off in a sea-fight that lasted a day. Not until a Spanish galley appeared on the eastern horizon did the enemy sail away northward. But one of the yards had been splintered by the enemy gun-fire, and a splinter had broken the cover of the glass chest. Here was fresh concern for Desclieux. Would it be all right if he were to keep the plant wrapped up in his own cloak? No, it needed concentrated sunlight, and not, like an animal, the warmth of a winter coat. Desclieux, therefore, with the aid of the ship's carpenter, had his frame remade, so that his treasure might continue to flourish in concentrated sunlight.

Now, however, it was Neptune's turn to blow his shell-trumpet. He sent a storm like that described by Virgil to agitate the unhappy ship, so that the remade forcing-house was shattered to pieces, and its contents were sprinkled with salt. Boreas did his fell work in turn. Then, as an added plague, came the doldrums. Day after day, beneath the bell-glass of the sky, the vessel with its precious freight lay "as idle as a painted ship upon a painted ocean." Now the spray of the coffee-shrub had more than enough sun, but was short of water. Desclieux shared his meagre ration with his treasure. At length, however, a favourable wind came, the ship pursued its westward course, and one moonlit night, when all on board were near to perishing from thirst, the silvery leaves of palm-trees hove in sight. They had reached the Antilles. The coffee-plant had been saved.

> Happy Martinique! Hospitable land!
> In a new world, you were the first

> To gather and to fertilize this delightful Asiatic berry,
> And, in a French soil, to ripen its ambrosia!

Thus sang Esmenard of the happy event in verses that were less happy. Anyhow, the important point was that the coffee-plant was uninjured. Desclieux entrusted it to the favourable soil, and, twenty months later, was able to garner the first harvest. The coffee-beans were supplied to intellectuals, physicians, and other persons of standing; but also to the planters of the island, who were quick to realize the value of the opportunity thus provided, and to dream golden dreams. "The culture of coffee is gradually spreading here," wrote Desclieux to Fréron, "for I have been supplying my friends with fruit from the new plants that have thriven in the shadow of the first one I imported. In course of time Guadeloupe and Santo Domingo discovered the fruitful shrub. The progress of coffee in Martinique was favoured by the extreme mortality among the cocoa-trees. This has been attributed by some to the recent volcanic eruption; by others, to the severity of the last rainy season, which continued for a whole three months this winter. Anyhow, when the planters found that the cocoa-tree had failed them as a source of livelihood, they turned to coffee-planting. Ere long this became their sole crop, and was a tremendous success. Within three years, there were many millions of coffee-shrubs on our island." Returning once more to France on furlough, Captain Desclieux was presented to Louis XV, who appointed him governor of the Antilles.

Before he died on November 30, 1774, at the age of eighty-eight, he had become a knight of the Order of St. Louis. *L'Année littéraire*, a periodical that often attacked the destructive tendencies of the Encyclopædists, devoted a long poem to the memory of Desclieux, who had been an ardent monarchist.

> Thou diest, thou diest, venerable sire,
> And art unaware of our sad plight!
> For kings and for subjects alike,
> Atropos, the Parca, makes the tomb yawn.
> Fellow-countryman and hero, in the springtime of thy life,
> Undaunted didst thou steer thy ship through the storm,
> Conveying to the new world the glorious plant
> That gives our blood fresh life
> And enriches our fatherland.
> The colonists bewail thee like children weeping a father lost!

Whites and Blacks of Martinique, a mourning chorus,
Lament thy departure, most affectionate of parents.

A heroic idyll found its term in these verses. *L'Année littéraire*, whose express aim it was to contrast Desclieux' aristocratic existence with the "impudent cosmopolitan ideals of a rout of philosophers," forgot that it was not only monarchists who drank coffee, but also the apostles of the Enlightenment. These latter, above all. . . .

"Coffee is the revolution!"

Michelet, the historian, did not write the foregoing words; but he came very near to doing so when he made coffee responsible for that "explosion étincelante," for that fulminating explosion of the intellectual life of the eighteenth century, when "l'esprit jaillit, spontané, comme il peut." ". . . for at length the tavern has been dethroned, the detestable tavern where, half a century ago, our young folks rioted among wine-tubs and harlots. Fewer drunken songs o' night-time, fewer nobles lying in the gutter. . . . Coffee, the sobering beverage, a mighty nutriment of the brain, unlike spirituous liquors, increases purity and clarity; coffee, which clears the imagination of fogs and heavy vapours; which illumines the reality of things with the white light of truth; anti-erotic coffee, which at length substitutes stimulation of the mind for stimulation of the sexual faculties! . . . The strong coffee of San Domingo, which Buffon, Diderot, and Rousseau drank, redoubled the ardour of their ardent souls—and the prophets who assembled day after day in the Café Procope saw, with penetrating glance, in the depths of their black drink the illumination of the year of the revolution."

It is self-evident that intellectual movements would never have brought about the revolution unless they had been mounted upon vigorous economic steeds. Coffee, however, and the coffee-houses in which it was consumed, were meeting-points between literature and economics, were the posting-stations at which mental discontent rubbed shoulders with material. We have seen that in the cafés men of all sorts assembled. Among the frequenters, therefore, there were also men of the two privileged classes, the priesthood and the nobility. But the nobles and priests in all France did not number as many as one hundred thousand, whereas the populace, the Third Estate, comprised

four-and-twenty million. Consequently the great majority of the frequenters of the Parisian coffee-houses were bourgeois, petty artisans,
and manual workers, who were one and all discontented. Their fathers
and their grandfathers had likewise been discontented: the fathers with
Louis XV, the grandfathers with Louis XIV. What had they to expect
from Louis XVI? Could he lift from their necks the fearful burden of
taxation imposed by his ancestors? In those days every movement of the
common man, every breath he drew, was taxed. The bankrupt towns
were in despair, and despair was intensified by that of the bankrupt
peasantry. What was the use of hard work? The logic of work is that
one works to avoid starving. But whoever worked in the France of
those days had to hand over so large a proportion of the fruit of his
toil to the king, the intendants, and the tax concessionnaires, that he remained hungry when all was said and done.

Dull despair prevailed. But now the bourgeois, slow thinkers and
unready talkers, came into touch with the penmen over the steaming
coffee-cups; rubbed elbows with these strange types who could think,
talk, and write for four-and-twenty hours a day. These glib lawyers,
these authors and journalists, were not only familiar with the woes of
the mute masses, but played upon their woes as musicians play upon
instruments. In their orations and writings, the widespread distresses,
the social and economic miseries of the time became vocal; their words
were as powerful as had been Joshua's trumpets before Jericho. The
walls quaked!

The walls fell. The Bastille was stormed. It was taken as the first
spoil of that explosive mixture from which our world can no longer
be freed, the mixture which, as Michelet puts it, "united within itself
the reality of things with the truth of the spirit." It was a mingling of
philosophic and economic thought.

The revolution was nothing other than the explosive encounter of
economic unfreedom and philosophic freedom of thought.

The French monarchy was overthrown by the clubs—the clubs which
were a British invention! Now these were closely connected with the
coffee-houses. The Bourbons or their police, warned by their study of
the history of England, realized often enough what would happen
when subjects stayed awake all night instead of going quietly to bed
and to sleep.

It is of unrivalled value
In maladies of the heart;
The pineal gland
Is fortified by it.

is what we read in a strophe about coffee that was sung in the streets
of Paris long before the revolution. In very truth, if the pineal gland
(supposed by the ancients to be the seat of the soul) could be, as
alleged, stimulated by coffee, then this stimulated machine would manufacture "public opinion," that is to say, criticism and political fervour.

The police authorities had often before been concerned about the
coffee-houses. Argenson, a minister of state, appointed special inspectors to supervise what went on in them. As a rule, the authorities
were easy-going enough in this matter, but from time to time they displayed remarkable energy. For instance, Denoux, the public prosecutor,
was arrested in a café near the Pont Neuf and sent to the Bastille because he had "let his tongue wag too freely." He had been denounced
for this by Cardinal Dubois. However, Argenson, who was friendly
with Denoux, soon released the prisoner.

The government thus knew what had been going on for fifty years
in the cafés; but it almost seemed as if the authorities regarded these
"talking-shops" as safety-valves which it would be inexpedient to
close. Thus the state desisted from its endeavour to police the cafés,
and was more concerned about early closing than about shutting them
up altogether. One might have thought that since coffee-house keepers
had become suspect, the number of licences would have been reduced
instead of being increased. Here, however, the greed of the budget was
a safeguard for the coffee-house keepers. The treasury was hard up,
and could not dispense with this source of revenue.

One who studies the images of the great revolution with a seeing
eye, catches glimpses of the night-life of Paris of that period. He dis-
cerns violet-tinted darkness, punctuated by the glare of torches, and
relieved by faces that grow red in their light. At no other time has
history been so much a product of the night. Speeches and orators, the
law-courts, political discussions, and hysterical tribunes of the people
—the whole revolution, the *Carmagnole*, and the *Ça Ira*, went arm in
arm with insomnia. Coffee disseminated the art of being wakeful by

night as well as by day. . . . As we look back it seems as if then no one could ever have gone to sleep.

There can be no doubt that in 1793, at the climax of the Terror, people drank more coffee than had been drunk ten or twenty years earlier. The Terror was already a stimulant; and the scent of blood tensed the nerves even more than did the aroma of coffee. "Liberty, brothers, is a woman with whom one cohabits best amid ruins!" This utterance of Desmoulins no longer smacks of the coffee-house. Coffee is like literature; both are in pursuit of a new order—but Desmoulins' words threaten chaos. Now, in chaos we need no beverage.

On the night before execution, neither the public at large nor the Gironde nor the Mountain needed coffee to keep them awake. Nevertheless, perhaps they did drink it. In that supreme hour, they saw the gates of hell yawning. Let me quote once more what Homer wrote of nepenthe: "A drug to lull all pain and anger, and bring forgetfulness of every sorrow. Whoso should drink a draught of it when it is mingled in the bowl, on that day he would let no tear fall down his cheek, not though his mother and his father died, not though men slew his brother or dear son with the sword before his face, and his own eyes beheld it."

14

Luxuries and Potentates

IT was characteristic of eighteenth-century France that the terms "coffee" and "enlightenment" were practically synonymous. When Pietro Verri, an Italian domiciled in Paris, founded a literary and philosophical periodical in the French capital, he christened it "Il Caffè" without more ado, although the contents had no concern with coffee as a beverage.

What about Germany? As if the Rhine had been wider than it is today, it was then usual in Germany to look askance at everything French. Or, to say the least, Germany's attitude towards France was ambiguous. Modern historians are apt to tell us that at the close of the seventeenth century and the beginning of the eighteenth, German burghers turned their eyes longingly towards France. But why, in that case, were German pamphlets of the day so unanimously anti-French in tone? For decades the Germans remained profoundly mortified because the castle of Heidelberg had been blown up by the generals of Louis XIV; and, for the very reason that news spread slowly in those times, such a catastrophe as the devastation of the Palatinate produced greater and more enduring effects upon the popular mind. Had the Germans really been such enthusiastic admirers of France as one might gather from the fashion-plates of the period, what could account for the frenzied enthusiasm of the German nation when the troops of Frederick the Great defeated the French at Rossbach (1757)?

In all earnestness one must admit that it was an advertisement of dubious value to declare that a commodity had been "made in France." Such a label might inspire admiration, but it was just as likely to inspire aversion. The national legend concerning Kolshitsky and his heroic deeds, the legend associated with the introduction of coffee into

Europe, did not spread far beyond Vienna. In High Germany and central Germany all that people could see was that coffee came from France! Only to professed cosmopolitans were French wares congenial —in places where an internationalized and uniform code of manners and customs was in vogue. That meant at the courts of the rulers! Among the treasures preserved in Dresden from the days of Augustus the Strong, we find a coffee-pot made by Melchior Dinglinger, a bombastically barbarian vessel almost sublime in its uniqueness. No one nowadays would want to drink coffee poured out of a utensil having so ornate an aspect of royal snobbery. The belly of this coffee-pot is encircled by strange emblems of gold and enamel—crocodiles, serpents, and cocks. Such an orgy of bad taste reminds us of the chimera slain by Bellerophon, "a fire-breathing monster, with a lion's head, a serpent's tail, and a goat's middle." Use and shape could not contrast more hopelessly.

It was, therefore, from the royal and grand-ducal courts that, towards 1730, a knowledge of the use of coffee began to make its way among the higher circles of the bourgeoisie. Not without difficulty, however. One of the fundamental characteristics of snobbery is that the most exalted snobs wish to defend their customs from imitators, so that we find it perfectly logical when the bishop of Paderborn threatened middle-class coffee-drinkers not only with high fines but also with a sojourn in the stocks. Still, in regions where there was exceptionally brisk intercourse with the outer world, coffee-drinking began to spread, apart from a desire to imitate the habits of the great and in defiance of prohibitions issued by the authorities.

There were in the Germany of that epoch only two towns freely visited by foreigners throughout the year. These metropolises were Hamburg and Leipzig. As early as 1690, Hamburg was distinguished by the foundation of a coffee-house. Not, indeed, to cater to the enjoyment of its own citizens. The place was opened to fulfil the demands of English merchants and seamen; and, it need hardly be said, the necessary supplies did not come overland from Venice through Nürnberg, but by water from London. When, a few decades later, the realm of Brother Coffee collapsed, the custom of coffee-drinking, not having secured a good hold in Hamburg, fell into desuetude there. In Leipzig, on the other hand, a city of fairs and one much frequented by foreigners, coffee-drinking was sooner and more firmly established. We learn of the importance of Leipzig in central-European life from Goethe's *Memories of Youth*. This was the first metropolis, the first town of importance, visited by the lad of sixteen. True, at the date when young Goethe came to Leipzig, the fortunes of the city had already passed their climax. The war indemnities exacted by the Prussians had done damage that seemed wellnigh irreparable. All the same, down to about 1750 Leipzig set the tone for Germany, being wealthier and more influential than Berlin or its nearest rival, Dresden, the official capital of Saxony. Staple-right, situation upon a leading commercial route, and the importance of its fair, gave to Leipzig a prestige and an aspect which justified its friendly nickname of "little Paris." The importance of the place was intensified when it became the centre of the German book-printing trade in place of Frankfort-on-Main. This made it the haunt of men of letters as well as of merchants.

No less celebrated than the gardens that framed the city of Leipzig (the Rosental was even more renowned for its elegance than the Vienna Prater) were Leipzig's eight coffee-houses. The Kaffeebaum was frequented by students who, incredible as it may seem, were no longer exclusive devotees of beer. To Richter's came all those who had business at the fair, sellers and buyers, many of them foreigners: Russians, Poles, and Frenchmen. Above all, among its habitués were to be found the Saxon scholars who, like Zachariae the satirist, towered head and shoulders above the beer-swilling students and the "braggarts of Jena." Coffee was quick to play its part. In a tranquil Germany, which had not hitherto been prone to value any sort of intellectual extravagance, there was born "Saxon turgidity," the tongue of the German rococo, which found expression in six-footed Alexandrines.

Those who decry this style for its spiritless baldness are apt to forget that German classical literature could not be created out of the baroque desert. The purifying decades of the intermediate Gottsched epoch, the thin stratum of the German rococo, were of great importance to German literary evolution. The praise of coffee in Alexandrines is more readable than the exordium penned sixty years later in hexameters by Rector Johann Heinrich Voss. The coffee scene in that writer's *Luise* is an anachronism. It was certainly out of date, in the year 1800, to style coffee "a heating Moorish beverage." The way Voss ignores the effect of coffee on the intelligence makes his description humdrum.

Hardly less philistine, though with flashes of humour and genius, is the famous *Coffee Cantata* by Johann Sebastian Bach. Of course, having no sense of humour, Voss failed to realize that in genre works humour and pathos must be conjoined. Impudent, broad, and withal comic, yet dignified, is Bach's cantata. It is composed with the wit of a paterfamilias endowed with genius.

Bach's inspiration came from one of the *Parisian Fables* of Picander:

> The news comes from Paris: A few short days ago
> An edict was issued. The king, you Germans must know,
> Declared his will thuswise: "We have, to our grief and pain,
> Learned that coffee wreaks ruin and does terrific bane.
> To heal the grievous disaster, We hereby declare
> That none to drink this same coffee in future shall dare,
> Save Us and Our court, and the greatly privileged few
> To whom, in Our royal kindness, We leave may endue.
> Without such a permit, the drink is unlawful."
> Hereupon there resounded a clamour most awful.
> "Alas!" cried the women, "take rather our bread.
> Can't live without coffee. We'll all soon be dead!"
> But the king would not budge, nor his edict revise;
> And, lo, as predicted, his subjects died off like flies;
> Interments were wholesale, as if from the pest;
> Girls, grannies, and mothers with babes at the breast,
> Until the king, becoming more and more afraid,
> At length cancelled his edict, and then the plague was stayed.

This skit relates, of course, to the disturbance that raged round coffee in the early part of the reign of Louis XV, when a state monopoly was established. Picander's somewhat dull and indubitably lame poem, published in 1727, seems to have pleased Bach so much that he asked the author to write him a libretto for a new cantata which was to deal with the "caffeomania of women." It was common in those days for composers to write music as a sort of arabesque surrounding the concerns of folk-life. There was a *Wine and Beer Pæan;* an extremely realistic *Dentist Cantata,* punctuated with screams and groans; a cat-and-dog piece entitled *Night-Watchman Love;* a *Worm-Tablet Round;* and many other pieces of the same sort. In Bach's *Coffee Cantata,*

Father Oldways wants to break his daughter Lieschen of the coffee habit, since, like most of the women of Leipzig, she has become a coffee-addict. Threats prove futile, until he has recourse to the formidable menace: "Either you give up coffee or I will marry you off to a husband who will take the matter in hand." But Lieschen cheats her father. While he is hunting round for a son-in-law, she spreads abroad the news:

> No lover shall woo me
> Unless I have his pledge,
> Written in the marriage settlement,
> That he will allow me
> To drink coffee when I please.

It need hardly be said that the music is well calculated to set off the words. In any case the *Coffee Cantata* is a document in the history of civilization. It would, however, be a mistake to infer from it that towards the year 1740 in other parts of Germany than Leipzig young women of the middle-classes could drink as much coffee as they pleased. Life was simple and luxuries were scarce in the Germany of those days, for various reasons. Although in his fable Picander makes the sovereign responsible for the prohibition of coffee, the rulers were not exclusively to blame for the straitened economic conditions of the epoch. The causes of unfreedom had often to be looked for in other quarters. For instance, in the German corporative spirit.

By the time when "liberating coffee" had become a commodity, it was itself no longer free. It belonged, first of all, to the planter, then to the trader, then to the consumer—and, more than to all three of these, to the king. Unless it belonged to the guild, which was often more tyrannical than the state!

Not only in France, but elsewhere as well, princes and potentates were on bad terms with the guilds, and worked against them, often for excellent reasons.

Guilds, which had been of great utility, giving handicraft prestige and guaranteeing quality of output, had, in the course of centuries, petrified into trade monopolies.

At the outset it had been necessary for the craft-guilds to forbid free competition, since that was the only way of restricting the activities of bunglers. Nevertheless, the trustifying of urban handicrafts that

was characteristic of the industrial history of the seventeenth and
eighteenth centuries was necessarily distasteful to the rulers. It con-
flicted with the guiding principle of the governments of those days.
For enlighted absolutism was highly concerned about fostering the
growth of population. This latter rivalled afforestation in importance,
being regarded by sovereign princes as essential to the development of
the economic life of their realms. Down to the year 1800, owing to
devastating wars and widespread pestilences, Europe remained thinly
populated. The inhabitants of Germany and Austria taken together
numbered no more than five-and-twenty millions; while the population
of England was only six millions. These low figures are the more remarkable since families were much larger than they are today. It was
usual for a married couple to have eight, ten, twelve, or even fifteen
children. Yet Europe remained sparsely peopled! Why? Owing to the
bad sanitary conditions that prevailed before the rise of modern hygiene,
half and more than half of the members of these large families died
before attaining maturity.

Social factors, too, were in great measure responsible for the slow-
ness of the growth of population. The craftsmen had formed rings
into which admission was extremely difficult, with the result that
immigration was hampered no less than freedom of occupation. Here
was reason enough why thoughtful princes should be antagonistic to
guilds and other monopolies. What was the use of looking eagerly
across the frontier for the likelihood that, say, the archbishop of
Salzburg, a prince-archbishop, would expel his Protestant subjects, if,
when a far-seeing ruler was about to net this catch of industrious
persons, the master-craftsmen of his own realm were to insist upon the
privileges of their guilds?

Hence the cry: "Down with the guilds!" A good many of the arbitrary measures of the rulers of those days were, in truth, advantageous
to the population at large.

Like other guilds, the Viennese guild of coffee-boilers experienced
many ups and downs during the pendulum swings from coercion to
freedom, and from freedom back to coercion. The Viennese guild of
coffee-boilers was one of the latest. When Kolshitsky began to popular-
ize the use of coffee, the Viennese bakers' guild had already been in

existence for five hundred years. We learn from *Enikel's Chronicle*, that at Christmas in the year 1217 the bakers took corporative action against Duke Leopold von Babenberg. But it was in the declining days of the guilds that the coffee-boilers' guild was founded. By the year 1700, a good many people had come to think ill of any restraint upon freedom of occupation.

Yet it was natural enough that the coffee-boilers should want their "secret" to become a privileged craft. They were not dwelling in the East, where Mohammed and the Koran had forbidden the use of alcoholic liquors. Very different were conditions in Vienna. There, from the outset, the vintners declared war against coffee. According to documents unearthed from the archives in the year 1933, Kolshitsky had to wait for years before being allowed to practise his craft. Permission was not granted him until, in numerous letters and petitions, he had reminded the town-council of his glorious services! But, in a contradictory spirit, "the trade" tried to force Kolshitsky to enrol himself under its banner. The guild of the "water-burners," insisted the tavern-keepers, had the chartered right of preparing beverages "with the aid of fire" —and this specification included *Mokka* as well as distilled liquors.

We do not know whether street brawls took place between the employees of the coffee-boilers, on the one hand, and those of the distillers, on the other; but it is likely enough. Ere this there had been many guild battles in Vienna. Flour wars between bakers and millers raged so fiercely that the streets and the squares were often whitened as if there had been a snow-storm. Quarrels between distillers and coffee-boilers waxed so fierce, both brandy and coffee being in great demand, that the law-courts were frequently called in to settle the disputes. In the year 1750, Maria Theresa, a wise sovereign and materfamilias, put an end to the conflict by a Solomonic decision: she "permitted"—that is, ordered—the coffee-boilers to provide spirituous liquors as well as coffee in future; and at the same time she permitted the sellers of alcoholic liquors to prepare coffee. Thereupon peace was restored by the formation of a guild of distillers and boilers.

It is true that Maria Theresa's action did not introduce "freedom of trade and occupation," but it put an end to a vexatious monopoly. From the date of the empress's edict, people could drink coffee in public whenever and wherever they pleased. They had long since been able to make coffee for themselves at home, but the edict encouraged the development of the coffee-house frequenter.

Another step taken at that date served to promote the drinking of coffee—a step that was extremely ill-advised. I refer to the tax on alcoholic beverages imposed by Maria Theresa (1779) in accordance with a proposal made by Councillor Greiner. The empress was guided by the wish to transfer taxation from the shoulders of the poor to the shoulders of the rich, and chose this injudicious method.

As a preliminary, various taxes were abolished which were considered to press heavily upon the poor. This was, naturally, a popular measure. The consequent loss of revenue was to be made good by the new taxes on liquor. Councillor Greiner justified his advice on the ground that anyone who chose could avoid taxation by abstaining from alcoholic beverages. Above all, he declared, the poor, whose limited means made it impossible for them to drink such beverages, would be exempt from taxation. It seems hardly credible that Maria Theresa, towards the end of her long reign, should have agreed to so amateurish a proposal. The upshot was that in a land where wine was exceedingly cheap and was the ordinary beverage of the population, it was greatly increased in price.

The new tax made the empress unpopular, but it certainly favoured the drinking of coffee, which, being non-alcoholic, was left untaxed.

Maria Theresa's liquor tax was a typical luxury-tax of the wrong kind. It was not followed up by other luxury-taxes. Austria was never a puritanical country, and none of its sovereigns ever ruled it in a Draconian spirit. They were always inspired with kindly sentiment towards their subjects.

The sociology of Sonnenfels, a noted political philosopher during the days of Emperor Joseph II, was almost eudemonist. Sonnenfels assumed that man should try to obtain more than mere necessities, and that he has a right to more! "The needs of man," he wrote, "are extremely restricted if we use the term 'needs' in the narrowest sense. If, however, people were to be confined to the satisfaction of bare need, their activities would likewise be exiguous. That would be most undesirable! An increase of need is characteristic of the growth of comfort and the provision of superfluity—these two together comprising what we term luxury. To rail against luxury and ostentation is, therefore, misguided, except in so far as we wish to hinder extravagance."

Under the regime of a statesman holding such views, it was only to be expected that the import duties upon "articles of luxury" (Sonnenfels was thinking of such foreign goods as pickled herrings, coffee, and southern wines) would remain moderate. People must not be prevented from satisfying their natural desire for good things. In an age that was in most respects illiberal, the advantages that would accrue to the State from a liberal economic order were already beginning to be recognized. "Liberty multiplies desires." A cheerful citizen would consume more and would work better than one who was gloomy and oppressed.

Like other apostles of enlightenment, Sonnenfels was an adversary of the guilds. They prevented freedom of occupation, and thus checked the growth of population! In those days, an increase in population was not merely one of the chief aims of the state, but also, as Sonnenfels in his eudemonism, in his desire to promote general happiness, was ready to prove to all and sundry, would redound to the interest of individuals:

"The larger the population, the greater its stability. This is one of the first principles of politics.

"The larger the population upon whose support a ruler can count, the less has the latter to fear from his subjects. This is one of the first principles of the promotion of public order.

"The more people, the more needs to be satisfied; the more hands there are, the more abundant the possibilities of creating the wares necessary for domestic and foreign trade. This is one of the first principles of political economy.

"The more citizens there are, the more persons to contribute to public revenue, and consequently the smaller the amount that has to be demanded from each individual. This is one of the first principles of sound taxation."

These four "rational principles" for a policy that would increase population are of dubious validity, and were supported by an extremely lame logic. But they were characteristically Austrian in their good-nature.

Very different was the Prussian creed, as formulated by Johann Gottlieb Fichte in relation to the problem of superfluity. In his *Der geschlossene Handelsstaat*, published in the year 1800, he flatly repudiated the right to luxury and display, and advocated a planned economy:

"All must first be well fed and properly housed before anyone sets about decorating his habitation; all must first be comfortably and warmly clad before anyone tries to dress splendidly. There must be no luxury in a state where agriculture is still backward, and where there is still a lack of hands for the simplest mechanical crafts. A man does not excuse himself adequately for the indulgence of luxurious tastes by saying, 'I can pay for what I want.' It is unjust that anyone should be able to pay for things he does not really need, and the money with which he pays for luxuries is not rightfully or reasonably his own."

There is an echo of Luther's zeal in these words. Above all, however, Fichte was inspired by reminiscences of an outstanding man who had passed away more recently—Frederick the Great.

Sonnenfels and Joseph II were not soldiers like their arch-enemy Frederick II of Prussia. The hardships of his life had made King Frederick a stoic rather than an epicurean. Experience had determined his attitude towards "superfluities."

In his early years, indeed, he had been an epicurean. That was when he was only crown-prince at Rheinsberg; when his humanism was not the outcome of ripe observation, but was the expression of his natural philosophical promptings. Why should he not allow himself and the world at large the happiness of luxury? Writing to Voltaire, he said: "I like the French love of pleasure. It pleases me to think that four hundred thousand town-dwellers are concerned only to enjoy themselves, and know practically nothing of the seamy side of life; that proves to me that these four hundred thousand persons are happy. . . . It seems to me that every ruler must do his utmost to make his subjects happy, even if he cannot make them wealthy; for there is no doubt that there can be content without wealth. A man, for instance, at a banquet or at the theatre, one who can mingle freely with congenial associates—such a man, at such times, is happy, and takes home with him a number of impressions that have fertilized his spirit. We must therefore do our utmost to provide for these masses many such moments of refreshment, which can sweeten the bitterness of life, or can make people forget their troubles for a time! The most tangible good in life is pleasure; and therefore we do good, much good, when we provide a large community with possibilities for enjoying itself."

Words of a green youth, wishing to supply circuses in abundance, because he has never known the need for bread! But when, during long years of warfare, the crude need for bread had been brought home to the lonely monarch, he ceased to dream of making his people happy by "spectacles and superfluities." Still less did he continue to think it a king's duty to act as a purveyor of pleasure.

When Frederick the Great returned home on the evening of March 30, 1763, though only fifty-one, he was already an old man. Seven years of warfare had aged him as much as seventy might have done. The well-ordered country he had once thought of establishing no longer existed even in his dreams. He had won a province, and had lost everything else. Financial devastation was obvious as far as the eye could reach.

With the native force of genius, Frederick now devoted himself to the task of reconstruction. This was a war that lasted more than seven years. It began on the day when the king converted his warchest into a peace-chest. The eastern provinces had been laid waste by the Russians. Frederick sent hundreds of thousands of gold pieces rolling thither, and bestowed his cavalry horses upon the impoverished peasants. In the towns, he provided subsidies for manufacturing industry. Just as a hundred years before Colbert, in France, had conjured manufactures out of the ground, so now in Berlin, Breslau, and Königsberg thriving factories appeared as if by magic. The old man on the throne set his subjects an example by working twelve hours a day himself. The "excessive diligence" of the Prussians had come into its own.

Great financial schemes were drawn up. The new industrial policy must be safeguarded by a protective system. As a mercantilist, the king laid stress, above all, upon a favourable balance of trade. Exports began to exceed imports. Silesian linen was sent to Russia. Only two articles of daily use took the form of costly imports. These were things paid for in Prussian thalers, which had much better, thought Frederick, have been kept in the country. All the same, they were things for which the monarch himself had a taste: good tobacco and good coffee.

As regards tobacco, the problem was not difficult to solve. He had tobacco planted in his own land. Certain kinds throve well enough, others not so well. One day Frederick asked Achard, the chemist, whether it was not possible "to discover a sauce which, without being in any way injurious, could improve Prussian-grown tobacco so that it would rival Virginian in flavour." But no such sauce could be found; and everyone who could afford it smoked imported tobacco.

Even Frederick had no scruples about establishing a state monopoly in coffee and tobacco. He regarded them as luxuries that could bear high taxation, since in any case the poor among his subjects could not afford to buy them. That was the way in which he justified a policy that was ill-conceived and unsuccessful. Following the French precedent, the monarch farmed out both these monopolies. He was influenced, no doubt, by his usual tendency to overvalue all that was French. Just as in youth he had believed that only in Paris good plays could be seen and good poetry written, so, in his old age, he swore by French political economy.

Frederick prepared a sackful of troubles for himself and his country through the malpractices of the French lessees of the monopolies. (One of them, it was currently reported, was a bankrupt from Marseille.) As with all hide-bound mercantilists, nationalist aims were more important to him than nationalist means, with the result that he used means that were anything but nationalist. One of the main principles of mercantilism was: "Skilled workers must be imported whenever they are needed." Since the king was convinced that French officials would work in monopolies better than his German subjects (who were, in his estimation, clumsy, inexperienced, and too good-natured), the king filled two hundred posts in his monopoly services with French officials. The upshot was a manifest recalcitrance on the part of the Prussian burghers, who could not understand to what end they had conquered the French at Rossbach and elsewhere if the vanquished were to occupy lucrative and respected posts. High-handed actions on the part of the foreign monopolist officials, which might have been overlooked if they had been committed by Prussians, became a serious grievance when committed by Frenchmen.

The habit of coffee-drinking became established later in Berlin than in Hamburg and Leipzig, these latter towns being centres of foreign intercourse in northern Germany. It was plain enough, as the outcome of a careful inquiry that the king instituted, that in Prussian towns there was a growing demand for the anti-Bacchic beverage; and this was surely a good thing, in view of the fact that his subjects must work harder if they were to increase their output. Still, Frederick pulled a wry face when he learned that seven hundred thousand thalers or more were going abroad year by year to pay for coffee, the money being sent chiefly to Holland. Meanwhile there was a corresponding decline in the brewing trade. We cannot doubt that Frederick knew well enough that his subjects drank coffee in order to work better and for longer hours. Still, he was vexed to discover that the increase in the consumption of coffee was set off by a decline in the consumption of beer. When, however, he reacted by imposing a tax of eight silver groschen per pound of imported coffee, it was only to find that he had equipped his state with a new industry—that of smuggling! The "hole in the West" began at Emden, and extended up the Rhine as far as Cleves. There was also a "hole in the North," through which coffee found its way illicitly in to Prussia, across Swedish Pomerania. The most earnest attempts were made to stop such abuses. Revenue officers were multiplied. Many of these "coffee-watchmen" were in league with the smugglers, and shared their ill-gotten gains.

With French subtlety, the monopoly administration now advocated a new expedient to stop smuggling. The coffee that was imported above-board was to go straight to the roasting-houses that the king had established, and none but roasted coffee was to be sold. This provided a check upon the consumption of smuggled coffee. If a house-owner or an innkeeper were to roast smuggled coffee, the volatile oils, the pyridine and the furfural, would assail the nostrils of the neighbours and the police, acquainting them with the fact that there was illicit coffee on the premises, and the smuggled goods could be promptly confiscated. The king was assured that this measure would not interfere in any way with trade. Frederick agreed to this plan when it was explained to him that the new method of control would provide employ-

ment for time-expired soldiers. Now there were to be seen veterans
from the Seven Years War ferreting about in town and countryside—
all of them replicas of Frederick, wearing uniforms, sporting pigtails,
carrying crutch-sticks—a sad spectacle. In the towns that were big
enough to have a public opinion, in Berlin, Breslau, and Königsberg,
there were loud complaints when members of this guild of "coffee-
smellers" made their way into private houses, impounded coffee-pots,
searched the store-rooms, making a mess and giving trouble. In the
countryside people were more dutiful; but the gentry of the regions
of Lauenburg and Bütow gave the royal customs service to understand
that they would promptly expel any coffee-spy who should venture to
set foot upon Pomeranian estates.

The surveillance thus exercised over consumers became preposterous,
with the natural result that trade fell off. By now, the import duty imposed on coffee had been increased to one thaler per pound. When
coffee could not be sold at the consequent high price, the duty was
reduced by one-half. That did not help matters. People began to use
coffee substitutes. The curtain had risen on the first act of a tragi-
comedy. In the dispute between coffee-drinkers and potentates, a laughing third character, chicory, had entered the stage.

It was no easy matter to tell the truth to a king who was not only
extremely authoritarian, but was also a man of genius. His minister
Heinitz ventured to do so. Heinitz was bold enough, in a detailed memorial, to denounce the mismanagement of the coffee-monopoly. He
showed that the ostensible increase of revenue derived from the monopoly by the state was really useless. The 96,000 thalers derived from
the tax upon coffee was only a spurious gain, for while the returns had
increased in a ratio of five to seven, expenditure upon the coffee-
monopoly had increased in a ratio of three to ten.

Frederick the Great was extremely annoyed, but all the same, as a
result of Heinitz' intervention, no more French officials were appointed. Three months before the death of Frederick II, the crown
prince, subsequently to ascend the throne as Frederick William II, who
had J. C. Wöllner as chief adviser, determined to abolish the coffee-
monopoly. Lest Frederick the Great should be too much mortified,
everything was arranged on the quiet. "I do not think that I am doing
wrong," wrote Wöllner in a letter accompanying his memorial, "in

working secretly for Your Highness in this matter, and, for the nonce, inscribing my opinion in a memorial for Your Highness's eyes alone." In this memorial, Wöllner described the coffee-monopoly as "extremely harassing to merchants, bringing about a decline in the trade and a decay of the fairs, interfering with transport, and swelling the army of officials, to the great alarm of the working-classes. There has resulted a marked increase in the cost of administration, while salaries and royalties are paid mainly to foreigners."

As soon as Frederick William II mounted the throne, he issued an edict considerably reducing the tax on coffee. "To remove all desire and inclination for fraud," on July 1, 1787, the decree insisting that coffee should be roasted only in the state roasting-houses was quashed.

Mirabeau penned a savage epitaph upon the outworn financial system of monopolies and tax-farming. It was strange that a Frenchman, in his *Monarchie prussienne sous Frédéric le Grand*, should write such a tribute to the greatest of all francophils. Yet not so strange after all, for three years later the charged political and economic atmosphere that lowered over Europe was to burst in a tremendous thunderstorm. Old-time France, so much admired in its day, the France of the *ancien régime* that had given birth to the institution of farming the taxes, perished very soon after its admirer Frederick of Prussia had passed away. A new generation had been born, the generation of those who were in revolt against the system according to which:

> The king bars the bridges and the roads,
> And saith: "The tithe is mine!"

15

Napoleon's Alliance with Chicory

THE bad old days of tyranny were over and done with. So believed the French until, after a brief frenzy of liberty, there appeared a new and mighty tyrant, Napoleon, the man of genius.

One of the first things the French forfeited in their craze for freedom was their best colony, their coffee-paradise of Santo Domingo. Ripples from the tidal wave that had made an end of authoritarianism in Paris ran swiftly over the surface of the sea to break upon the shores of the French Indies. In these colonies, Negroes and mulattoes took the talk of freedom at its face value. Among their palms, they erected a tree of liberty, crowning it, like the French, with a Phrygian cap; they encircled it with a park of artillery, and gaily shot down their white masters. France for the French? Well and good! But in that case, Haiti for the Negroes!

The crime of the French absolute monarchy, which had colonized its West Indian possessions with kidnapped Africans, was now avenged upon its successor, the republic. The excellent coffee of Santo Domingo had been used by Montesquieu, Rousseau, Diderot, and other eighteenth-century writers to keep their brains lively. But the Blacks who now made themselves lords of the island owned the coffee-plantations, and they sent no coffee to France. The frequenters of the Café Procope sat before empty cups, unless they were sufficiently well-to-do to pay for the more expensive coffee from Java.

Since about 1740, the French Indies had been a premier source of supply. Two-thirds of all the coffee drunk in Europe came from the Antilles. The revolution in Santo Domingo not only severed for a considerable time the political ties with France, but also put an end to coffee-planting, which was the chief local source of wealth. The Negro liberator, Toussaint Louverture, who headed the insurrection, would have saved the plantations had he been able; but the rebellious slaves regarded these plantations as symbols of their slavery, with the result that, not content with massacring their some-time masters, they burned the crops.

After 1791, coffee-growing came to an end in Haiti and Santo Domingo, their places as sources of supply being taken by Java. The fruit of Desclieux' pioneer work had been destroyed. Henceforward, the Dutch Indies, and not the Antilles, provided fully two-thirds of the coffee that was consumed throughout the world. The total production fell off, and this enabled the Hollanders to jack up prices. All the better for England! The lords of the Anglo-Indian tea plantations could undersell coffee, and could market their tea better than before.

Among the hundred grievances Napoleon harboured against England was the loss of the good coffee of Santo Domingo—or, rather, the trading advantage England derived from the revolution in Haiti. Indeed, his grievances against England were manifold and worldwide. During the last years in St. Helena, the dethroned emperor came clearly to recognize that all his other troubles and combats had been no more than preliminary skirmishes for the final tussle with England, in which he was so cruelly defeated.

Yet from the first he realized that England was the arch-enemy.

How long had he waited in camp at Boulogne, hoping for a miracle that would enable him to cross the Channel and land in England? Would not the waters divide, as of old the waters of the Red Sea had divided, that his army might march on dry ground to invade England? Alas, there was to be no miracle; so, unwillingly, and often bored, he fought other enemies who were not English. Britannia ruled the waves he could not cross. Sea-power made Britain invincible.

On one occasion he successfully took to the water. Early in his career, when he was still more the romanticist than the statesman, he crossed the Mediterranean to Egypt. Thiers has pointed out how inadequately, from the military standpoint, this Egyptian expedition was prepared. Could it be shown as any better, politically considered? Was General Bonaparte well advised to deprive France of her best army for two long years in order to found a chimerical colony in Egypt? Since France was unable to hold her own against Britain on the seas, this colony could not remain in permanent connexion with French seaports. Nevertheless, though fundamentally preposterous from the outlook of the soldier and from that of the statesman, Napoleon's Egyptian campaign was the opening of his fabulous glory. The nations were fired by its romantic aspect. Here was a man setting out towards India, at the head of a French army; a man treading in the footsteps of Alexander the Great. Cairo, the pyramids, Suez, were but steps on the road to Hindustan.

Francis I, Henry IV, Louis XIV, Mazarin, would probably have clapped General Bonaparte into the Bastille if he had propounded to them a scheme for the conquest of Egypt. What could seem more disadvantageous to France than to wage war against the Turks? Defeat would be disastrous, but victory hardly less so. Wars against the Turks were for Austrians and Russians, to whom a weakening of the sultan would be helpful. The French, on the other hand, needed a powerful Turkey as a tacit ally against central Europe.

Nevertheless Napoleon undertook the conquest of Egypt, and the world was greatly impressed by his deeds in the ancient land of the Nile. Why? Because the world has always idolized romanticist will— and such was the obvious inspiration of the Egyptian campaign. Later, at Boulogne, Napoleon was but thirty miles from England; but in Egypt, General Bonaparte was aiming at remote Hindustan, and Hindustan was England! Hindustan was the mystical source of British wealth, of British power. The sea-route to the East Indies was Britannia's, now that Britannia, having vanquished the Portuguese and the Dutch, ruled the waves. But the land-route to India was not under her command, the route that led by way of Egypt and Araby!

When, later, political realism gained the upper hand in Napoleon's mind, he fled from Egypt. He no longer possessed a fleet, for Nelson had destroyed the French fleet in Aboukir Bay. Nothing was left to him but two small vessels. Regarding himself as more important than his army, Napoleon left his army to its own devices in Egypt, just as he forsook the shattered remnants of the Grand Army in Russia thirteen years later. What had really been his aim in going to Egypt? Letting his imagination run riot, he actually forgot France for the moment. The night before the battle of Acre, he declared: "If all goes well, I shall make myself pasha of Syria, shall march upon Damascus and Aleppo. . . . I shall reach Constantinople and uproot the Turkish empire. In the East I shall found a new empire, which will make my name glorious for ever!" Later, when he had become emperor in the West, on the evening before the battle of Austerlitz he reverted to these wish-dreams. While breathing the sober atmosphere of the Moravian plains, he delivered himself as follows to the members of his staff: "If, in 1799, I had taken Acre, I should have turned Mohammedan, and probably my army with me. . . . I should not have been here to fight tomorrow in Moravia. Instead, like Alexander, I should have fought a battle at Issus, should have made myself supreme sultan of the East, and should have returned to Europe by way of Byzantium. I should have founded a new religion to replace that of Mohammed; should have been mounted on an elephant, wearing a turban on my head, and holding in my hands my new Koran."

At a later date, speaking of his experiences during the Egyptian campaign, he said: "I always had seven coffee-pots on the boil while I was discussing with the Turks, for I had to stay awake all night talking over religious matters with them." Emperor of the West and of the East! To go to India in the footsteps of Alexander! What a strange hotchpotch of mysticism, self-idolization, priestcraft, and highly practical genius. For always those twenty to thirty nautical miles were to cut off his armies from Britain. He could fight only on land. The naval disasters in the battles of the Nile and Trafalgar ruined the possibilities of success on the high seas.

India, where at noon the sun touched the zenith, so that its perpendicular rays encouraged the growth not only of vegetation, but of gold likewise! Asia was always the goal of his ambition, Asia counted more for him than Europe. Just as at the opening of his career he hazarded destruction by his expedition to Egypt, so, in the end, did he destroy himself by his expedition to Russia. For it was rather an expedition than a campaign. In 1797 he went to Africa as a detour on the way to Asia. In 1812 he chose an even less practicable detour, the northern route by way of Moscow. Bubonic plague proved an insuperable obstacle to General Bonaparte in Egypt and Syria, putting an end to his attempts to invade India as a new Alexander. It was the Muscovite winter that compelled Emperor Napoleon to turn back from his second eastern raid. Never was he to see Hindustan, never was he to drive his foes the British out of India. Once only did he, for a time, grasp his formidable enemy by the throat, so that the spices of India no longer found a market in Europe. It was in the year 1806, midway between his overture in Egypt and his disastrous finale in Muscovy, that he seemed to be making headway against England. This was by means of the blockade which became known as the Continental System.

The Berlin Decree, issued at Charlottenburg on November 21, 1806, the decree by which a blockade was declared against the British Isles, was a measure of war economics. As such, we can compare it with like measures of earlier and later dates. Especially it has been compared with the blockade of the Central Powers by the Allies from 1914 to 1918. But the Continental System, which closed the seaports of the Continent, of France and her feudatories (among which Russia was soon to be numbered) to British ships, was a grander scheme. Grander both geographically and politically. Geographically, because in those days the world, which knew nothing of steamships or railways or airplanes, was much larger than it is today. Politically, because Europe was never so centralized as under Emperor Napoleon—not even in the days of Charlemagne.

Napoleon had, in his own person, become Europe. The exclusion of England from Europe, the pointing of a finger from the Continent to indicate to the British Isles that henceforward they might consider themselves isolated in the desert of the Atlantic, was symbolic of the man who undertook it. It was not merely a "system," which may be sound or unsound. It was not a purely intellectual product, but was the outcome of Napoleon's "sensibilité d'Etat." Intelligence apart, he possessed this "state sense" as a sixth sense. For Napoleon, politics were not only a logical and practical activity, they were also his bodily and mental reaction to the daily situation. There was a psycho-physical identity between himself and the organism of the State.

On that foggy morning of November 21, when, in a Prussian castle, he signed his name to a document, his anger became creative. The hostility which throughout life he cherished against Britain found vent in momentous written characters. Therewith, simultaneously, mighty gates, so to say, were lowered in front of the mouths of the Elbe, the Weser, the Oder, and the Vistula. The ports of Naples, Marseille, and Barcelona were closed. St. Petersburg, Königsburg, Danzig, and Amsterdam were defended as if by casemates.

For a time the Continental System was marvellously effective, producing results which hardly anyone but Napoleon, with the imagination of genius, could have foreseen. The Continent was to be organized industrially as if England did not exist.

Had Napoleon failed to realize that, when British commodities were excluded from his empire, all foreign commodities would be excluded? England had the monopoly of the carrying trade. One who established a blockade of goods brought in English bottoms, was primarily blockading himself. No vessel flying the French flag could steer a course for Hamburg, Bordeaux, or Ragusa, without a ninety per cent chance of being captured as a prize by the English. The huge mass of territories lying between Illyria and Scandinavia was no longer refreshed by the introduction of wares from overseas. It was isolated. Continental Europe was left to itself.

Napoleon had realized well enough what would happen. Reiterating his old war-cry "Activité, activité, vitesse!" he planted his feet firmly on the ground, and insisted that the Continent must produce for itself all that it had hitherto imported from England and the colonies. The emperor knew that the contemplated ruin of the English carrying trade would not advantage the French carrying trade, since the French navy and the French mercantile marine had been driven off the seas. There was to be no more overseas trade, so far as the Continent was concerned. His policy was determined by the position of France. As early as 1806, during a reception at the Chamber of Commerce in Paris, he prophetically declared: "Our world is continually changing. In former days, if we desired to be rich, we had to own colonies, to establish ourselves in India and the Antilles, in Central America, in Santo Domingo. These times are over and done with. Today we must become manufacturers, must be able to provide for ourselves what we used to get from elsewhere. We must, let me insist, provide our own indigo, rice, and sugar.

Manufacturing industry is at least as valuable as commerce used to be. While I am trying to gain the command of the seas, the industries of France will be developed or will be created."

"Tout cela, nous le faisons nous-mêmes!" We shall make everything for ourselves! These bold words are charged with a tremor of expectation. Man is to show himself mightier than destiny, which has allotted different climates to different parts of the world, dividing it into different zones. The faculties of the soil are determined by the direction of the sun's rays, which fall perpendicularly in the tropics and aslant in the temperate zones; but man's inventive spirit rebels against fate's decrees. He wants to harvest melons from pine-trees; and, if possible, to make bread out of reeds. With the decreeing of the Continental System, Prometheus was reborn; Prometheus, who made for himself whatever he wanted; who invented, built, and dared; who did not ask for gifts from the gods, because he wished to be independent of the gods.

"Tout cela, nous le faisons nous-mêmes!" Nothing has such deep roots that we cannot make it for ourselves. In Verona, Napoleon visited the magnificent Roman amphitheatre. His eyes shone covetously, and the flame of his enthusiasm kindled the imagination of his companion Marmont. Five days later, Marmont wrote to his father: "In Verona we saw the loveliest monument of antiquity, in a perfect state of preservation; the Roman circus providing seats for 80,000 spectators. The sight of it expands the mind and stimulates the fancy. We, too, are worthy of such a monument. Something of the same kind must be built in Paris." . . . "Activité, activité, vitesse!" . . . With energy and speed, the emperor's subjects set themselves to work to realize the teaching of the new Prometheus. Colbert's vision of an industrialized France was child's play when compared with the great forcing-house into which the country was transformed by the Continental System.

All kinds of Manchester goods, woollen and cotton textiles, every sort of piqué, muslin, fustian, dimity, and nankeen, must henceforward be made in France—or French substitutes be found. Hardware, dinner-services, knives, everything that can be made of steel, tin, copper, pig-iron, and pewter, were henceforward to be produced by French factories. Tanned leather, carts and carriages, saddles and harness, ribbons, hats, chiffons and shawls, glassware, pottery of all possible kinds, must be manufactured out of nothing by French hands. They must be! A crowd of inventors, of chemists and physicists, of ambitious scientists, hurried to explore untrodden paths. To Oberkampf, the industrial magnate, Napoleon said: "Tous les deux, nous faisons la guerre à l'Angleterre, mais la vôtre est encore la meilleure."

Thus industry became a titan. The Continental System surrounded France with a barrier more insuperable than that of a high tariff. No British-manufactured articles could any longer disturb the French market. But where were raw materials to come from? Could they be charmed into existence? Surely that was as difficult as it would be to make the sun shine down vertically at noon in the forty-sixth parallel of latitude? No, not so difficult as that! One of the raw materials of which there was the most urgent need, now that overseas imports had been suppressed, was sugar. In the year 1504, sugar-cane had been introduced from Cyprus into the West Indies, and only in this new home had people learned the art of sugar-boiling. Two and a half centuries later, in 1750, Marggraf, a Berlin chemist, showed that beet-root contains a sweet substance, probably identical with sugar; but the discovery was overlooked. Now, however, when cane sugar could no longer be imported from the West Indies, Napoleon got wind of the matter. He reminded his subjects of the possibilities of the sugar-beet. Thanks to additional discoveries made by Achard (1753–1821), another German chemist, it became possible for Europe to supply itself with sugar from home-grown crops.

France even began to cultivate its own cotton. The minister of the interior imported cotton-seeds from Spain and southern Italy, and distributed them among the *départements*. A premium was offered per kilogram of cotton that had been carded and was ready for spinning. Everywhere the emperor was ready to stimulate the cotton industry by appropriate commendations. A Society for the Encouragement of National Industry was founded. Jacquard, a Lyons mechanic, was granted three thousand francs for the invention of an improved loom; another industrial worker, Almeyras, invented an improved carding-machine. The government offered a hundred thousand francs to anyone who should discover an indigenous plant that would furnish a dye akin to indigo; the same amount to the discoverer of a native vegetable dye suitable for wool, cotton, linen, and silk. No less than a million was promised to one who should invent the best machine for spinning flax; the text of this offer was translated into all European languages and posted everywhere.

Prior to the establishment of the Continental System, neither in France nor elsewhere had there existed a special Ministry of Commerce. Commerce and agriculture were within the province of the Ministry of the Interior. Now industrial and agricultural production increased so enormously that two special ministries had to be established, this happening at the outset of the nineteenth century. Soon the century became characterized by a phenomenal division of labour. The barriers imposed by the Continental System were responsible for extreme specialization of industry.

The Continental System was an ideology even more than it was an economic edict. The barriers it erected interfered with worldwide thought. The ideas of millions of human beings became restricted to the regions in which they lived. Thought, investigation, production, were localized. The Continental System was the foundation of many of the inventions of the nineteenth century.

Not in France alone! The Chinese Wall with which the emperor of the French surrounded Europe acted as a stimulus to the British mind no less than to that of the French. It had before this been discovered in England that during the manufacture of coal-tar out of coal an inflammable gas was given off; but little attention was paid to the matter until necessity became the mother of invention. After nightfall, people still lighted their houses with candles made of tallow imported from Russia.

The Russian tallow industry had been one of the most flourishing industries in the pre-Napoleonic world. In 1803, the annual export of raw tallow from Russia was worth ten and a half million roubles, and in addition half a million tallow candles were sent across the Russian frontier. Now, when tallow could no longer be imported from St. Petersburg, was London to suffer darkness? Not a bit of it. As early as 1807, Londoners began to light their houses with gas.

Thus did an evil system promote the work of civilization.

Napoleon himself said (adapting from Thomas Paine) that it is but one step from the sublime to the ridiculous. In the year 1808, the Chamber of Commerce in Toulouse offered rewards: first to anyone who should succeed in making artificially certain drugs which had hitherto been imported, notably quinine; secondly to anyone who should be able to manufacture "certain comestibles to which people have become accustomed, such substances as sugar and coffee, without any falling-off in their quality and at a price which does not exceed the average price of the days before the war."

Though it was still a century before the modern plethora of synthetic drugs, a good many native substitutes could be found, even as beet-root sugar could take the place of cane sugar. A coffee-substitute was a more difficult matter. There did not exist in France any plant (or, at any rate, no such plant is as yet known) that combined the peculiar virtues of coffee, providing wakefulness at will and capable of supplying the aromatics produced in the coffee-bean by roasting it. Trimethyldioxypurin in combination with ether, phenol, furfural—in a word, a substance having the formula $C_8H_{10}N_4O_2$—could be produced only by a plant that grew in the damp, warm, porous soil of the tropical or sub-tropical belt. The soil of Europe said no to the beckoning of Napoleon's imperious finger.

At that time, during the first decade of the nineteenth century, the qualities of coffee had become almost as widely recognized as they are today. As a stimulant, it was indispensable in the fat years, when people could feed liberally, since coffee is a digestive aid. But coffee was no less necessary in the lean years, inasmuch as by its effect on the nervous system, and by its quickening of the heart's action, it can produce a specious sensation of satiety. No matter whether Napoleon prized coffee chiefly as a stimulant, or chiefly for this faculty it has of making underfed people feel that they have dined well, he regarded it as essential that a substitute for coffee should be provided for popular use. That was why the emperor entered into one of his questionable but momentous alliances, the alliance with chicory.

Chicory is an innocent and insignificant plant. It has a long, brown root, which exudes a bitter juice when freshly cut. There is nothing in this bitter juice to act as a stimulant; it contains neither trimethyldioxy-purin nor aromatic oils. The blue-flowering chicory is an ordinary European plant, which flourishes in temperate climes and is free from wonder-working influences derived from a tropical soil. When God made it, long ages ago, it never dreamed of its high destiny, never dreamed that in days to come it would be used by millions as a coffee-substitute. As substitute for a far more wonderful creation—for which, in actual fact, there is no substitute.

The idea of using roasted chicory roots as a substitute for coffee did not originate with Napoleon, nor indeed with a Frenchman. It was born in Germany. Various German industrialists had been on the look-out for a coffee-substitute, until at length, in 1770, Major Christian von Heine and his associate Gottlieb Förster secured an exclusive privilege for a chicory-powder factory. In the *Braunschweiger Anzeiger* of 1772 we read that the new enterprise was proving a great success. Before long chicory was being grown throughout Prussia, and factories for roasting and grinding chicory roots were established. All over Germany, Förster and Heine's ground chicory was sold in packets, having as trade-mark on the cover a vignette of a German farmer sowing chicory-seed, and waving away ships freighted with coffee-beans. Beneath was the legend:

> Without you,
> Healthy and rich!

To what is this success to be ascribed? How had it been possible to induce the populace to drink the new beverage, an infusion of chicory, which was certainly not coffee?

Heine and Förster understood the psychology of their fellow-countrymen. First of all, since everybody else was drinking coffee, the Germans wanted to be in the swim. But the high tax that even the most insignificant potentate imposed on "articles of luxury" made it impossible for the masses to drink real coffee. Those who were bold enough to roast and powder a bitter-tasting root, to say confidently "This is coffee," and to sell it at a very low price, were doing a good turn to the petty bourgeois, who are of the same type the world over. These petty bourgeois were being invited to become confederates in a falsification—but it soon became apparent that the falsification was both physiologically and morally justified.

The reader must not forget that though by this time coffee was widely drunk in Germany, being prized for its taste and its aroma, the Germans were afraid of its effect. They were alarmed at the wakefulness and restlessness produced by coffee. Now chicory provided them with a means for drinking a beverage that they could call "coffee," but that did not have the, to them, undesirable effect. Especially for social purposes, from the German outlook true coffee imported from the tropics had a grave drawback. It could not be drunk in large quantities, hour after hour, as the Germans were accustomed to drink beer and wine; for intemperance in the use of coffee produces palpitation. Those who replaced genuine coffee as a beverage by chicory were using a substitute that enabled them to keep money in their pockets, and that, so they believed, improved their health.

The fable that chicory juice is an extremely wholesome beverage dates back to the wife of one of the first manufacturers of chicory as a coffee-substitute. She had had personal experience of its beneficial influence. Major Heine's lady had been robbed by a "party of French cavalrymen." Thereafter the lady suffered from nervous shock, and her doctor prescribed a decoction of chicory-root as a calmative. This medicament had to be taken for several weeks. The taste of the decoction of the unroasted root was so disagreeable that the patient decided to roast it "as if it had been coffee." That was the origin of chicory as a coffee-substitute, and of the legend that it "strengthens the nerves."

There is pleasure in renunciation. The puritan method of political thought had seeped so far down among the bourgeoisie that townsfolk no longer ignored the problem of imports and the consequent influx of money with a possibly unfavourable balance of trade. Restriction of the import of luxuries, a restriction that Justus Möser had again and again recommended, was in conformity with the asceticism of German-Protestant feeling.

Napoleon now turned to account this readiness of decent folk "to undergo bodily privation in pursuit of a higher aim." The movement was not confined to Germany. In France as well, chicory-planting began to flourish. A hundred years later, of course, in the days of the great war, the industry of providing substitutes became far more extensive than anything that had flourished in Napoleon's time. We learn from a publication of the year 1917 that the unhappy Germans could not get even chicory. They made coffee-substitutes out of Jerusalem artichokes and dahlia tubers, out of dandelion roots, out of comfrey roots, burrs, and chrysanthemum seeds. It was made from monkey-nuts, vetch, chick-peas, carob-beans, horse-chestnuts, asparagus seeds, and asparagus stalks. The roots of reeds were used, so was linseed, so was arrow-head, so was cane, so was bracken, and so were various bulbs. Other ingredients of "coffee-substitute" were quaker-grass roots, parsnips, swedes, juniper berries, sloes, elder-berries and rowan berries, barberries, hips and haws, cranberries, mulberries, holly berries, box seeds, pumpkin seeds, gherkins, sunflower seeds, and hemp seeds. So were the seeds of the lime tree, the acacia, the laburnum, of gorse, flax, and broom. Indeed, "coffee" was made out of the lees of wine and beer —had to be made, lest the populace, deprived of a drink that at least bore the name of coffee, might use roasted wheat to prepare the beverage instead of reserving this carefully rationed product for the making of bread!

Well, Napoleon was primarily responsible for all this, since he popularized chicory, the ancestor of such substitutes. The great emperor entered into an alliance with the modest petty bourgeoise, Dame Chicory, in order, by commands and threats, to impose upon Europe his will that a decoction of roasted and ground chicory roots should pass for coffee. His orders were heard at long range. The fine coffee-plantations in the French Antilles had been for the most part destroyed by the insurgent Negro population, and what coffee remained to be shipped was captured by the British. The coffee of the Dutch East Indies was, some of it, in Javanese store-houses; some of it in London repositories; while some was still brought from Batavia to London in lone ships over which the Union Jack waved, making it unattainable to the Parisians. The Turks, the Egyptians, and the Syrians smiled. They had good reason for doing so, since Arabian coffee, the parent of all the coffees in the world, had come into its own once more. Napoleon's writ did not run in the southeastern Mediterranean. But in Hamburg, in Breslau and Warsaw, in Milan, Genoa, and Bordeaux, people's nostrils dilated as they sniffed the breeze to see whether it bore the aroma of that ethereal oil with which the vision of liberty was anointed.

Liberty came at last. The Russian winter, which in the year 1812 broke the ring Napoleon had welded around Europe and made an end of his plans for a raid into Asia, broke the Continental System likewise, and flung its fragments into the sea. It had been in a bad way for some time. Like all systems that are too extensive and too fine-meshed, this widespread scheme of prohibition had made people who were forced to live under it restless. Few men are idealists, or will tolerate for long a coercion that runs counter to their interests.

No doubt it was agreeable to French nationalist vanity to know that France could get along without England, but nevertheless, rich profits could be earned by smugglers; for the "allies of France" (as, by a euphemism, the subjugated nations were termed) did not share this vanity. Discontent spread quickly from the rest of Europe into France itself. "Victory" that is accompanied by growing privations is hard for the victors to bear. Despite so much "encouragement" of domestic industry, the exclusion of British commodities involved undeniable hardships. The public likes to maintain its customary standard of life. In France, no less than elsewhere in Europe, smuggled English goods found ready purchasers. Even when the heavy profits earned by the smugglers had been paid, the English could supply necessities and luxuries that were cheaper and better than the products of French industry!

But it was not contraband that made the first hopeless breach in the Continental System. Napoleon was the master of many legions, and could use formidable means to enforce his will. He did not hesitate to avail himself of them. On all hands could be seen the smoke and the flames arising from bonfires of confiscated English smuggled goods. No, it was the French state that allowed itself to be "corrupted" by the English. England needed grain, of which France possessed a superfluity, and England paid hard cash. When the French treasury became aware of the influx of British gold, and realized that the stream might be greatly increased, instead of intensifying the strictness of import prohibition, it clapped on high import duties. These duties were to serve the purposes both of protection and of revenue. They protected home industry, indeed, but they provided the government with so much money that it was decided to issue "licences for import."

The exchequer was gaining its ends. Enormous were the sums paid by French and also by German firms for "trading licences." England, in her turn, when she realized what great advantages the French exchequer was deriving from import duties and licences, began to blockade the continent, and to forbid the export of many articles.

Thus by the logic of events, which differs from the logic of genius, Napoleon's France and Pitt's England had long before exchanged roles when, on April 23, 1814, King Louis XVIII cancelled the law by which the Continental System had been established. That system, by then, existed only in name.

With other commodities, coffee was freed.

Parisian café under the Empire (1805)

Coffee-house of 1848

New Year's present for the coffee-house waiter (Vienna, 1840)

Coffee-mill as a mitrailleuse (Franco-Prussian War cartoon)

Families may brew coffee here" (middle of the nineteenth century)

BOOK FOUR

Coffee in the Nineteenth Century

16

The Advance of Tea

THE barrier which, for seven years, Napoleon's Continental System established between Britain and the Continent knocked the bottom out of the coffee-market. Coffee prices have seldom been steady for long, but never were they so tumultuously disturbed as during this period. From 1806 onwards, since the stores of coffee that continued to accumulate in London could no longer be exported, they rose mountain high. Any attempt to maintain prices was foredoomed to failure. No one knew how long the Continental System would remain in being, nor how strictly the emperor would enforce it. Coffee can be kept in good condition for a considerable time, but not for ever. The price of coffee in London consequently came down with a run. Cheap though this staple had now become, the English could not make up their minds to use their own coffee. For too long they had been accustomed to tea. Coffee, which in the repositories was slowly losing its flavour, was in the perilous position of a commodity hoarded by middlemen who can find no market for it. England did not in a year consume more than ten thousand hundredweight of coffee, but there was a thousand times that amount in store. Not all of it in England, of course, but at least in the hands of British merchants overseas. It happened to be called "coffee," but it was in reality a medium of exchange. London, which was the great clearing-house of the world, financed the coffee trade as it financed all other trades. In its merchant vessels it sent machinery and manufactured articles to the hot coffee-growing countries, to Java and Arabia and America, receiving coffee in payment. Exporters everywhere drew upon the merchant bankers of London.

Thus coffee was, substantially, a form of money, but it was money that fluctuated in value. When Prussia, Austria, Russia, and Sweden won the Battle of the Nations near Leipzig in October 1813, they were not fighting primarily to assist British export trade, but, nevertheless, the liberation of the London stocks of goods was an obvious outcome. Except for the Peninsular Campaign, Britain had hitherto prudently refrained from participating in the operations against Napoleon on land. It was natural, however, that the emperor's escape from Elba and return to Paris should have stirred England out of her reserve. She could not face the possibility of a re-establishment of the Continental System, of a repetition of the years from 1806 to 1813. Driven by necessity, she sent an expeditionary force to the Continent, and Wellington won the Battle of Waterloo.

In January 1813, the price of coffee in London fell to forty shillings a hundredweight. On the Hamburg exchange, coffee had been quoted at over five hundred shillings the hundredweight. This was no more than a fancy price, for a hundredweight of coffee could not be got together anywhere on the Continent. What the smugglers, facing terrible risks, were able to ship across the Channel and the North Sea did not amount to more than a few handfuls of coffee-beans at a time. But when King Louis XVIII abolished the Continental System, prices quickly rose in London and fell in Hamburg to meet one another. The situation of the market was favourable, and a prompt increase in the consumption of coffee might have been expected throughout Europe. Strangely enough, this did not occur. Hamburgers would not, in the long run, content themselves with greatly lowered prices, nor would London merchants be satisfied with a reasonable rise in the price of coffee. They wanted prices that would make good their losses during long years. The upshot of the chaffering between the Continental middlemen and the British, and of their failure to come to an agreement now that British groceries were once more freely admitted to the Continent, was a boom in the tea-market.

But the rise in the consumption of tea on the mainland of Europe during the first decade of the Restoration was partly determined by other causes than commercial ones.

In the Napoleonic era, Russia had been for a time allied with France, and then had become one of her most formidable adversaries. Russia had, to begin with, participated willingly enough in Emperor Napoleon's commercial war against Britain, closing her harbours to British ships, and therefore to commodities brought round the Cape from Hindustan. Unceasingly, however, throughout the years of the blockade, caravan traffic across Asia continued. While in the rest of Europe the stimulating beverages to which people had become accustomed were no longer obtainable, it was otherwise in Russia. There tea was still to be had, tea which, like coffee, contained trimethyldioxypurin. Tea relieved both thirst and hunger, and was also a remedy for excessive cold or excessive heat. Nobles and serfs alike drank tea. What had been carried across the snows and across the blazing deserts from China to Russia was a fraternal link uniting all classes of the Russian people. The northern route led by Kiakhta and Omsk; the southern route, by way of Bukhara and Tashkent.

The Russians had conquered France, and as a result, tea suddenly became a Paris fashion. The green-clad Alexander, the mightiest of the allied rulers, and his suite of Russian officers—men who tramped along the boulevards wearing top-boots ornamented with clanking spurs— all drank tea. They brought with them the romance and the far-flung distances of the Russian steppes. For years after this incursion, Parisian life had a Russian note. Never before had the French seen so many Russians. At the courts of Catherine I and Catherine II people had thought, conversed, and loved in the French manner. But now Russianism was the mode in France. The army of the victorious Alexander brought with it the ideas and customs of Russia.

For a long while there existed mystical ties between St. Petersburg and Berlin. Through the instrumentality of Frau von Krüdener, the tsar, with his literary tastes, exercised a considerable influence in German intellectual circles. Now the wave flowed over Paris. This was strange, for one might have expected the vanquished to be hostile to anything that reminded them of their conquerors—but it was a remarkable proof of suppleness in the French character. Hardly was Napoleon crushed when, easily and lightly, Paris renounced the literary trappings of the First Empire, to become Bourbon and Christo-Romantic.

Throughout Europe, the Christo-Romanticists drank tea. This infusion influenced poetry, opinions, conversation. It promoted gentleness and thoughtfulness, but also emotionalism and sentimentality. Chateaubriand, the leading light of the new poetic world, read his epics aloud at the famous Parisian tea-parties. He read well, but when he reached a climax in one of his descriptions of *Weltschmerz* he was likely to be so carried away by his own eloquence as to burst into tears. Even when the reading was over, his tears would drop into his teacup. Such scenes were repulsive to those who were out of tune with the Restoration epoch, to Italian carbonari, to Spanish revolutionists, to enthusiasts who were ready to fight for the liberation of Greece. In a word, the political opponents of "a Europe that had gone to sleep" remained true to the ardours of coffee.

As far as Germany was concerned, it was especially in the circles that were out of sympathy with beer-drinking students that tea was widely consumed. Even before the inauguration of the Continental System, before 1806, tea had been a favourite beverage in the literary salons of Berlin—English tea imported by way of Hamburg.

It need hardly be said that Britons travelling on the Continent were great propagandists for tea. After the downfall of Napoleon, when a German tour became the vogue for Londoners, the English who went up the Rhine on their way to Switzerland wanted tea-rooms, so tea-rooms were provided for these travellers with money to spend. Even in typical coffee-drinking countries like Austria and Italy, Englishmen insisted on being supplied with Ceylon tea. But they were not able to impose their beverage upon the inhabitants. In Italy today, according to the latest statistics, the consumption of tea is no more than one ounce per annum per head of population. The quantity is so small that we may assume the only tea-drinkers in Italy to be British visitors.

Nevertheless, tea made headway in Germany both before and after the Napoleonic epoch, as we can learn from the literature of the period. Uhland wrote a poem in praise of tea. The evening tea-parties that became fashionable in literary circles were gently ridiculed by that prince of satirists, Heinrich Heine.

17

Pleasures of the Ladies of Berlin

ET it would be an illusion to suppose that in those days more
tea than coffee was drunk in Germany. The reverse was true,
and herein we have an elementary instance of how the writers
of history err when they depend mainly on "literary evidence." Such
evidence is all we have to rely upon as regards the greater part of antiquity. But when we come to the nineteenth century, we are guided
by figures relating to economic life, by the science of statistics.

During the year 1841, Hamburg imported 36,000 tons of coffee, but
only 137 tons of tea. The figures show indisputably the interesting fact
that two hundred and seventy times more coffee was imported than
tea.

The figures are remarkable even though the difference between the
consumption of tea and coffee was not so extensive as they might seem
to imply. From a given weight of leaves, six times as many cups of tea
can be prepared as of coffee from the same weight of beans. Allowing
for this fact, however, we learn that forty-five times as much coffee
was consumed as tea.

The port of Hamburg, of course, did not supply German territory
exclusively, being in part a place of transit trade supplying various
regions in northern and eastern Europe. Still, since this applied both to
tea and to coffee, the consumption of the respective beverages in Germany was not notably affected by the consideration.

Forty-five times as much coffee was drunk in Germany, as compared
with tea. At the first glance this seems barely credible. Where were
these great quantities of coffee consumed? In the public life of the
country there is little vestige of anything of the kind. Coffee-drinking
did not leave any noteworthy traces in the street life of Berlin during

those days. About the middle of the nineteenth century, when there were numerous coffee-houses in the streets of Paris, and a still larger number in the streets of Vienna, there were hardly any such places in Berlin. The Prussian capital was abundantly supplied with eating-houses, beer-saloons, wine-shops of all sorts and sizes, but had very few coffee-houses. Since we know that at that date, in literary circles, tea

Stabtverorbneter **Cichorie.**
Meine Herren! es ift allerbings
in vielen Lebensmitteln Theuerung,
aber es gibt ein unfehlbares Mittel
bagegen, ich meine bie Surrogate.
(Mit 100 gegen 1 Stimme abgelehnt).

MUNICIPAL COUNCILLOR CHICORY

Gentlemen! It is true that there is a general rise in prices, but we have an infallible remedy—the use of substitutes. (One vote in their favour.)

(*Coffee famine cartoon, 1855*)

was the principal beverage, we have to ask who, during the epoch in question, were the consumers of these vast quantities of coffee?

Women, chiefly! Women of the middle-class, who played no part in the salons or in literary circles, and of whose life little record remains. It was the wives of worthy German burghers who drank coffee. The women of this class would on Monday go to visit Kätchen; on Tuesday, Lottchen; on Wednesday, Gretchen; and so on. When they had finished their daily round of housework, when the needs of husband and children had been attended to, these good women foregathered to drink coffee together. Over their coffee and their cakes they chattered and they sewed. From the plump coffee-pot there flowed a continuous stream into coffee-cups and thence into stomachs.

It is part of the nature of coffee that it can never become the favourite beverage of women. It makes the intelligence wakeful and critical. It stimulates to a reconstruction of the world. Its effects on the brain are antagonistic to the longing for harmony and peace which is characteristic of the best of women. If, during the period we are now considering, and thenceforward down to the opening of the great war, it was chiefly women who drank coffee in Germany, we infer that the coffee must have been extremely weak. The beverage must have been so watery that it could have had little effect in producing the cerebral excitement characteristic of the coffee-drinker. Among German women it was a social drink of which from ten to twelve cups could be consumed in an afternoon without risk—little more than bitter hot water, strongly sweetened. The large supplies of coffee that found their way into the stomachs of the Berliners were copiously diluted.

As aforesaid, this diluted beverage was consumed chiefly by women —and, in man-ruled Germany, their husbands, their fathers, their brothers, and their sons made fun of them for it. Two new terms were introduced into the German language by the practice, and remain current to this day: "*Kaffeeklatsch*" and "*Kaffeeschwester*." The former word means the gossip or scandal talked by women at a coffee-party; and the latter, primarily a person who is fond of coffee, and secondarily a gossip or a scandal-monger. Coffee was regarded by the men as a "woman's drink," and this idea finds vent in numerous caricatures of the period.

Part of the joke is, however, that men drank coffee, too, though not much in Germany as a social beverage. They all wanted it, and still want it, for breakfast; and any considerable increase in the price of coffee, such as occurred in 1855, evoked loud protests. Witness the caricature showing a race run by the necessities of life to attain the highest price, coffee taking the lead. Next comes a sugar-loaf, followed by an oil-butt and a pepper-sack.

"In the thirties," writes Helmuth von Moltke (the elder), "much political talk went on in the saloons, in the theatres, and in the beer-saloons." It is eminently characteristic of Berlin that he should make no mention of coffee-houses. There were, in fact, very few coffee-houses in Berlin. In Paris, Milan, Vienna, and Venice—to name only the chief focuses of European unrest—coffee-houses at that date had a strong political flavour. "The Café Florian in Venice," writes Balzac in his tale *Massimilla Doni*, "is a strange place. . . . It is at one and the same

"THE WETTER, THE BETTER"

Even the granite basin before the Old Museum must serve the Berlin nurse-maids in their rage for coffee.

(*Cartoon of the 1850's*)

time a lawyer's office, an exchange, a theatre foyer, a club, and a reading-room. . . . Of course it is crowded with political spies, but their presence serves only to stimulate the acuteness of the Venetians, who have been accustomed to be overlooked by these gentry for centuries past." In Berlin, on the other hand, coffee was far too private a concern to become associated with politics, so eminently public. Coffee-drinking, for the Germans, was one of the privacies of domestic life.

What the men of Berlin drank in public was beer. For the lower orders there was "white beer," an effervescent beverage containing very little alcohol, being hardly more intoxicating than diluted fruit-juice.

It was the favourite tipple of cab-drivers and of handicraftsmen of one sort and another. The Berliners have a dry humour of their own, and this "white beer," now dying out, seemed to stimulate it as they quaffed vast quantities from huge glass beakers resembling gold-fish-bowls, and not infrequently used as such.

Before 1890, coffee-houses of the Viennese type scarcely existed in Berlin. How could they, since the Viennese way of doing business in a café, where the greater part of the day was spent, was repugnant to the Berliners? The "public-houses" of Berlin were beer-saloons. Beer provided rest, amusement, and comfort, when men got together after the day's work was over. Coffee came in as a bad second, being regarded as a trifle ridiculous, if only because of its exotic origin. There is a remarkable caricature that was printed during the war of 1870. As is well known, during the war the Prussians made great fun of the mitrailleuse, a French innovation in artillery. The cut shows a French artilleryman turning the crank of a mitrailleuse in which coffee is being ground.

Grinding coffee, especially by a man, always seemed funny to the Berliners. This was presumably an exemplification of the overbearingly masculine attitude of Germans towards their women, and of the fact that the preparation of coffee, in contrast with the preparation of beer, was regarded as a feminine occupation. An English caricature of about the same date (1869), when the bicycle had recently come into use, shows an English cyclist—velocipedist he would then have been called—whose back wheel is connected by cranks and a lever with a coffee-mill behind his saddle. In nineteenth-century England, coffee-houses were as rare as in northern Germany of the period.

Although Berlin business folk regarded public coffee-drinking with good-natured contempt, coffee was nevertheless drunk in considerable quantities publicly in the German capital. Behind a screen! The Berliners drank coffee in confectioners' shops.

The "Konditorei," or pastry-cook's, was, in truth, the creation of the women of Berlin. Although middle-class German women did not mix well in society, the confectioners' shops were meeting-places for both sexes. This went on for decades, and indeed, among the few vestiges of the comparatively recent past in Berlin, are the pastry-cooks' or confectioners' shops, with their threadbare plush sofas and their strange aroma of burnt sugar and the punch with which the fruit-tarts are flavoured.

BICYCLE COFFEE-MILL
(*English cartoon, 1869*)

Characteristically, where women ruled, much coffee was drunk, but it was bad coffee. Furthermore, the beverage was flanked by piles of cakes and tartlets. The pastries of Berlin deserve to be better known than they are. There is, in truth, a "Berlinese style," in pastry, although the world at large thinks only of a Parisian or a Viennese style. The confectionery of Berlin is solid stuff, which has been made out of an extremely substantial dough. The icing is almost as thick as armour-plate. The Parisian epicure's notion that one should rise from one's meal with a light stomach is not suited to the Berlinese character. "Everything you eat must be as solid as the sands of Brandenburg," was meant as a commendation of the pastry-cook's art in Berlin. It applies to almost all the wares of the Berlin confectioner—wares for which no name exists in other languages than German. Fine, filling pastries, made toothsome by liberal quantities of whipped cream. The preamble to a large proportion of Berlin weddings used to be a tryst in a pastry-cook's shop.

For these were the only places in which, without losing caste, German lads and lasses of good family could make assignations. Here, woman held sway. She was responsible for the fact that the cakes were so strong and the coffee so weak!

Small confectioners' shops were as numerous in Berlin (since many bakers were pastry-cooks as well) as coffee-houses were in Vienna. But there were bigger establishments of the kind that were not the haunt of lovers. They were for middle-aged people, persons of rank and station. The most celebrated was Kranzler's, situated at that important street-corner in Berlin, where the Friedrichsstrasse impinges upon Unter den Linden. In no other town in the world would a pastry-cook have established himself here instead of a coffee-house keeper. Two busy streams of wayfarers jostled one another, but Kranzler's remained Kranzler's, an oasis of peace.

As famous as Kranzler's were Josty's and Stehely's. These much-visited confectioners, one of them in the Jägerstrasse and the other in the Potsdamerplatz, these social centres, were, characteristically enough, not run by natives of Berlin. The history of the French capital was repeating itself almost two centuries later in the history of the capital of Prussia. Just as long before, in Paris, the first to open coffee-houses had been Armenians and Persians, so did Josty and Stehely come north from the classic land of sugar-bakery, from Grisons. "Josty" would seem to have been the German-Swiss variant of the Rhaeto-Romanic "Giusti." The name Stehely is still common in Switzerland under the form of Stehelis or Stäheli. It was a new thing for Germans of position to eat cakes and pastries in public. During the Napoleonic epoch, Friedrich Ludwig Jahn had knocked a piece of cake out of the mouth of a boy who, thought Jahn, ought to have been eating bread. In those days, "luxury" was regarded as un-Prussian and effeminate. With the aid of the confectioners, a less harsh time followed upon the iron age of Fichte.

Still, it was but slowly that the Berliners learned to prize the milder European climate into which they had been introduced by their sudden acquisition of wealth and by the new standing of Prussia as a world state. But this newly acquired wealth gave them a chance of getting away from Berlin now and again! Before 1870, an annual summer holiday in the country or at the sea-side, which had long since become a commonplace for the well-to-do of other metropolises, had been regarded as an almost chimerical luxury for the average citizen of Berlin. A townsman was a townsman, a countryman was a countryman, that was all there was to say about the matter. Nevertheless, the good people of Berlin had always longed for things out of their reach. To the Viennese, whose hills and brooks thrust their way into the town, it seemed natural enough that a Schubert should be born in their city. Much more enigmatic was the birth of a Mendelssohn, upon whose ears the strains of his *Sommernachtstraum* suddenly fell in central Berlin, in a stone house in the Leipzigerplatz. Characteristically Berlinese was his music, the expression of a yearning for distant nature!

When, towards the middle of the nineteenth century, twenty years before the fashion of summer excursions began, the Berliners discovered the environs of their city, the Kaffeeschwestern led the way. Had it not been for the Kaffeeschwestern, who could not get on without their abundance of weak coffee, the natural beauties of Charlottenburg, Wilmersdorf, Schöneberg, Stralau-Rummelburg, Pankow, and Niederschöneweide would never have been discovered. Beer, which during the heat of summer made men bad walkers, beer, which made excursions costly because it necessitated the hiring of huge breaks, was a bad travelling-companion. It was otherwise with coffee. To the great delight of the good wives, the city soon became encircled with coffee-gardens. Beside some marshy backwater over which the flies hovered, or where beech woods were interspersed with pine groves, one could sit on a rustic seat in front of a rustic table. "Families can make their coffee here!" would be the sign. Such signs are to be seen in the outskirts of Berlin even today. They show the true function of woman in the Berlinese family. A frugal supper enhanced the enjoyment of nature, while the setting sun displayed its carmine glories. For the atmosphere of Berlin produces at nightfall a colouring even more splendid than that of the steppes.

18

Coffee-House Frequenters in Austria

ORE coffee entered northern Germany by way of Hamburg than entered the Danubian monarchy by way of Trieste. Statistics show that Germany consumed more than Austria. But in Germany, coffee remained inconspicuous, almost invisible. It was elsewhere than in Germany that coffee and its use took visible shape, becoming a distinct factor in Austrian social life.

What the prefects or lords-lieutenant were, politically considered, in the new Austro-Hungarian empire, the coffee-houses were, considered socially. They bore witness to unity of manners and customs. Just as in the Imperium Romanum one encountered the military milestones every thousand double paces along the high road, so, throughout Austria-Hungary, among the territories inhabited by various nationalities, one encountered the prefectoral headquarters built of yellow sandstone and fitted with green shutters—and coffee-houses after the Viennese model. For official business, for registration and the like, the burghers' life centred round the prefecture. There the emperor's subjects were kept under supervision, for administrative purposes; but in other respects their existence circled round the coffee-houses. The administrative offices and the coffee-houses were among the chief determinative factors in the lives of Austro-Hungarians. The better the relations between these two departments, the more genial the association between officialdom and non-officialdom, the more harmoniously flowed the existence of the monarchy.

It was an agreeable enough life! Foreigners found it charmingly attractive. No matter whether the stranger entered Austria from the north, at Bodenbach on the Elbe, or landed at a village in Istria after a Mediterranean voyage, or made his way into Vorarlberg after a so-

journ in highly civilized and comfortable Switzerland, or entered Buko-
vina coming by train from Russia, he instantly became aware of the
smell of coffee, an agreeable testimony to the habits of the Austrians.
Germans, Hungarians, Italians, and Slavs, in other respects often at odds,
were unified at least by the approved Viennese method of making and
drinking coffee. A "Viennese breakfast" denoted coffee with a crescent-
shaped roll, served by a friendly waiter. There was nothing like this
outside the royal and imperial frontier. A waiter who was "Vienna-
trained," even though the man had never been in Vienna, was a product
of Austro-Hungarian unification, almost as much as if he had been a
soldier fighting under the Austro-Hungarian flag. When the incoming
express drew to a stop and one of these waiters, with deft movements,
acting on a stage created by his own imagination, drew near, the traveller instantly felt that with such a servitor and such a breakfast the day
had begun pleasantly. Yes, this was really Austria!

The Austrian coffee-house was invented in Vienna. It spread into
neighbouring territories in the wake of the conquering armies of the
Habsburgs.

As soon as, in the middle of the eighteenth century, Maria Theresa
had first combated and then destroyed the corporative avarice of the
coffee-boilers, the coffee-house industry began to flourish with tropical
luxuriance. It paid well! There is no record of a coffee-house proprietor
going bankrupt in the Vienna of Joseph II. On the contrary, one could
see three coffee-houses side by side in Leopoldstadt. The urge to sit
down in a coffee-house was so powerful among the Viennese that many
foreigners were inclined to think that every block of flats in Vienna
had a coffee-room of its own, as an atrium, a vestibule, for the use of
all the families domiciled therein!

Had not this instinct been so deeply rooted in the life of the Viennese,
the conviction that everyone had a right to his private coffee-house, to
a place which, though public, was a sort of annex to his own dwelling,
it would be impossible to explain the multiplication of little cafés in the
city of Vienna. At his café, the Viennese feels that he is simultaneously
at home and taking part in public life. He is no longer confined within
the four walls of his own domicile, and yet he is in a place more peculiar to himself than the street. His relations with the waiter, the

young lady at the pay-desk, and the man who makes the coffee, are of a quasi-familiar nature.

Together with his quantum of the stimulating beverage, there is brought to him a newspaper fresh from the press, with its atmosphere of the wide world. The Viennese citizen breakfasts in a coffee-house. Thus his day begins filled with images and possibilities. What he makes out of these possibilities is his own concern. Many quit the café to go about their various affairs. Many remain sitting where they are, hypnotized by the murmuring sea of newspapers. No press is so chatty and alluring as that of Vienna.

A great deal of water has run under the bridges between 1780 and the present day. Civilizations have completely changed their visage. Forms of government have decayed, empires have perished, kings have been dethroned. Tallow candles were replaced by gas; then came carbon-arc lights; then tungsten incandescents; and then flood-lighting as the modern form of electric illumination. Only the most conservative people have clung to the habits of a century and a half ago. The Viennese clings to his coffee-house.

He goes there thrice a day. First of all in the morning, between eight and nine. Then at three o'clock in the afternoon, for the "small black," which he drinks soon after his mid-day meal. Then in the evening, between nine and ten. At the first visit, as aforesaid, he gets into touch with the outer world by reading the newspapers, and does not talk much; but the evening visit is devoted to social intercourse, to friendly conversation.

"Coffee-house three times a day" is a fixed prescription. But the length of the visit varies. Although the Viennese punctuates his day by spells in the coffee-house, these spells may be short or long. Sometimes they are so greatly extended that they overlap, especially when he has found it possible to transfer part of his business life to his café. So numerous are the coffee-houses that there is no shortage of space in them. An habitué can write his letters there, or find a convenient corner for a private negotiation. I have spoken of the Viennese as conservative; and, in very truth, many of the cafés of the Austrian capital retain the function such places had in the London of 1680. They are business resorts. Whereas in London this sort of thing came to an end nigh upon two centuries ago, the Viennese coffee-houses continue, as of old, to play the part of exchanges. Of course a merchant with a large business learned long ago to transfer his affairs to his private office. Fifty years back, to do such a thing in Vienna would have been regarded as "putting on side." The Viennese "city man" was looked up by other Viennese in "his" coffee-house. This was a place that seemed to be democratically accessible to every visitor; but where, nevertheless, the staff could, at a hint, make fine distinctions when the host wanted the reception to be cordial or otherwise; when the guest was to be courted or cold-shouldered; when the standing of the man of business who was receiving visitors was to be shown in a more exalted light than would have been possible in his office. Only to outward seeming were these coffee-houses neutral ground. They were and are attuned to the qualities of particular sorts of men, who know one another by repute. "That is a man from my coffee-house!" a Viennese will say during a Sunday walk in the Wiener Wald, when he encounters an acquaintance whose name perhaps he does not know.

The proprietor and the waiter showed great discrimination in their treatment of the guests. They played as if upon a piano by making delicate distinctions in their attention to this, that, and the other customer, and in the deference they showed to persons with official titles. The frequenters were appropriately flattered, a well-to-do member of the middle-class being unjustifiably addressed as "von," an intellectual being belauded as "Professor" or "Doctor." The "attachment" of a coffee-house keeper to his respective guests was not solely determined by material causes. It did not depend upon the amount of the particular bill. Regular visitors were those most affectionately received, and to lose a guest of long standing was and is regarded as a disaster, a misfortune, a mortification.

The affection is mutual. I know a paper-merchant whose business went down so that he had to remove to a distant quarter of the town, but he continued for twenty years thereafter to frequent his familiar coffee-house. When I asked him the reason for this strange and unpractical behaviour, he replied that he could not stomach the idea of hurting his host's feelings by making a change. . . . The high respect paid to the coffee-house keepers of Vienna has often aroused a smile, perhaps unjustly. Assuredly a Viennese coffee-house keeper who for thirty or forty years in succession has ministered to the comfort of his fellow-citizens during the many hours they pass in public is entitled to all respect. Tokens of honour were almost too conspicuous upon the breast of Ludwig Riedl! A good many foreign princes also bestowed decorations upon the man who ran the favourite coffee-house of Emperor Francis Joseph. They would have been hard put to it to give a reason for doing so. It was the thing to do, and that was the long and short of it. The proprietor of the Café de l'Europe assembled upon his breast, as a symbol of the coffee-house industry, tokens of the reverence the Viennese feel for themselves and their peculiar type of civilization. It delighted them that a coffee-house keeper should be honoured—all the more because his business was carried on where the cathedral of St. Stephen's throws its shadow at noon.

There were two things which primarily attracted the Viennese into coffee-houses.

The first lure was billiards. The billiard-tables were longer than those of today, furnished with very heavy legs, screwed to the floor. The game played upon these tables was not billiards, but pool. When a ball was pocketed, a bell rang. The table was lighted with candles, and on the floor was a stool which the marker could mount when the candles needed snuffing. The cost of a game of billiards was four kreuzer, the price of a couple of litres of wine. Though the charge was thus high, the billiard-tables were greatly patronized. When, towards 1810, Napoleon's officers introduced "French billiards," a game played upon a table without pockets, masters in the art of this cannon game developed in Vienna. The most famous resort for billiard-players was Hugelmann's coffee-house close to Ferdinand Bridge.

The second attraction was a more notable one. It occurred to a man named Cramer to have the latest newspapers lying about on the tables of his coffee-house. He was inspired by the notion that merchants and men-of-letters, intellectuals and officials, are eager for the latest news, and that the provision of newspapers for public reading would save their pockets. Cramer did things on the grand scale. He subscribed to almost all the dailies and weeklies published in the German tongue, providing also Italian, French, and English newspapers and magazines. The cost was heavy, but the venture paid amazingly. Cramer's Café became transformed into a reading-room, and the impatience of the incessant stream of newcomers saw to it that guests should not sit too long over their papers. Thus the goddess of curiosity had made her way into the coffee-house. There she remained. There are newspaper-addicts everywhere, but especially in Vienna. Newspapers are the opium of the Viennese.

Until recently the Parisian coffee-house keeper supplied no newspapers to his customers, and even now, except for those left there by the guests, the number of journals on the tables is scanty. Therein lies a notable distinction between a French café and an Austrian one. Although the modern Parisians drink a good deal of coffee, nowadays (unless the café is also a restaurant), their stay in the coffee-house is short. Small cafés are extremely numerous in Paris, and they supply alcoholic liquors as well as coffee. The proprietors speed the circulation of their customers by furnishing coffee and other drinks at the bar at far lower prices than are paid by persons who sit down at the tables. When you sit at a table, to avoid the possibility of dispute the enhanced price of your coffee or other drinks is often stamped on the saucer!

The furnishing of the coffee-houses was, to begin with, extremely simple. The only adornment was to put up on the walls a few mirrors with rococo frames. But even this seemed splendid for those days. When, subsequently, the voice of Rousseau reached Vienna from France, demanding a "return to nature," and when the Viennese discovered the Prater, they built among rustling trees three coffee-houses which became centres of social life. The distance between them and the distance from the town became symbolical of distance in general. People took note of the time required to reach the first coffee-house. On the way to these resorts, the Viennese learned how to ride and to drive. Furious driving, originally a Hungarian practice, now became one of the favourite sports in Vienna.

The final defeat of Napoleon brought wealth to the Austrian bourgeoisie, which had hitherto lived frugally. One of the outcomes of the consequent expansion was, in the year 1820, the opening of the Silver Coffee-House in the Plankengasse. The host, Ignaz Neuner, provided silver utensils and table-service, and even had the hangers for hats and overcoats made of silver. There were three rooms in the café. One of them was for billiard-players, the second for chess-players, and the

BEETHOVEN URGES GRILLPARZER TO SEEK HIM AT THE COFFEE-HOUSE
("Opposite the Golden Pear—but alone and without a tiresome appendix.")

third (how great an innovation!) was a ladies' room. Prior to 1840, very few Viennese ladies entered a coffee-house. Only through much reading of foreign literature could they be brought to this emancipation and to adopting so masculine a practice. At Neuner's, however, they were to be found—in the famous Silver Coffee-House which was, above all, the café of Austrian poetry. Grillparzer and Lenau were among its frequenters. We are told of Lenau that for more than twelve years he was to be seen every day at Neuner's, sometimes in melancholy mood, sometimes genial, sometimes manfully fighting down his inward disquiet. He was a fine billiard-player. He held his billiard cue like St. George's spear, though the dragon was invisible. It was far from his beloved coffee-house that the dragon of lunacy at length claimed him for its own.

Of course the Viennese coffee-houses were not exempt from the old-standing enmity of governments against the political activities of coffee-house frequenters. We find again and again in history that the "spirit of the coffee-houses" becomes especially powerful after defeat. Political agitators are stimulated by the overthrow of national armies in war. Thus, very soon after the retreat of Kara Mustafa from Vienna, somewhere about 1690, the coffee-houses of Constantinople were closed, as being centres of agitation. For centuries, coffee has been a support to citizens in their revolts against authority. The Madrid revolution began in the Café Lorenzoni; and in Northern Italy the revolts against Austrian rule at Venice, Padua, Verona, and other towns were almost always the outcome of coffee-house conspiracies. In one of her Italian novels, *Federigo Gonfalonière*, Ricarda Huch describes the program of the young Milanese intellectuals in the year 1820. It contains the following demands: gas-lighting in the houses and streets, newspapers, public baths, and, above all, "coffee-houses, in which newspapers shall be provided, and where interesting persons can exchange ideas." Coffee "dilates the blood-vessels." It sounds like a joke, but is true, that Baptista d'Andrade, the Brazilian chemist, was able to distil from one hundred litres of coffee-berries ten grammes of explosive, a variety of nitromannite.

The idea of awakening, of a "rising"—the notion of the Italian revival, the "risorgimento," is physiologically coincident with the chemical effect of coffee upon the human organism.

Even in the gentler climate of Vienna, an explosive mood prevailed against Metternich. The discharge occurred in 1848. A year before, the Café Griensteidl had been founded. This promptly became the head-quarters of the malcontent nationalists and democrats, who were opposed to the conservative supporters of the government, frequenters of the Café Daum, hard by. The Austrian police were so suspicious of the Griensteidlians, that they bribed one of the waiters at the café, a man named Schorsch, to act as a spy upon the habitués, and to report many of their incautious utterances. When this transpired, there was an internal revolution in the Café Griensteidl. Schorsch was promptly given the sack, and the comic papers of Vienna made fun of the matter. In 1862, when one of the north-German governments was secretly recruiting volunteers in Vienna to help in the invasion of Denmark, there were again troubles in the Café Griensteidl; and once more, in 1870, there were feuds between francophils and germanophils. But the police soon put a stop to the attempts of these factions to re-fight the Battle of Sedan in the cafés!

19

Speculation and the Spanish Crisis

T HE nineteenth century had a different relationship towards coffee from that which had respectively obtained in the two preceding centuries.

Whereas the seventeenth century valued coffee for the most part as a medicament, as a quickener of the circulation and as an anti-Bacchic remedy, the eighteenth century looked upon it as an intellectual stimulant. Coffee, said Montesquieu, sometimes enables very stupid people to do clever things.

The attitude of the nineteenth century was a much more comprehensive one. For it, coffee was primarily, secondarily, and all the time an energizer. The nineteenth century was the epoch of unparalleled achievement. The industrial era, in great measure inaugurated by the Continental System and continuing to flourish abundantly when that system had been overthrown, demanded, in theory at least, a twenty-four-hour working day. This could only be realized through the aid of coffee, which was therefore consumed freely by the masses. During the nineteenth century, the working-classes drank coffee. Coffee, often very badly prepared, was a prerequisite to the activity of factories and workshops.

Indeed, during the nineteenth century, coffee began to show a new visage. It speciously presented itself as competent "to solve the social problem." It came to be regarded as the antagonist of hunger. During the dispute which those who imported coffee into Europe carried on for so long against the high tariff imposed upon this staple, it was again and again declared that: "Coffee is a popular nutrient, and must therefore not be highly taxed." From the medical standpoint, the statement is false. Coffee has no nutritive value whatever, and one who should try to live upon it would soon starve to death. Sociologically considered, however, there was something to be said for the argument. Coffee produces a fallacious sense that hunger has been satisfied. It "helps people to bear scarcity of food." Coffee alleviates the pangs of hunger. Napoleon was one of the first men of note who recognized the widespread importance of coffee in war-time. Throughout the nineteenth century, coffee was "the soldiers' drink." A beleaguered fortress in which there was no coffee was foredoomed to destruction just as if there had been a shortage of ammunition. During the war of 1914–1918, the beleaguered fortress of Germany became painfully aware of this.

Coffee, then, though not a nutrient, is valuable, nay indispensable, to the worker as an energizer of the labour process. As soon as this became recognized, it was natural that coffee should be one of the chief pawns in the game of financial speculation, which loves to play with the necessities of life, or with articles that are believed to be such.

Coffee had become one of the necessities of life!

In the years when the Continental System was in force, and when no coffee could be imported, such small quantities as were in store or could be smuggled in commanded fantastic prices. Throughout the nineteenth century, the memory of this remained alive in the minds of speculators, who were aware that, given certain conditions, a fortune could be made out of coffee. Its price on the exchanges depended upon the relation between supply and demand. Prices soared in times of scarcity.

A good example of jiggery-pokery in such matters, of the way in which speculators turned passing political conditions to account, is furnished by the remarkable story of the tension between France and Spain in the year 1823.

At the beginning of this year, war was imminent in western Europe. Why? The Spaniards, a strange people, prone to swift vacillations, sometimes fervent on behalf of the Catholic cause, and sometimes eager for revolution, had, for years, been in an uproar. To begin with, inspired by their Christian sentiments, they fought against Napoleon, the antichrist of the North. They took up arms on behalf of the pious king, Ferdinand of Bourbon. Yet hardly was Ferdinand back in the country, than they changed their minds. Now they were zealous for the confiscation of ecclesiastical estates, for a declaration of the Rights of Man, for popular liberties, parliamentary government—in a word, for every-thing that the French revolution, which they had so strenuously re-sisted, had brought into being northward of the Pyrenees. Now Europe, which had been contemplating Ferdinand and his Spaniards with scorn-ful amusement, was horrified. Was there not something in the wind which recalled the great revolution of 1793? Was the monarch about to be arrested, deposed, perhaps executed? Tsar Alexander was especially concerned. He was farthest away from the seat of disturbance, but had the most sensitive nerves. Alarmed again and again by reports from Metternich, he considered it incumbent upon him to save monarchy in Spain, to fight once more against the revolution, to maintain the legit-imist principle, to send a Russian army to Madrid. At the meetings of the monarchs in Troppau, Laibach, and Verona, where intervention in southern Europe (for there were disturbances in Italy as well) was discussed, it was unanimously agreed to suppress the Spanish revolution.

But who could bell the cat? Who was to coerce the Spaniards to good behaviour?

France!

Louis XVIII, and Chateaubriand as well, would seem to have proposed that the French fleur-de-lis, the banner that thirty years before had been contemptuously torn down by the men of the Parisian Terror, should, now that it had been rehoisted, be triumphantly borne to Madrid. What a splendid idea! New France, the France of the restored Bourbons, monarchical and Christian France, was to show herself the supreme champion of legitimism. Besides, Ferdinand VII and Louis XVIII were both Bourbons, and therefore distant cousins. Blood is thicker than water.

The tacit mandate that Russia, Austria, and Prussia conferred upon conquered France eight years after her supreme humiliation, this mis-sion to play the victor in Spain, was pleasing to French national vanity. First of all, on the pretext that Spanish revolutionists were sowing dis-quiet in southern France, a police cordon was established along the frontier. Then troops were sent to guard the passes, it being alleged that yellow fever prevailed in Spain. More and yet more battalions were dispatched to the south. At length everyone expected war. Peo-ple were only waiting for the declaration of King Louis XVIII, as soon as he returned from Verona.

The king read the Speech from the Throne on January 28, 1823. It was moderate in form, but the contents signified war. Louis declared that he had done everything he could to make sure that, henceforward, France should not be disturbed by Spanish propaganda. But the folly of Madrid destroyed all hopes of peace. He was compelled, therefore, he said, to recall his ambassador. One hundred thousand Frenchmen, under the command of a prince of the blood royal, were ready, God willing, to maintain monarchy in Spain, and to reconcile that country with Europe.

The Speech from the Throne was accepted by a decisive majority in the Chamber. Shouts were raised: "Long live the King and all the Bourbons!" The ambassadors of the European powers were looking on like gods of destiny. With one exception, the British ambassador! The British government, in which the whig, George Canning, was secretary for foreign affairs, was not inclined to smile at the notion that, only ten years after England had protected Spain against Napoleonic usurpation, Frenchmen, though royalist, should once more conquer Madrid. In contrast with the deputies, the public of Paris, the French populace, showed little enthusiasm. Those who held national securities were dismayed. One hundred francs in the national debt was quoted at seventy-seven, and most other securities fell in proportion. When the names of the generals were announced who, under Angoulême, were to lead the invasion of Spain—some of them were Napoleonic marshals, such as Oudinot—confidence was somewhat restored.

In these circumstances, speculators began to play for a rise in prices, especially in the prices of imports. King Louis XVIII, in his Speech from the Throne, had declared that French naval stations were adequately fortified, and that a number of cruisers had been equipped to protect marine commerce. Among all the rhetorical flourishes in the speech of this obese and undependable man, this seemed the most alarming. Almost as alarming, however, was the next, to the effect that "if war should prove unavoidable, its area will be restricted and its duration shortened as much as possible." What did that really mean? Perhaps that England was planning to withdraw from any sort of collaboration with the Alliance, Prussia, Russia, Austria, France, and to make common cause with revolutionary Spain? In that case the war might last for a very long time. As early as January 30, mounted couriers were galloping across Europe from exchange to exchange, to Amsterdam, Hamburg, Vienna, St. Petersburg, Berlin, Frankfort-on-Main, and, on the western side of the Channel, to London. "Buy coffee!" was the watchword. "Within a few weeks there will be no more to be had, since the sea-routes will be closed!" Even if there was not to be a naval war between equally matched forces, the danger of privateering was very great. Neither Spanish nor French merchantmen freighted from coffee-growing countries would dare to keep the seas. While there was a general fall in securities, the price of coffee rose rapidly. Large sums were invested in coffee on the exchanges.

But what had become of the presupposition upon which these transactions had been based: the war? After all, there was no war! The faithless Chamber, which had so recently applauded the king, was now listening, with malicious delight, to the speeches of the opposition. Duvergier de Huranne proved that intervention in Spain would be unpatriotic and scandalous. Sebastiani outdid the previous speaker by asking the nation what interest it could have in espousing the cause of the Holy Alliance, the former enemy of France, which had so unexpectedly shown an interest in Spain. Lainé, Lesaigneur, and Cabanon laid stress upon the injury which a war would do to trade. In the upper house, too, there suddenly appeared many adversaries of the war. Talleyrand, now seventy years of age, roused himself out of his apathy to show, with shrewd arguments, that absolutism in Spain was not genuinely legitimist or, rather, was not strictly lawful, since popular councils had already existed in Aragon of old. Napoleon, said the Emperor's sometime right-hand man, had really ensured his downfall through fighting a war with Spain, and the restored French monarchy would do well to avoid following his example. He himself, Talleyrand, Prince of Benevento, had, in 1809, warned Napoleon against the Spanish adventure. Perhaps King Louis would pay heed to a similar warning now!

This speech, delivered by Talleyrand in his caustic and intentionally tedious manner, produced an immense effect. It seemed barely credible that after hearing such words the Chamber would vote the war credits. On February 25 there was an oratorical duel between Chateaubriand, who belonged to the extreme Right, and Manuel, the leader of the Left.

Manuel went so far as to rail not only against the advocates of war, but against the Bourbons themselves and Louis XVIII. Until this sitting of the Chamber, coffee speculators had, in fear and trembling, maintained the price of coffee. They had been hoping for a war; but now, exactly four weeks after the king's Speech from the Throne, they believed that there would be no war.

Instead of a war, something else came. Coffee! Coffee from all directions! The seas were no longer dangerous, so, during March, trading ships in abundance arrived from America. Supplies of coffee were

WHAT THE ARMY NEEDS MOST . . .
provided Prussia should become involved
in the Crimean War.

(*Cartoon, 1855*)

shipped from Mexico, the Antilles, Jamaica; and the vessels brought news that a huge Brazilian harvest was expected. Prices, which had been artificially sustained, fell with a rush. There were failures in London, Paris, Frankfort, Berlin, and St. Petersburg; a mercantile crash of gigantic proportions led to hundreds of suicides. Millionaires became paupers.

Then, when the earth was still fresh upon the tombs of these victims of speculation, war was, after all, declared between France and Spain. A short, local war, such as the king had predicted. An almost bloodless war, in which the British took no part. On April 7 the Duke of Angoulême's army crossed the Bidassoa, which, for twelve miles of its course, forms the boundary between France and Spain.

But the victims of the coffee crisis did not hear the martial tramp of the French regiments as these entered Madrid.

Overseas Harvests, World Markets, and Prices

THE happiness of countless thousands in Europe, their lives, their wealth, and their health, depended upon the harvest in coffee-growing countries.

Vacillations in the price of this staple were not due exclusively to the machinations of speculators. They depended also upon the nature of the coffee-shrub and upon the nature of man. The mutual relationships between these respective natures, the way they reacted upon each other, determined whether, as far as coffee was concerned, a year should be a year of plenty or a year of famine.

It worked as follows. The harvest was sold for cash. The planter, naturally, had a strong motive for investing as much as he could of this cash in new plantations. His material benefit from the harvest was like money won at the gaming-table, which always incites gamesters to hazard it once more. In extending their plantations, planters took no heed of the commercial side of the question, forgetting that since markets first existed they have always been subject to the iron law of supply and demand.

Thoughtlessly, therefore, the planters extended their enterprises, with the inevitable result of over-production. Confident that prices would be maintained, they grew more and ever more coffee, to learn, in their despair, that each new million sacks had the effect of reducing profits instead of increasing them.

Was this the immediate effect? Unfortunately not. The planters were given time to persist in their mistaken courses. Had they been taught within a year that they were on the wrong track, the crisis would have been less catastrophic.

The nature of the coffee-shrub is such that it does not begin to bear fruit until after the lapse of four barren years! During these four years, in which no return could be expected, the planters had no direct evidence that their reckless extension of plantations would recoil upon their own heads, so they continued to put more and more land under cultivation. It was after the lapse of four years that over-production became manifest. In the fifth, sixth, seventh, and eighth years, larger and ever larger quantities of coffee were poured into the market. Prices thereupon crashed. In the seventh year, the psychological consequences became manifest. There was a panic among the planters; the new plantations were neglected; workers were discharged; coffee fell into disrepute because "it did not pay"; landowners turned their attention to maize, cotton, or stock-raising. Then the price of coffee began to recover. Supply was falling short of demand. The planters found, to their astonishment, that their worthless coffee could once more be sold for good money. Here was a stimulus to fresh plantation, and the cycle was resumed—*da capo*.

Approximately every seven years the life of a coffee-planter completes this predestined cycle. Seven years are a long time, and memories are short. Men forget their mistakes, and make them once more. Again and again this happened. Throughout the nineteenth century we can trace the history of this anarchic succession of over-production and under-production of coffee. Delight in a year when prices have been high is translated into an undue extension of planting, which, four years later, leads to the recurrence of rock-bottom prices. Then there is a panic. In the seventh year, the pendulum swings back once more towards the side of extended planting.

In 1790, when the revolution put an end for a time to coffee-planting in Santo Domingo, there was a shortage of coffee in the world. Prices rose, so that there might have been expected extreme over-production towards 1799. The Napoleonic wars prevented this. Although prices were high, the planters did not venture to go on producing a commodity that was continually exposed to capture upon the high seas. This state of affairs lasted until 1813. Very soon after sea traffic had been freed from its hazards, under-production took effect in a rise of prices, and, at the beginning of the eighteen-twenties, over-production in the West Indian plantations was the inevitable consequence. Except for the perturbations produced by wars, and especially by the American Civil

War, decade after decade was characterized by a regular succession of over-production and under-production, with intermediate years when, for a brief period, there was a balance.

In the year 1903, at a congress of representatives from coffee-producing lands, held in New York, a retrospect of nineteenth-century experience was drawn up, to the following effect: "Very remarkable is the way in which, for some decades, at least since the War of Secession, but before this as well, crises of over-production and under-production have regularly alternated; periods of very high profits and periods disastrous to the planters. This anarchy is, in both cases, the outcome of extravagant views; of enthusiasm, which leads to excessive planting, and then to moral depression, the result of which is that large areas are left uncultivated. . . . The coffee-planter's life is characterized by decennial crises. For what reason? The planters do not know one another, and do not take counsel together. . . . They make no attempt to consolidate the market."

Often enough, in the tropics, a white coffee-planter was several days' journey from his nearest neighbour, with whom he might have exchanged ideas. This isolation was supposed, by those who assembled at the aforesaid congress, to account for the failure to organize coffee-planting in the nineteenth century. The isolated planter, left entirely to his own devices, and connected with the outer world by nothing more than the news which reached him concerning the price of coffee, acted upon the impulses of the moment.

He acted foolishly, to his own detriment. Nevertheless—and herein lies the tragic element—his actions were logically accordant with the laws of political economy.

Classical economists formulated the "law of gravitation of prices." The law finds expression in the relationship of the coffee-planter to his own product. How does the law run?

"The market price of a product tends always to gravitate towards the natural price."

What does that mean? First of all, the natural price is the price determined by the cost of production. The market price, on the other hand, is the price that depends upon the number and the eagerness of buyers and sellers in the market. When supply is scanty, the market price rises. Thereupon, this high price acts like a magnet attracting capital and labour. The planters would be superhuman if their intelligence enabled them to resist what is as irresistible as gravitation. Since they do not resist, the result is inevitable. Increased application of capital and labour increases production, and thus augments the supply until there are more sellers than buyers, and prices fall. They fall so low that the returns do not suffice to pay the interest on capital and the wages of labour. Thereupon capital and labour are withdrawn from this field of production.

In European lands, a sort of inertia prevents a too rapid change between the opening and closing of factories and workshops, between the engagement and discharge of workers. But in tropical countries (where as yet, for the most part, social legislation and labour-protection laws are unknown) such fluctuations occur with amazing speed. Coffee has always been a ticklish commodity. Its troubles have not been merely due to speculators in the European market, but to the vagaries of the coffee-planting States.

The coffee-bean is smooth and slippery!

When the Arabs lost the supremacy they once held in supplying coffee to the world, the Dutch were, for a long time, the chief sellers of coffee.

Amsterdam—in this respect a suburb of Batavia—was, of course, the principal place to which produce was shipped from the Dutch Indies. Still, Rotterdam came in as a good second. How did the magnates of the Dutch East India Company dispose of their coffee? Mostly by auction. Thus, in 1712, the first shipment of coffee from Java, eight hundred ninety-four sacks, was sold by auction in Amsterdam.

In every auction there is an element of uncertainty, of surprise. If you go into a shop to buy half a pound of coffee priced at three shillings, and cannot get it because somebody else offers four shillings, you will feel yourself back in primitive times. Are there no longer any fixed prices? Actually, it need hardly be said, in retail trade that sort of thing does not happen. For half a pound of coffee, as for other goods, there is a specified price.

Wholesale trade is different. Here coffee is too great a dignitary to be controlled by rules and regulations. The uncertainties of sale by auction correspond to the caprices of coffee's abundance, to the quantities that have been shipped and to the quantities that are stored in warehouses.

Through auctions, the magnates of the Dutch East India Company secured what they wanted, which was that their warehouses should not remain glutted with coffee. Many buyers came to the salesroom, and, amid the excitement of competition, paid higher prices than they would have paid if their heads had kept cool. Still, there were disadvantages in the system. When the attendance at an auction was scanty, lower prices might prevail than corresponded to the true state of the market.

The Dutch did not remain for ever the dictators of the market. Other colonies than those of the Netherlands came into the field. Towards the end of the eighteenth century, the French were the most important coffee-brokers. Shipments from the French Indies were sold by auction in Bordeaux. Then Havre, being much nearer Paris, came to the fore in this matter. After that, both Holland and France were outpaced by England as rulers in the coffee-market. After the close of the Napoleonic wars, London could dictate prices. Then, towards 1850, the New York market became no less important than that of London, for the United States had developed into a great consumer of coffee, absorbing a considerable part of the harvest of the new coffee-growing giant, Brazil. Now Hamburg came third in the list after London and New York. The rise of the Hamburg coffee-market to importance was closely connected with the extension of coffee-planting in Brazil.

In Hamburg, coffee was seldom sold by auction. There the produce exchange decided matters. There was a good reason for this, inasmuch as auctions of produce are difficult to arrange except as regards the products of the auctioning country's own colonies. No doubt the example of London can be quoted to refute this dictum. The British empire produces much tea, and Britain consumes comparatively little coffee, but nevertheless large quantities of coffee were auctioned in London.

Why? Because London was the banker of the world. At any rate it was the banker of many coffee-growing countries. There was so much capital seeking investment in the London market, that exporters of coffee could reckon with fair confidence upon the disposal of their goods. Even if no English out-and-out buyers were forthcoming, there would be London firms to bid at auction in order to reship coffee to the continent. Moreover, London was the best place in which to sell coffee on commission. It was a place where banks would lend money upon shipments, so that the shipper could get his cash without waiting for the produce to be sold.

The earlier London auctions took place in certain coffee-houses, and were popularly known as "auction by candle." The auctioneer had a lighted candle-stump on his desk, and continued to receive bids as long as the candle was burning. When it flickered out, the lot was knocked down to the last bidder.

During the nineteenth century these auctions assumed very peculiar features. No outsider could take a hand in the game, because he could not understand the dialect. The auction-room had a slang of its own. One who intended to become a coffee-broker, had to serve years of apprenticeship before he could "know the ropes."

The coffee that was to be sold by auction was divided into lots, graded by quality and in accordance with the place of origin. Samples of each lot were exposed for inspection. Lists of these lots, containing a precise description of the wares, were sent round to the dealers. One who did not wish to bid in person at the auction would go to the salesroom, examine samples, roast small quantities, make coffee and taste it, and then give a purchasing broker his instructions. The actual buyer would make secret signs to the broker while the auction was in progress.

The genuine buyers were dealers who really wanted to get coffee in order to sell it again. But among the bidders were speculators who had no intention of buying, and only wished to keep up prices.

A produce exchange is a market where goods are sold without being actually on the premises. A coffee exchange is such a market, where coffee is sold, although there is no coffee there. It is a part of our manifold human nature that we are influenced by absent things. A man may have a peculiarly active faith—or the reverse—in things unseen, which are known to him only by repute. The rise and fall of prices in a produce exchange depends, in the last analysis, upon the workings of the human imagination.

A shortage in supply would, in any case, raise prices without the intervention of speculators. Still, in such circumstances, speculators seize their opportunity, combining with financiers to form a ring, in order to maintain high prices as long as possible. Before the 'seventies, when there were no submarine cables, few steamships, and the telephone had not yet been invented, such a ring would buy all the coffee in the market, and run up prices to a fancy level. Wholesale traders had to pay whatever the ring demanded. Its activities were only frustrated when unexpected shipments arrived.

In 1823, as already related, when the tension between France and Spain did not culminate in war so soon as had been anticipated, there was for a time such a fanciful rise in prices. Then the bottom dropped out of the market, and many of the speculators, being ruined, committed suicide. In the beginning of the eighteen-seventies, there was a similar swindle, when exaggerated tidings of a failure in the coffee-crop were disseminated. The price of coffee soared to a higher level than it had reached for fifty years. When large quantities of the staple now began to pour in from across the seas, the bears in the coffee-market seized their opportunity, laid a counter-mine, defeated the bulls, and forced the price of coffee below the figure warranted by the actual situation. In 1874, submarine cables were laid down from South America to New York and from New York to London. Thenceforward, the daily receipt of messages in the market modified the technique of speculation. Prices were regulated, not by actual shipments, but by expected harvests. News from Brazil concerning frost and rainfall or favourable weather while the crops were ripening came to play a great part in the game.

In 1888, an ill-conceived attempt to raise prices glutted Havre with supplies of coffee. Catastrophe was imminent. To avoid disaster, the bulls tried to enlist the aid of capital from elsewhere. The attempt took the form of trading in "futures." This helped the speculators, with the aid of extraneous capital, to avoid having to unload their stocks of coffee at knock-down prices; but the result further showed that capital thus used was strong enough to distribute the produce of the harvest quietly and equably throughout the ensuing year.

The introduction of dealing in futures in the coffee trade was natural enough. Coffee, though used in much the same quantities throughout the year, is marketed in vast amounts at a particular season when the staple has been produced in distant lands. The function of commerce is to bridge differences in time and space. Capital could not fulfil this important function without the aid of the "time-bargain," as dealing futures is sometimes called. The capital invested in time-bargains renders possible a coalescence of the funds of numerous gamblers who are not genuine traders, in the sense of performing some function in relation to the commodity, but wish only to earn profits. One who enters into a time-bargain contracts to sell stocks, shares, or a commodity such as coffee, for a stipulated price at a future time. But the speculator is not interested in a genuine deal with the commodity in question. He does not aspire to handle coffee, not being a real merchant; he wants only to earn a profit from his contract when the term expires—or before. He hopes to gain out of the difference between the price at which he has agreed to sell months ahead and the price which now rules in the market.

German merchants were slow to follow the example set them by Havre. But the Hamburg exchange had to introduce trading in futures when it saw, year after year, all the capital available for trading or speculation in coffee flow away to Havre.

Time-bargains were, indeed, originally devised, not to promote speculation, but to hinder it. With their aid, a prudent merchant could ensure himself against the risk to which he was exposed from future fluctuations in prices. These prices were unknown. By covering purchases or sales in the futures market, by "hedging" in fact, he was able to safeguard his position. But who were his partners in this matter? Speculators, of course! Since these speculators absolved the merchant from risk, they quickly gained control of the market.

Thus, very soon after the introduction of time-bargains into the Hamburg produce exchange, excesses of speculation ensued. There was an unhealthy swing of prices from high to low and from low back to high again, so that ten times as much "paper coffee" changed hands as there was coffee actually produced. That was in the year 1888, when sixty-one million sacks of coffee were bought and sold in seven futures markets, although the harvest amounted to only six million sacks. Gaming-houses where roulette was played had been closed, but people could gamble as much as they liked in time-bargains. What distinguished the time-bargain market from the gaming-house was that in the former the lowest possible stake was five hundred sacks of coffee, and that one could gamble without staking anything in hard cash.

It was no longer the traditional oscillation of the balance between supply and demand that now led to fluctuations in the price of coffee. These latter were determined by the shrewdness and the boldness of rival groups, the bulls and the bears.

"Overseas harvests and speculation," writes Hans Roth, "affect the movements of the world markets as the winds affect the waves of the sea. Crests and depressions follow each other in a perpetual rhythm. Only when the wind blows against the current of the waters are the big waves broken up into the little ones of a choppy sea. If, on the other hand, the wind and the current are in the same direction, the waves grow higher. When the wind rises to a storm, the waves grow mountains high, and break at their crests. There you have an image of the contest between the bulls and the bears, of the great battles in the exchange. The wreckage after the storm takes the form of bankruptcies and repudiation of contracts."

These kinds of storms, however, are seen only at or near the surface. The consumer, dwelling at peace in the depths, knows nothing of this turmoil on the surface. Were it otherwise, the consumption of coffee would soon come to an end.

Genuine wholesale dealers within any country are influenced only to a moderate extent by wild fluctuations in the produce exchange. There are other factors besides the price in the world market that determine the wholesale price of coffee in England, Germany, or France. Freightage, customs dues, and other overhead charges do not vary with the fluctuations in the original price of coffee, or at any rate they vary less extensively and swiftly, and the extent of the fluctuations is thereby damped down.

Besides, the trader must not expect too much from the consumer. The majority of petty buyers want to go on buying the kinds of coffee with which they are familiar and to buy them at the accustomed prices. To the unskilled eye, all coffees are alike, so the purchaser regards the price of a coffee as a measure and a guarantee of quality. The individual purchaser reacts against a rise in price by restricting his personal consumption. That is only natural. Oddly enough, however, he is also estranged by a fall in the price of coffee, if that fall affects only certain varieties of coffee, and not coffee in general. "Why is coffee cheaper?" you may hear him ask, with suspicion in his voice. Even when a low price is due to exceptionally large harvests or to other conditions affecting the world market, it is difficult to persuade the purchaser that anything but a decline in quality can account for a decline in price. The retail price must remain stable, if the retailer is to dispose of his stock successfully. The price at which he has bought will differ to a varying degree from the price at which he sells, since the price at which he buys depends upon vacillating conditions in the world market. The larger the difference between purchasing and selling price, the better for the dealer. At times, however, this difference becomes smaller and smaller, until at length the retail trader cannot make any profit. To help himself out of the difficulty, he sells inferior kinds of coffee at the old price. Of course the purchaser must not know anything about this. The retailer's art lies in a skilful blending which will deceive the consumer's palate.

The retailer must also tickle his customers' imagination. He will give his blends of coffee fancy names, which in most cases have nothing to do with the origin of the coffee that is being sold, or with its accepted destination in the trade. Most of the purchasers are women, and they are attracted by pretty names. To call a blend "pearl coffee" may tickle their fancy so much as to make them willing to pay a higher price.

The name "mocha" has a wonder-working influence. Arabia cannot produce nearly as much mocha as the public demands. Brazil has here come to the coffee-merchant's aid. During the rainy season, coffee is shipped on old-style windjammers to Arabia, by the longest route, round the Cape of Good Hope. It reaches port as wet as a soaked sponge. The damp and the long voyage have spoiled its aroma. Doctored and dried under the Arabian sun, and rechristened with the money-making name of mocha, it is now shipped on steamers to be sold in the great markets of the West.

We are coming to the realm of jests and anecdotes. Of course coffee can be as sophisticated as wine. Even if the history of the coffee-trade were not fully known, one could guess as much. There are, indeed, as many jokes about humbugging with coffee as there are about the spurious labels on wine-bottles.

One of the greatest revolutions in the coffee-trade occurred in 1906, when a caffeine-free coffee was put on the market. What do we mean by "caffeine-free" coffee? Since, in the seventeenth century, coffee helped to wean the English from drunkenness, and the movement spread from England to Germany, Scandinavia, and the rest of northern Europe, coffee has often been styled "the puritans' drink." The enemies of wine, beer, spirits, and intoxicating beverages generally, had armed themselves with this puritans' decoction.

Now, persistence as well as seriousness are characteristic of the puritan temperament. The waves of puritan thought flowed on. It was only natural that what had led the puritans, aided by coffee, to carry on a campaign against alcohol, should further lead them to attack the excessive craving of human beings for caffeine.

The self-composed epitaph, attributed by some to Balzac, and by others to Voltaire, "He lived and he died through thirty thousand cups of coffee," though penned in jest, gave many people cause to think. Did the writer mean that coffee was a slow poison? Might it not be that the enormous expenditure of energy demanded by the new times, multiplying achievement, simultaneously cut short the life of the individual? Was not this tropical luxuriance of achievement, with a reduced duration of life, symbolized by caffeine?

During the first years of the twentieth century many began to entertain such thoughts. The friends of coffee tried to reassure doubters by reminding them of Fontenelle, a great consumer of coffee, who lived until he almost became a centenarian. But Fontenelle, said the objectors, had been an exception. The escape of one individual from the deleterious effects of coffee could not guarantee the harmlessness of the beverage for ordinary persons. In any case, far more coffee than ever was now being drunk as a spur to flagging energies. Doctors were almost unanimous in their condemnation of the speeding-up of modern life. Whereas those who died prematurely in former days had often died as victims of beer, wine, opium, or tobacco, in the twentieth century, despite its wonderful achievements, there were manifest the stigmata of nervous insomnia, palpitation, restlessness—in a word, pandemic signs of coffee-poisoning.

Superadded to these considerations was the desire that everything men did should be done by their own unaided powers. It was regarded by many, on general principles, as inadvisable that mental activity should be stimulated by drugs. Just as, at all times, there have been persons who demanded "intoxication without wine," so now there were persons who demanded "wakefulness without caffeine." The supply of coffee-substitutes, which began during the Seven Years War, reached its climax in Germany at the opening of the twentieth century. Those who could not afford to buy genuine coffee bought and drank the word coffee at least—"coffee" preceded by another word linked to "coffee" with a hyphen—some such word as "wheat," "chicory," "malt," "acorn," or "fig." Generally speaking, the second component of this hyphened word was a phantom. The "coffee" element in the "acorn-coffee," etc., was non-existent.

One point, however, becomes plain to those who study economic psychology. If it be possible to sell to millions a coffee which is not coffee at all and which is devoid of the stimulant trimethyldioxypurin, this must be because there is a growing repugnance to the stimulating effect of caffeine. The recognition of the fact guided the work now undertaken by a young merchant of Bremen, Ludwig Roselius by name. His attitude towards coffee was twofold. Being an honest trader, he did not wish to sell as "coffee" something that was not coffee. On the other hand, for personal reasons, he was an enemy of coffee. His father, a coffee-taster by profession, had died prematurely, and Ludwig ascribed the death to coffee-poisoning. As a safeguard against overdosage with caffeine, coffee-tasters and tea-tasters spit out the fluid when they have tasted it; but, willy-nilly, they are likely to swallow a little, and persons who are exceptionally sensitive to caffeine have sometimes to abandon the profession. Ludwig Roselius' belief that his father had died from coffee-poisoning led him to study the possible deleterious effects of coffee in other persons—perhaps as the result of a fairly common idiosyncrasy. He came to regard coffee as one of the causes of heart trouble, gout, and, arteriosclerosis. In diabetes and liver troubles, doctors have long been accustomed to forbid the use of coffee. There can be no question that various ailments, major and minor, have become more common since the middle of the nineteenth century, when a great increase in the consumption of coffee began.

Influenced by these considerations, young Roselius set to work, with the characteristic German perseverance, upon an investigation which was to lead to great results. He wanted to produce a caffeine-free coffee. It was to be genuine coffee, with the aroma and other agreeable qualities preserved, but to be free from the trimethyldioxypurin which is dangerous to the continually growing number of neurotics.

Sufferers from coffee were to be relieved of their troubles without any decline in the consumption of coffee. Those who had abandoned coffee in favour of substitutes were to be recalled to the use of the Arabian berry. No one, henceforward, was to be compelled to renounce the enjoyment of coffee, or to adopt an ascetic life for reasons of health, or forced to accept an unsatisfactory substitute. Roselius was convinced that if he could produce a caffeine-free coffee, this new coffee would no longer be frowned upon by medical opponents of the ordinary beverage.

When, in the year 1820, Goethe sent Ferdinand Runge, the analytical chemist of Jena, a boxful of coffee-beans, the poet was giving away something for which he had no use. To the Dionysiac son of the antique world, the Black Apollo who was the spirit of coffee seemed repugnant. Goethe, as a lover of good wine, wrote several diatribes against coffee. Perhaps the most unwarranted of these is to be found in his last letter to Frau von Stein, under date June 1, 1789, in which he ascribes the loving woman's distresses and reproaches to insomnia produced by coffee. When, thirty years later, Goethe sent a supply of coffee-beans to a chemist, it was certainly not done that Runge might have coffee to drink, but in the hope that his friend would analyse the beans. In actual fact, Runge discovered the demon that lurked in them; he was the first to extract caffeine from coffee.

This analytical feat caused considerable excitement in the early part of the nineteenth century. First of all for pharmaceutical reasons. Caffeine, the purified drug, was now made available for prescribers and was stored by apothecaries. The solution of the industrial problem, as far as coffee-salesmen were concerned, was reserved for a considerably later date. How could caffeine be extracted from coffee-beans without destroying the other qualities that made it possible to prepare an agreeable beverage from these beans? That was what Ludwig Roselius set himself to discover.

His new process for the extraction of caffeine from coffee produced the alkaloid in such large quantities that its price, which before the war was thirty-six marks per kilogram, has now fallen to six marks. But Roselius was even more interested in the other aspects of his process; the decaffeinized coffee was still coffee. That was the result he achieved after lengthy and laborious investigation.

Roselius set out from the fundamental experience that the taste and aroma of coffee are developed while the bean is being roasted. He therefore extracted the caffeine from unroasted beans. Since the grinding of raw beans is difficult, and since they have a very hard shell, he subjected them to a preliminary treatment, a "disintegrating process." By this the cells were opened. He exposed the beans to superheated steam, which was acid or alkaline as their quality varied. When, after this preliminary treatment, the beans were subjected to the action of solvents of caffeine, about twenty-nine parts in thirty of the caffeine could be extracted without simultaneously extracting the aromatic substances in the beans.

Thereafter, they could be roasted in the usual manner to develop their aroma.

In the year 1906, Ludwig Roselius founded a joint-stock company to work his patents, with the result that by the year 1912, Bremen came near to challenge Hamburg as a centre of the coffee trade. From the Bremen factory a lively propaganda has gone forth throughout the world in favour of the use of caffeine-free coffee.

Brazilian Dictatorship

Soil, Empire, and the Labour Problem

T HE historian of coffee will, down to 1850, be chiefly concerned with consumers. But from the middle of the nineteenth century onwards, production was so mightily increased, and the problem of the coffee-growing lands became so serious, that our attention is perforce directed towards producers.

By 1850, the building of railways had made the Old World wellnigh uniform. There might still be differences in the way in which coffee was drunk in Palermo and in Stockholm. These differences, however, were unimportant. The decisive fact in the history of coffee is that, during the middle of the nineteenth century, this plant became synonymous with destiny for a whole continent.

In the story of coffee, the twentieth century—or, at any rate, the first third thereof—denotes the dictatorship of Brazil. Brazil is the largest state on the South American continent, comprising eighteen and a half millions of square kilometres, more than five and a half million square miles, sixteen times as large as France, and, as a dominion under one government, exceeded in size only by Russia, Canada, and China. In 1906 it produced as much as ninety-seven per cent of all the coffee grown throughout the world. The momentous result was the dictatorship of Brazil as a coffee-growing country; but in Brazil itself coffee was dictator. Coffee was master. Capricious as a volcano, a cyclone, or an earthquake, coffee was not wholly a blessing.

One who speaks of coffee in Brazil, of the last half-century of coffee-growing there, is compelled to use words and images that in other respects seem only appropriate to the taming of natural forces.

In 1926, the Brazilian government celebrated the bicentenary of the introduction of coffee-planting into Brazil. The fixing of the date of the latter event by the choice of the year 1726 was somewhat arbitrary.

It seems probable that all the coffee-plants on the South American continent are descendants of the famous shoot brought by Lieutenant Desclieux from France to Martinique. We know for certain that Desclieux's voyage took place in 1723. Since, as aforesaid, there are four barren years after coffee has been planted, we can hardly suppose that coffee-planting can have begun in Brazil before 1728.

By that time, the Dutch were planting coffee in South America. These plantations were in Dutch Guiana. Eastward of Dutch Guiana lay French Guiana, and the two colonies were so jealous of each other that the governors forbade, under pain of death, the export of coffee-berries. A foolish prohibition, since coffee, the "wonderful shrub," was already being grown in Guiana under both the Dutch and the French flags.

Still, the prohibition had some sense as against third parties. Except for the French and the Dutch, no one was to grow coffee on the American continent. At this juncture, by a strange chance, when there was a dispute between the French and the Dutch as to the delimitation of their respective territories, they called in a Brazilian to adjudicate, an official from Para, Palheta by name. This gentleman made love to the wife of the governor of French Guiana. At a banquet, under the eyes of her unsuspecting husband, she gave Palheta a huge bouquet, in whose interior a handful of ripe coffee-berries was concealed. Thus Palheta was able to evade the prohibition on export, and to sail off with his treasure to the mouth of the Amazon, where the coffee-berries were planted, and flourished abundantly.

Such is the Brazilian saga. For those who are romantically inclined, the value of coffee is naturally enhanced by the thought that its introduction to Brazil was effected in so gallant a fashion. The only demonstrable fact, however, is that coffee-planting in Brazil began at Para, and spread thence southward.

Long before this, in the Far East, in Java and Indonesia, the Dutch had dispossessed the Portuguese. By one of time's revenges, it was a Portuguese—for Brazil was then a Portuguese colony—who tapped a main source of Dutch wealth by transferring coffee from Surinam to Portuguese territory. Thenceforward, coffee began "to talk Portuguese."

The southward march of coffee from Para to what is now the heart of the coffee-country, the plateau of São Paulo, took more than fifty

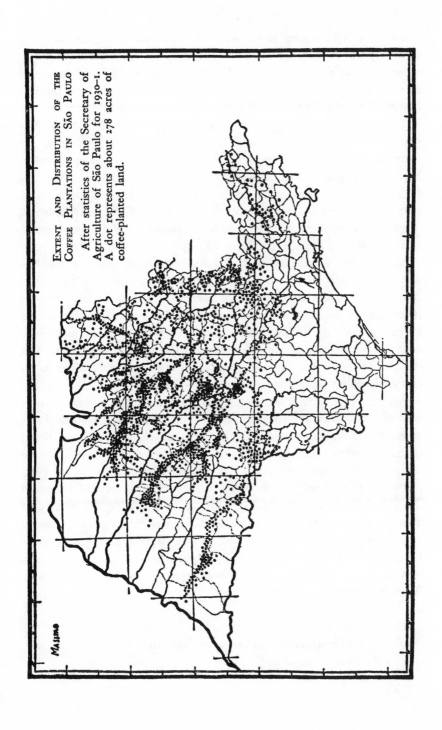

EXTENT AND DISTRIBUTION OF THE
COFFEE PLANTATIONS IN SÃO PAULO

After statistics of the Secretary of
Agriculture of São Paulo for 1930–1.
A dot represents about 278 acres of
coffee-planted land.

years. That was a long time, even when we take into consideration how vast are the distances in Brazil. In truth, the Brazilians were not in a hurry to set about coffee-planting. Brazil cultivated sugar-cane, and in such enormous quantities as to dictate to the world sugar-market. During the eighteenth century it was sugar that "talked Portuguese."

Then a comet appeared in the skies of the sugar-world. It was Napoleon, whose campaign against the British carrying trade took the form of an endeavour to make the European continent independent as regards sugar-production. The reader will remember that Napoleon had luck in this matter, being able to turn the Prussian discovery of sugar in beet-root to account for the promotion of his Continental System. Therewith cane sugar was dethroned, and Brazil could no longer maintain her place as premier producer of sugar in the world. Since, however, Napoleon's "alliance with chicory" was a comparative failure—because neither chicory nor any of the other suggested coffee-substitutes grown in the temperate zone contained a trace of caffeine—the Brazilians were quick to realize that they must replace sugar-growing by coffee-growing. Like so many other salient facts of the nineteenth century, the almost exclusive devotion of Brazil to coffee-growing was the outcome of Napoleon's activities. It was an indirect answer to his economic policy.

Prior to the establishment of the Continental System, Brazil's export of coffee was so small that not until 1818 do we find any statistical references to Brazil as a coffee-producing country. In that year, Brazil marketed seventy-five thousand sacks. More than five and a half million kilograms of coffee were being shipped to Europe from various parts of the world, and only the intrigues of speculators prevented a crash in the price. Not until 1823 did the Brazilian harvest begin seriously to affect European prices of coffee, when the coffee exchanges were taking advantage of the imminence of war between France and Spain to bear the market.

Now everyone in Europe who was interested in coffee knew that Brazil had to be taken into account.

There were three factors that combined to promote the victory of Brazil as a coffee-producing country: the soil, the form of government, and local labour conditions.

Coffee in Brazil was, for the most part, planted on virgin soil, where the humus was rich and porous, favoured by many centuries of tropical sunshine. The planters, attended by their slaves, made their way into the primeval forests, felled the huge trees with axes, and, with billhooks, cleared away the lianas with which the living tree-trunks and the dead were ensnared. Day after day the forest resounded to the noise made by the invaders, until, on the selected area, not a tree was left standing. The waist-high stubble of undergrowth, over which brightly coloured butterflies fluttered and amid which spotted orchids gleamed, rotted and dried week after week beneath the burning sun. Even the snakes fled into the shade of the surrounding uncleared forest. They sensed the imminent "roça," the burning, and fled from the peril.

When the felled tree-trunks had been sufficiently sunned, the roça began. The fires that were lighted consumed the tree-trunks and the stumps, with the exception of specimens of one particular tree which the Indians named the "iron tree." Its blue-black wood was resistant to fire. All the rest, however, were destroyed, leaving the newly cleared land covered with a layer of silvery ashes. Ghastly was the aspect of this grey clearing, surrounded on all sides by the imperishable forest. In that damp, hothouse atmosphere, the unfelled titans were immune to forest fires.

The ashes were cleared away, and coffee was planted in a procreative volcanic soil admirably suited to it. It flourished abundantly. Soon a neighbouring area of forest shared the fate of the first.

Through a region extending over more than twenty degrees of latitude, from Para on the equator to São Paulo on the tropic of Capricorn, the devouring roça did its work. With planned conflagrations, the way was prepared for coffee-planting.

In this long-enduring campaign on behalf of coffee against the primeval forest, the colonists soon learned how to find the best sites for their plantations. Among the trees which showed that the soil would be favourable the most notable were the white cedar, the wild white fig-tree, the white palm, and the heliocarpus. The most fruitful region was the plateau of São Paulo. It soon came to be called the "terra roxa," the red earth, although its colour was rather chocolate than red. Often, here, one can walk for miles across loam that looks as artificial as freshly ground cocoa. At sunset the earth shines with a violet light which, though reflected, looks as if it emanated from the soil.

In São Paulo, coffee-planting speedily became a science. The seed was taken only from the best plants. Then the first planting was made in nurseries, where the young shrubs were allowed to grow to the height of a foot or two before they were transplanted to their permanent site. They were spaced out at distances of twelve feet, so that they should not rob one another of light. Manuring and weeding were very carefully attended to.

The terra roxa, an earth rich in humus, containing much nitrogen, phosphoric acid, lime, and potash, is of recent volcanic origin, produced by the disintegration of basalt and trachyte. It yields abundant harvests. The variety of chemicals withdrawn during the growth of the coffee-shrub is restored when the husks fall. Thus the land is inexhaustible.

The climate as well as the soil has contributed to make of Brazil the principal coffee-growing country in the world. Climatic conditions are so favourable that the coffee-shrubs could thrive without care. Even the shade-trees which, in other lands, are required for the protection of young coffee-plants, are needless in Brazil. The peculiar cloudiness of the atmosphere mitigates the drying effect of the sun. Above all, rain is frequent without being excessive, so that the trees have a sufficiency of water all the year round.

Once Brazil had entered the lists as a coffee-growing country, its competition was irresistible. Local labour-conditions were favourable, no less than soil and climate. Down to 1888, slavery persisted in Brazil. Even today, one who lands at Bahia, can, in an afternoon's walk, make the acquaintance of many old Negroes who, half a century ago, still worked in chains.

The slaves were imported from the west coat and from the east coast of Africa. Indisputably, the slave-trade and slave labour are the most odious and most cruel of all economic forms. Still, it cannot be denied that a Negro slave in Brazil was in many respects better off than a Negro, bound or free, in Anglo-Saxon countries. For—this is the important point—the Portuguese are free from race prejudice. The colonists brought few of their own womenkind with them to Brazil, and cohabited unrestrainedly with Indians and Negro women, so that, in the course of four centuries, the population of Brazil has come to consist largely of half-breeds. In a society so constituted, although the Negro was a slave, he was not as such despised. When he came to live in a town, he was comparatively well-off. His lazy master used him to earn money. The slave was not set free, but his servitude was a light one; the Negro became a handicraftsman, an inn-keeper, a stone-mason, a policeman. He had to hand over a percentage of his earnings to his master, but could keep the rest for himself.

It was only on the great plantations that the Negroes had an evil time. Even there, however, the self-interest of the planters checked excessive exploitation. Cruelty, beyond limits, would have recoiled upon their own heads. The slave-owners were enormously outnumbered; they could not have resisted a serious slave-rising, for the central government was far away. Moreover, miscegenation was rife. A planter had, as a rule, so many illegitimate children that the Negro families were allied to him in a way that prevented the extremity of mutual hatred between master and slave.

There were also many methods of emancipation, and widespread jobbery served to mitigate the hardships of a slave's life. All the same, there were hardships enough. For certain forms of labour, among which labour upon the plantations is one, the toil of slaves is cheaper than the toil of freemen. The long persistence of slavery in Brazil gave that country an irresistible advantage over its competitors.

In the end, the economic system, successful though it was, was changed with amazing suddenness. By one stroke of the pen, the emperor of Brazil, Pedro II, freed all the slaves. He was dethroned by a republican revolution next year, but emancipation held its ground.

The earlier revolution, thanks to which in 1822 Pedro I had become emperor of Brazil, making himself independent of Portugal, was traceable, like all the earlier revolutions of the nineteenth century, to the influence of Napoleon. In fact, Napoleon, indirectly at least, wrought changes in North and South America no less extensive than those he effected in Europe, Africa, and Asia. Everywhere the nations were magnetically transformed by his existence, now attracted and now repelled.

When his star was setting, the revolutionary wave, of which his rise to power had been the symbol, spread to America. In North America, revolution triumphed before the days of Napoleon. A French enthusiast, Lafayette, had fought on behalf of the American revolution. In the year of Napoleon's death, the republicans of Spanish America were fighting for freedom. The spirit of the Holy Alliance, which had conquered Napoleon, would not tolerate new republics anywhere upon the globe. Metternich was dreaming of intervention; the tsar was equipping a fleet which was to land at La Plata. Thereupon the spirit of Napoleon was resurrected in the Congress of the United States of America. In the eventful year 1823, only two years after Napoleon's death, was formulated the famous Monroe Doctrine, according to which no European intervention would henceforward be tolerated in America.

Even more remarkable than the revolt of the Spanish colonies was the way in which Portugal lost Brazil. This huge dominion had been fairly well governed. The ties between the various "captainates" and Lisbon had not been drawn too close. There had never been any such dispute as that between Britain and the North American coastal states. But there came a turn of events that was altogether unexpected, and was eminently calculated to inflate the Brazilians' sense of self-importance.

In November 1807, Junot, one of Napoleon's marshals, captured Lisbon, and literally drove the Portuguese royal family into the sea. They took refuge on British warships, which sailed with them to Rio. Thus Brazil became personally acquainted with its Portuguese rulers, who at a distance had been so greatly admired, but were now somewhat discredited refugees. Portugal had temporarily ceased to exist. Brazil had become Portugal.

The inevitable result was that the court of John VI became permeated with Brazilians. The colonists demanded rights, and the king had no option but to grant them. Hitherto, none but Portuguese ships had been allowed to enter Brazilian ports. Now, when the laws of Portugal had become visionary, Brazil insisted on being entitled to trade on equal terms with all friendly nations. The king, glad to have been able to find asylum from the Napoleonic storms in this great colony, agreed further, in the year 1815, that Brazil was to be regarded as a kingdom.

The Portuguese revolution of 1820 compelled John VI to return to

Europe. He left his son Dom Pedro behind him in Brazil as regent. Pedro, who understood the signs of the times, and wished to save the dynasty in America, severed the ties between Brazil and Portugal, and had himself crowned emperor on September 7, 1822. Had he not done this, he would doubtless have been expelled as the Spanish proconsuls were expelled from Argentina.

The establishment of a Brazilian empire was a clever move. Nevertheless, Brazil was a difficult country to rule. There were frontier disputes with the republics which had at one time been provinces of Spain, and there were antagonisms between the different parts of Brazil, often taking the form of open hostilities. The huge realm extended from north to south across thirty parallels of latitude. It contained almost all kinds of vegetation, and its inhabitants were of every tint of skin.

In 1831, Pedro I abdicated in favour of his son Pedro, a little boy of five. During the child's minority, Brazil was governed by regents; his majority was proclaimed on July 23, 1840, and he was crowned on July 18, 1841. Pedro II was an able, indeed, a wise ruler. This second —and last—emperor of Brazil was among the most notable and attractive personalities of the nineteenth century.

"An Athenian in South America," Pedro II cultivated the arts and sciences, and began to have Rio laid out as one of the most beautiful cities in the world. He established a strictly federal constitution, which flattered the vanity of Rio without affronting that of the widely separated parts of the realm. Traders and industrialists idolized Pedro. He built roads and railways, "because coffee must have an exit to the sea." Before his enterprises were fulfilled, the crops had been transported by teams of oxen, but now coffee could be shipped within a very few days after having been harvested. The Brazilian coffee-barons could make the best possible use of their cheap labour. The value of the exports from Brazil vied with that of those from any other country in the world.

His idealism and his culture played Emperor Pedro a trick. To this poet upon an imperial throne, this corresponding member of European academies, translator of Sully Prudhomme, Victor Hugo, and Longfellow, coffee had an exceptionally bitter taste, which was given to it by slavery. Emancipation? He ventured to lay an axe to the stem which sustained the economic life of the country.

In 1871 he promulgated the "lei do ventre livre," the "law of free birth." It ordained that no one could any longer be born to slavery in Brazil; the children of slaves were free. The practical effect of this would be that by 1900, when the older slaves would be dying off rapidly, slavery would be in course of extinction, slowly at first, then swiftly. The coffee-planters could adapt themselves to what was, after all, a distant prospect, without any immediate and grave disturbance of labour conditions upon their estates. But there were revolutionists at headquarters who considered that the proposed method of emancipation was too slow. When the emperor was visiting Europe for the sake of his health, in 1888, his daughter Izabel, who was acting as regent, promulgated the "lei aurea," the "golden law," whereby slavery was abolished forthwith, completely, and without compensation to the planters. These latter, not being in a position to pay adequate wages to their ex-slaves, rebelled against the emperor. Hitherto they had been loyal monarchists, full of respect and admiration for the man to whom they owed their roads and railways; but now, in their despair, they joined forces with the republicans. Army officers collaborated in the revolt, and on November 15, 1889, the Brazilian empire fell. Pedro, who had by now returned, was forced into exile. When the telegraph conveyed the news to other American capitals, the president of Venezuela, Rojas Paul, uttered the memorable words: "They have done away with the only republic that existed in America, the Brazilian empire!"

The planters did not venture upon the re-establishment of the slave-holding system. Still, they got out of their difficulties quickly enough. Nothing was needed to overcome the labour crisis but intensified immigration from Europe.

Slave-labour had been cheap, but it had been of poor quality. You cannot see more than a few paces in a coffee-plantation, and, when they were not under the eyes of the overseer, the Negroes took things easy. The planters had long known that European free labourers, though costly, worked much better than Negro slaves.

Heinrich Schüler, who has made a special study of the question, estimates that from 1820 down to the present day about six million persons have migrated to Brazil. He believes that fourteen millions of the population—nearly two-thirds of the total—consist of immigrants or the descendants of immigrants who have come to Brazil during the last hundred years. But from year to year the number of immigrants varied much, just as did their fortunes. While slavery was still in being, the free whites generally worked on the system known as metayage, receiving as their wages half the crops of the land they tilled. Thus the white immigrant was not a slave, but neither was he a free landowner, and he was therefore in an inferior social position. Metayage soon led to exploitation of the colonists, and the stream of immigration fell off. Von der Heydt's decree, issued in the year 1850, forbade Germans to emigrate to Brazil. This had important political consequences, for it directed German emigration towards the United States.

The evil repute into which Brazil fell as "a country of exploiters" led the Brazilian government to take action. It freed the immigrants from their contractual obligations, and did its utmost to create a class of free peasants. Every colonist received a house and a suitable area of tilled land where he could plant coffee-shrubs, and where between the rows of coffee he could cultivate cereals. His wife and children would work with him. If he were a thrifty man, he would soon be able to buy land for himself and become an independent planter. The most successful of such immigrants was the famous Francisco Schmidt. He came to Brazil as an ordinary labourer and set to work as a metayer. In the year 1918, the Schmidt family united their fifty-two "fazendas"—the largest coffee-plantation in the world—into a joint-stock company with a capital of fifteen million marks.

All the same, prior to 1888 the number of immigrants barely reached thirty thousand per annum. Then the emigration agents in Europe heard of the fall of the empire and the abolition of slavery in Brazil. Immediately the current of emigration became intensified. In 1888 the newcomers to Brazil numbered one hundred and thirty thousand; and in 1891, the figure rose to two hundred and twenty thousand. The "lei aurea," the emancipation edict, which for moral and political reasons was irrevocable, had been issued during a period of prosperity and high prices. The plantations were being greatly enlarged, and there was a shortage of labour. The republican government ably supported the planters, and helped to finance immigration from Europe.

Entrepreneurs in São Paulo founded a steamship line running from

Italian and other Mediterranean ports to Brazil. The number of Italian immigrants during 1888 equalled that of all the Germans who had come to the country since 1835. The outflow of Italians had to be restricted by the Italian government. The Italians were followed by Portuguese and by Spaniards. In Germany, on the other hand, the psychological after-effects of von der Heydt's decree were still operative. Among the two hundred and twenty thousand immigrants of the record year 1891, only forty-one hundred Germans came to Brazil.

Asia, as well as Europe, contributed its quota to the aid of Brazil. Japan, always on the look-out for living-room and for new markets, saw that there was a fine opportunity for instituting commercial relations. It guided the stream of Japanese emigration towards Brazil, to follow up men by Japanese manufactured goods. Brazil needed labour; and, since Japan was a country where very little coffee was drunk, the Brazilian planters hoped to get rid of some of their surplus in the Land of the Rising Sun. They were mistaken, for a tea-growing country would never become a coffee-consuming one.

On the Asiatic mainland, opposite Japan, was the huge realm of China, overstocked with yellow labour-power. Why should not China export coolies to Brazil? In the 1890's there was formed a syndicate in São Paulo to bring fifty thousand Chinese labourers to the centre of the Brazilian coffee industry. The planters proposed to advance money to defray the cost of the voyage and to guarantee a minimum wage. Chinese coolies were to contract for five years. The Peking government, however, was not satisfied with the conditions, and called the bargain off.

Since the demand for labour exceeded the supply, wages rose. Then, in the year 1900, the planters were hard hit by the fall in the price of coffee, and were unable to pay the wages they had promised. Italy took diplomatic steps on behalf of her subjects in the Brazilian plantations. The planters were in so desperate a position that the Brazilian government had to advance money. It hesitated for a time. But when Giolitti and Tittoni threatened to prohibit Italian emigration, Rio was compelled to come to terms with Italy.

It was in accordance with the law of coffee-crises that the Brazilian planters should be once more in a bad way towards the turn of the century. This time, however, the crisis was worse than usual, owing to the fall in the Brazilian monetary exchange.

What had happened to the milreis currency?

Immediately after the abdication of Emperor Pedro II, on November 15, 1889, Brazilian money began to totter. New York and London, although the former by hypothesis was republican in sentiment, and the latter—at that date—still quasi-republican as far as other lands were concerned, had regarded the dominion of the House of Braganza as a safeguard in Brazil. During the six years after Pedro was given his marching orders, the value of Brazilian currency in the international exchanges sank by two-thirds.

This fall in exchange was, to begin with, very much to the planters' taste. They sold their coffee for sterling in the London market. Prices were not high (if they had been, over-plantation would have begun again); still, a planter could now get three times as many milreis as he used to get for an English pound. The value of currency never falls so much or so quickly at home as it falls in the foreign money market, for a population is faithful to its own standard. Therefore it did not matter to the planters that they had to employ costly wage-labour instead of cheap slave-labour. They could get along all right, for a time.

But the coffee-barons were to find, as inflationists have always found, that the advantages of inflation lead to disaster. When the State, as was meet, determined to stabilize the currency, they perceived that their welfare had been illusory. It was, of course, necessary to arrest the fall in the milreis. Brazil had to pay the interest on her foreign loans in the currency of the creditor countries, and if bankruptcy was to be avoided, the purchasing power of the milreis must not be allowed to fall to zero. In 1898, Manual de Campos Salles, the new president, undertook, with the aid of the house of Rothschild in London, to steady the state finances. He succeeded so well, that the milreis was soon quoted at a better figure. But state bankruptcy was avoided at the cost of the ruin of the planters.

A considerable proportion of the plantation-hands took advantage of the rising exchange to book their passages for Europe and return home. A good many, however, procured well-paid work in Rio de Janeiro. Now that the state finances were on a sound footing, the building trade was busy; new quarters of the town were being laid out, and the docks were being enlarged. Thus the plantations were gradually deprived of their workers, and in the end this was advantageous, as a hindrance to crazy over-production. Not an adequate hindrance, however, for during the years of spurious money, when the planters had had such a lot of inflated milreis to play with, they had, after their usual custom, used their money to plant more and more land. Coffee was growing like a demon in a nightmare. Since there were no hands to harvest the crops, the berries fell to the ground as they ripened.

Owing to the rise in the Brazilian exchange and the decline in the price of coffee, the income of the planters was being steadily reduced. There could be no question of raising the price of coffee. The coffee planted on extended areas during the years of prosperity was lying in wait to prevent anything of that kind.

Catastrophe seemed inevitable.

The newspapers clamoured for a saviour. Not, in the sense of Europe, for a "deliverer from scarcity and need," but, on the contrary, for a "deliverer from superfluity." In numberless variations there now became current a proverb: "Terra rica—povo rico."

Wealthy land—poor plutocrats!

22

Ruin of the Plantations in Ceylon

ECONOMIC history is harder to write than any other kind of history. Why? Because in economic history the ostensibly lifeless makes vast claims, and because a living creature, man, is unimportant and powerless as against the might of commodities.

Was not man the creator of economics?

No, or only in part. Man is the father, the progenitor of economics, but nature is the mother. One who speaks of the growth of economic life, a life that is mysterious, peculiar to itself, and not always reasonable, is not speaking only or mainly about something that is the product of the human mind, but about something that depends quite as much upon the blind forces of inscrutable nature.

While in Brazil the soil, the form of government, and the power of human labour were wooing the terrible favour of coffee, what was the attitude of other colonial countries towards a phenomenon which to them represented not frightfulness, but fertility?

Not without a struggle had other tropical countries surrendered to Brazil the hegemony in the production of coffee.

Towards 1830, the race among the colonies for the premier position in this respect began. New names came to the front, and were soon forgotten.

The "favourite" in this competition had originally been Java. The island realm of the Dutch had long been settled by coffee-planters who, therefore, were no novices at the game. Their fathers, grandfathers, and great-grandfathers before them had been coffee-planters. Still, this did not prevent the relations between the coolies and their Dutch overlords from growing worse and worse. Coffee-growing in Java was a government monopoly; the natives were compelled, under the supervision of Dutch officials, to tend a definite number of bushes annually and to harvest the crops. Each family had to look after six hundred and fifty-five bushes. The yield of these "coffee-looms" was taken over by the government from the coolies at a fixed and very low price, the authorities then disposing of the crops by auction through the instrumentality of the Netherlands Trading Company. In addition to this coffee-growing, carried on by what was virtually forced labour, there existed voluntary cultivation in small areas that were the property of the Javanese, but naturally, in the circumstances, they lacked time and energy to attend to their private farms. Multatuli—the pen-name of Eduard Douwes Dekker (1820–1887)—in his autobiographical novel *Max Havelaar*, published in 1860, pilloried the administration of the Dutch Indies, describing the forced labour of the natives in plain terms as a corvée. Since their work was unwillingly performed, it was comparatively unproductive.

With the decline of Javanese production, Central America began to come to the fore. Three factors combined to stimulate the ambition of these petty states. First of all, the example of Brazil; second, the consideration that Central America was nearer to North America and its big markets for coffee than South America was; third, liberation from Spanish rule had awakened industrial ambition as well as stimulating national sentiment. The upshot was that Mexico, Costa Rica, El Salvador, and Guatemala became competitors of some importance. Venezuela, Ecuador, Colombia, and Peru followed suit. But all these countries put together were unable, despite their best efforts, to shake the supremacy of Brazil. In 1930, the total harvests of Central America and South America, Brazil apart, were only one-sixth of the Brazilian harvest.

During the nineteenth century, new coffee-growing areas came into the running in the Far East. The French began to plant coffee in Indo-China, and the British followed this example in the Straits Settlements. These efforts were attended with varying success. The United States of America, after the Spanish-American war, had its own coffee-plantations in the Philippines.

Very remarkable has been the history of coffee on the African continent. Africa was the original home of the coffee-plant. Two different kinds of coffee are indigenous to Africa. The transplanted Ethiopian coffee-bush was the source of Arabian coffee. On the west coast of Africa grew the Liberian coffee-tree, differing considerably from Ethiopian coffee. This West African tree sometimes grows to twice the height of the Arabian coffee-bush. Its leaves and its berries are more resistant, more robust, less susceptible to disease than those of the Arabian coffee-plant. When, during the nineteenth century, in many parts of the world the success of coffee-plantations was endangered by parasitic diseases, the Arabian bushes were replaced by Liberian, or by a hybrid of the two, the vigorous "robusta-bush." Sometimes these experiments were successful, but at other times the quality of the coffee fell off. No more than every kind of vine can be successfully grown in every vineyard, can every kind of coffee be successfully grown in every coffee-plantation. During recent decades, coffee has become less tasty, less aromatic, has, as connoisseurs say, become "smokier." This is because the planters have overlooked the importance of a sound relationship between soil and seed. Climatic or atmospheric conditions doubtless play a part as well as soil. To quote a saw from the brewing trade: "You cannot brew Milwaukee beer outside of Milwaukee."

Many investigators regard Africa as the coffee-country of the future. The French have greatly increased production in Madagascar, Guinea, and Somaliland. Good crops are being raised in the sometime German colonies. New coffee-countries are Kenya and Uganda. The Portuguese have had very remarkable success in Angola. Nevertheless, the African figures of coffee-production seen almost microscopic when compared with those of Brazil. In the year 1930, the whole African continent supplied only five hundred and forty thousand sacks, as against Brazil's twenty-nine million.

The rise and fall of coffee-countries, often going up like a rocket and coming down like the stick, was but a reflection of the "colonial nervousness" characteristic of the nineteenth century. "Put money in thy purse," was the motto; exploit the possibilities of newly acquired territories without thought of the future. Envy of neighbours has, in most cases, been the chief spur to colonial activity.

Each of the newly settled regions has its peculiar history, but none a history more peculiar than that of the coffee epic in Ceylon.

How did coffee-planting begin in Ceylon?

Like the rest of the Indies, in old colonial days Ceylon was discovered by the Portuguese. Then the Dutch dispossessed them.

When Napoleon's brother Louis became king of Holland, so that dynastic interests connected Holland with France, the time was ripe for Ceylon to fall a prey to Britain. In the Peace of Amiens (1803), Holland was forced to renounce Ceylon. England annexed the wealthy island.

The first British governor was struck by the fact that in certain districts the inhabitants did not drink tea, but coffee. This was strange, since the Cingalese were not Mohammedans but Buddhists, and Buddhists in general are tea-drinkers, not coffee-drinkers. Inquiry showed that the Dutch had brought coffee from Java fifty years before, and had inaugurated plantations. These had not been extensive, however, probably because the Hollanders did not wish Ceylon to become a formidable competitor to Java.

The British, the new owners of the island, had little interest in coffee-growing. Their only interest in coffee was as traders and as the bankers of the world. Still, political considerations compelled them to occupy themselves with coffee-growing in Ceylon. This came about because, in the course of the Napoleonic wars, the British had occupied Java, which they held from September 1811 to August 1814. Temporarily, therefore, they were masters of what was then the most important coffee-growing region in the world.

Though their tenure of power there was brief—for when the Napoleonic mess was cleared up, Java was restored to the Dutch—the English had, during these three years, become initiated into the mysteries of coffee-growing. They were quick to realize how similar were the climatic and agrarian conditions of Java and Ceylon. This made them wish to become coffee-planters in the latter island. Partly determinative was the fact that in the peninsula of Hindustan the consumption of coffee was increasing, at any rate among the Mohammedans. When in the year 1806 the British frigate *Panther* anchored in the port of Mocha, the officers noted that wearers of turbans abounded there. No less than two hundred and fifty merchants had come from Hindustan for cargoes of coffee to be shipped to their own country.

But if India now drank so much coffee, it would be better to grow the supply in a British colony. It would be better for political as well as for commercial reasons, inasmuch as the ties between the Indian Mohammedans and the Turkish caliphate were a source of anxiety to the British, and trading voyages from Hindustan to Arabia would tend to strengthen these ties. It would be much better if the Indian Mohammedans could get their coffee from Ceylon.

The soil of the island was extremely suitable, and the climate more stable than that of the adjoining mainland. The southwest monsoon ensured a regular rainfall; and even May, the hottest month, had its fires tempered by the insular position of Ceylon. The climate was mild as compared with that of the river-mouths and arid jungles of Hindustan proper.

For thousands of years the moist fertility of Ceylon had been known, not only to the natives but to the western world. The Hellenes wrote of Taprobane as a "garden-island." Five hundred years before Christ, the Hindu emperor Pandukabaya had begun terraced cultivation. During the subsequent two thousand five hundred years, despite continued tillings, the upper strata of the soil had not been exhausted. Gneiss, lava, and coral rag contributed to its richness.

In the year 1812, the export of coffee from Ceylon amounted to one hundred and fifty thousand kilograms. In 1837, it had risen to ten times as much. In 1845, it had reached fifteen million kilograms; in 1859, double that quantity; and in 1869, over fifty million kilograms. This was a success all the more remarkable since the cultivable area was not extremely large, being smaller than that of Java, to say nothing of Brazil.

The yield of coffee from Ceylon might have been yet further increased had not the Cingalese shown a growing disinclination for labour. Their own wants were few, for they could live upon rice and fruit; and, being pious Buddhists, they had religious objections to labour on the coffee-plantations. These scruples led, in 1848, to a rebellion against the strict regime of Governor Torrington.

Harsh measures were unavailing. From year to year, the natives showed themselves more and more disinclined for coffee-growing. Since they were paid for coffee by weight in Colombo, the capital, they had a way of boiling the berries beforehand to make them heavier and larger. Nevertheless, despite such pranks coffee-growing continued to thrive in Ceylon until in 1857 something ominous occurred.

That was the year of the Sepoy Rebellion, when Britain was hard put to it to maintain her grip on Hindustan. There were massacres of the whites in Cawnpore, Delhi, and elsewhere. During this period, strange birds visited Ceylon and feasted on the ripening berries. Similar invasions of crows had been recorded during the days of Dutch rule. While the English remained unperturbed, or dispersed the birds now and again by a sprinkling of grape-shot, the Cingalese looked anxiously in one another's brown faces. No doubt the birds would fly away again, but were they really birds? Were they not discontented spirits, whose crooked claws were a token of death and of a curse that had been decreed against the wealth of the English plantations?

The common folk of Ceylon who made a modest living in other ways than by coffee-planting—cotton-weavers and rice-growers, fishermen and sailors, makers of palm-oil and distillers of arrack, brickmakers and potters—praised the gods that they had nothing to do with coffee, which was doomed to destruction. But the English paid no heed. Wearing white topis and red tunics—red as if stained with blood—they returned from crushing the Indian mutiny. The excrement of the strange birds, the dung with which the plantations were freely besprinkled, did not differ from any other manure. The blue-eyed men, who cared nothing for omens, continued to hold sway over the island.

But ten years later, in 1867, the Cingalese began to whisper that a disease had attacked the coffee-shrubs. They showed one another leaves spotted with a red vesicular eruption, tiny vesicles at first, and only on the underside of the leaves. Hands and clothing, to which the spores clung, spread the disease everywhere. Three years later this rust had affected two-thirds of the plantations in the island. It attacked only the coffee-shrubs. Rice-fields and coco-nut-palms were unaffected. By the decree of destiny, the deadly organism was deadly only to the coffee-plant.

From the spores that settled on the leaves, a mycelium grew into the substance of the cells. A reddish-brown eruption covered the leaf and choked it. By 1870, this blight, *Hemileia vastatrix*, had stripped most of the shrubs.

Too late did the governmental authorities of Ceylon recognize the danger. At first they had regarded the blight as a local phenomenon. But when it spread all over the island they cabled to London for help. Botanical institutes throughout the world conducted experiments. But by the time a remedy was suggested, the malady was too widespread, destruction was too far advanced.

Experts from England fought the plague with sulphur and lime, with sulphate of iron and sulphate of copper, with tobacco sprays. Here and there they were successful. But since millions of coffee-trees had been infected, they could not cope with the evil. By the middle of the eighteen-eighties, *Hemileia vastatrix* had conquered. In the devastated coffee-plantations a new crop was grown—tea. India's sun and Buddha's heaven watched over the tea-plant. Its leaves were healthy. Patience and strength dwelt in their tissues. The tea-plant was a challenge to men to be as vigorous and simple as it itself was.

The last coffee-crop harvested in Ceylon was in the year 1900, and amounted to no more than seven thousand sacks. For years the island had been one of Brazil's rivals, but now was out of the running.

It had once more become a tea-growing country. In 1926, Ceylon led the world as a tea-producing land, exporting this product to the value of 213,000,000 rupees.

23

The Economic Struggle of Brazil

WHILE on the island of Ceylon a biochemical destroyer was calling a halt to the growth of coffee, the coffee-plantations continued to expand luxuriantly in Brazil. There no cry of alarm hindered advance. Year after year, in one province after another, the coffee-berries ripened. No matter that the harvest could not be reaped. The trees went on reproducing themselves. Perpetually they scattered new seed upon the land.

Besides, the planters were compelled to garner their crops, for they had workmen to pay and to keep busy. So, anxious at heart, the plantation-owners gave orders that the ripe berries should be picked, though they knew that they were being ruined thereby. What else could they do?

Six varieties were mainly planted, varieties as different as apples or roses that bear different names. Experts could recognize them from a distance by the position and aspect of the twigs. The favourite shrub was the "creolo," the "national coffee of Brazil." Next came the "bourbon," more valuable but more delicate, more sensitive to frost and wind; it was less long-lived than the "creolo," but bore more fruit. The "botucatu," or the "yellow," was the richest in caffeine. Its berries remained yellow until they ripened.

Java coffee, our old acquaintance of the Dutch Indies, was early transplanted to Brazil. The yield was good, but the taste was coarse. Then there was the largest of the Brazilian coffee-trees, the "maragogipe," which was grown in the Bahia district. It had abundant berries, and produced coffee of a good flavour.

The story of the harvesting was the same year after year. The blossoms were small, odorous, white. The calyx had five sepals; the corolla, five petals; the androecium, five stamens. After pollination, the fruit grew in the ovary. At first it was green, then yellow, then cherry-red. When signs of drying appeared in the berries, pickers came with their ladders. Cloths were spread round each tree. The harvest did not ripen everywhere at the same moment. That depended mainly upon altitude, being later in the mountains than in the valleys. At the drying-stations, the berries had to be sorted into "secco," "maduro," and "verde."

When the harvest had been garnered, the "preparation" followed, in accordance with either of two well-tried methods.

The first method was simple and inexpensive. After the berries had been dried for a while in the sun, they were pounded in wooden mortars to break the husks, from which the beans were then separated by sifting. The "wet process" was more thorough, but costlier, since it needed machinery. Through a pipe, the berries were poured into a pulping-machine, which detached the outer envelope of the fruit from the bean. The sugar-containing, sticky pulp having been detached, the beans were washed, and stored for a while in fermenting-tanks. Then, for three or four weeks, they were exposed to the sun on the great drying-terraces. Every evening they were raked together into a mound, and covered with coco-nut matting, palm leaves, or thin tin-plate, to keep off the dew. Early next morning, they were spread out once more in the sunshine. If rain threatened, the coffee was quickly shovelled into ventilated store-houses, where the drying process could continue.

When, after four weeks, the beans had acquired a "dureza vitrea," a glassy hardness, the experts knew that the process was finished, provided that the outer shell could no longer be scratched by the finger-nail, and that when the bean was struck by a hammer, it was not flattened, but remained resilient. The coffee was now ready for shipment. No, not quite. It still contained useless elements which added to its weight, and therefore to the cost of freightage. These were horny substances which had to be detached from the bean in another machine. With them was also removed the "silver-skin" that had continued to cling to the bean. Now at length the coffee was a finished commodity, ready for the market and for the world.

The "ensaccadores" packed it for transport to the coast. Sack after sack left the plantations. Shading his eyes with his hand, the white-clad planter sat watching the daily exit of his goods. Could he be expected to understand that he was ministering to his own destruction? Had the world been stood upon its head? Had a curse been uttered upon the sowing and harvesting of coffee?

In the year 1906, matters seemed to have reached this pass. The new harvest was reckoned at twenty million sacks. According to the logic of facts, the shipment of this harvest would bring down the price of coffee to zero.

What was the use of attempting to sell coffee which had become worthless? It might just as well be given away. Should the harvest be brought to market, chaos would ensue.

Ninety per cent of the popular wealth was inherent in coffee-growing. In the whirlpool that would result, not only would the planters be ruined, but practically the entire population. It seemed likely that Brazil would be destroyed by the greatest revolution that had ever been known in the world.

At length insight and courage were found to build an economic dam. The Convention of Taubaté marks a memorable day in the history of economics.

The idea of "valorization" originated in the mind of an Italo-Brazilian from São Paulo, a planter and merchant named Siciliano. He had carefully calculated the chances. If a prohibition of fresh planting were enforced throughout Brazil, the state, so Siciliano believed, could, without great risk, present itself to the planters as middleman, sequestrating the entire harvest, to sell it again at some later date when market conditions should have become favourable. We see that Siciliano had read the story of Joseph and Pharaoh to good purpose.

The respective state presidents of São Paulo, Rio de Janeiro, and Minas Geraes now assembled in the little town of Taubaté, between Rio and São Paulo, and there, in accordance with Siciliano's advice, arranged for a maintenance of prices, propaganda, strict regulation of the coffee-trade, and at the same time stabilization of the currency. But to Alves, the federal president of Brazil, state interference to the extent implied by stabilization of the currency seemed unduly bold. After lively disputes, he refused to sign the decree. All the planters of Brazil stood solidly behind the Convention. They regarded any delay in ratification as dangerous. The federal state of São Paulo, whose harvest had reached the fearful amount of fifteen million sacks, so that it was more interested than its neighbours in measures for the protection of the market, could not wait, and set about valorization alone.

In general, a state is supported by the financial strength of its citizens. Here, however, the state was supporting itself, at a great sacrifice, by saving its citizens from bankruptcy. The state did this by entering the market as a wholesale purchaser, and by buying their coffee from the planters at a price that could never have been maintained in a free market. Over-production had been so preposterous that, theoretically, coffee was not worth a farthing a pound. The state purchased the harvest and stored it away under lock and key. São Paulo was acting as Joseph had acted long before in Egypt when faced with a glut of grain. Joseph had withheld the superfluity from the market in order to release it by driblets in the later, lean years.

The planters stood behind the state and supported the measures adopted. Consumers were not so well content. Traders, above all, were disgruntled, declaring the governmental action to be nothing better than a commercial speculation. The authorities, they said, were trying to keep up the price of a commodity by artificial means, or, by an economic *coup de main*, to prevent the price from falling to its natural level.

Were these accusations justified? No. Who could tell whether, if the government, remaining true to liberal principles, had let matters alone, the market would have been left undisturbed to the interplay of supply and demand? Before this, speculators had effected a corner in coffee, releasing supplies into the market only when it suited their pockets. There could be little doubt that the same thing would have happened in the present case. In the year 1905, there had quietly been formed at Havre a syndicate to exert a permanent control over the coffee-market. The clamour for a free market was only a screen behind which financial groups and private capitalists wanted to play their own game with the chief product of a continent. Could these magnates of financial and commercial capital have had their way, the Brazilian planters would have been ruined, but the consumer would not have benefited in the least. What could it matter to consumers the world over whether the superfluity of coffee was kept away from the market by the São Paulo government or by a syndicate, or, in smaller quantities, by a few thousand coffee-dealers?

The government was not strong enough to do the work alone, and appealed for help to international capital. Help was given, for international capital was interested in the welfare of Brazil. Europeans had long since come to settle in Brazil as planters; European capitalists had made advances upon mortgage to Brazilian planters, and owned various Brazilian securities. Complete ruin of the coffee-planters of Brazil would have made shoes pinch in many other parts of the world. A revolution in Brazil—not one of the minor military revolutions that occur in Spanish America every ten years or so, but revolution on the grand scale, a war of social extermination—would have thrown back the country into a condition in which drought, the primeval forest, and the rivers would have come into their own once more. The purchasing power of the Brazilian market, so important to European producers, would have been destroyed for an indefinite period. If financial capital in the rest of the world now rallied to the help of Brazil, it was in order to avert the ruin of a country so gigantic that, as Albrecht Penck once said, "it will, perhaps, some day have a population of twelve hundred millions."

Among all those to whom appeal for help was made, Hermann Sielcken, a Hamburg merchant with a large business, was the first to see clearly how far the disturbances were likely to extend if Brazil were allowed to go down to ruin. He combined with a few other capitalists to form a financial group which, through Henry Schröder in London as intermediary, provided the first loan to the state of São Paulo. At a cost of three million sterling, São Paulo bought two million sacks of coffee from its own planters. This "valorization coffee" was shipped to New York, Hamburg, and Havre, to be stored there under seal. The firms owning the warehouses made advances to the São Paulo government on the security of the goods, thus providing means for continuing to buy coffee.

When still more money was required, the state of São Paulo farmed out one of its railways for a further loan of two million sterling. Valorization went on briskly. In the year 1908, eight million sacks of coffee were being kept under seal in the financiers' warehouses as security for their loans. To defray interest and other expenses, the São

Paulo government made the exporters pay a duty of three francs per sack at the time of shipment.

But the state of São Paulo was still the owner of this coffee, wherever it might be stored, whether in Hamburg, New York, Havre, or elsewhere. Brazil had to be enabled to keep the coffee in store until there should be a favourable turn in the market. In December 1908, the Brazilian government raised a loan of five million sterling to defray all previous valorization commitments and to enable the buying process to continue. The great financiers of the world had so much confidence, by this time, that the loan was over-subscribed on the first day. The security for the loan consisted of seven million sacks of government coffee in the warehouses, the stocks being administered by a committee of financiers, merchants, and government officials, meeting on equal terms.

The harvest of 1906, which had nearly submerged the country with its waves of coffee, was thus artificially cleared out of the way. Experience had taught that after a bumper harvest, for two years in succession the crops would be comparatively small. Like animals, plants are likely to be weakened for a time by excessive reproduction, and must restore their energies out of the air and the soil. On this occasion, however, experience was given the lie. The ensuing seasons, as the Brazilian planters noted with anxious hearts, were exceptionally favourable, with the result that the harvests of the years 1907 and 1908 were more considerable than had been hoped, so that the process of valorization had to be greatly protracted. It was not until February 1913 that the last sacks of government coffee were released from the warehouses and put on the market.

Thus for seven years the government sequestrated by purchase the principal product of the country. The seven-year term makes the parallel with Joseph in Egypt closer than ever. But Joseph stored grain, which is food. Unfortunately coffee is not an article of nutrition. At best, the money paid for it can be used to buy food.

The Brazilians were not wise enough to learn from the menace that had hung so long over their heads. Instead of setting to work, by degrees, to plant some other crop than coffee, they continued on their old ways. The evil had not been cut at the root, but was only superficially and temporarily pruned. The root continued to flourish luxuriantly, with the natural result that a few years later the crisis was redoubled.

This time it took on a new face, one which had never been regarded as possible, the face of 1914.

For a while the world went crash—at any rate, that political world which the nineteenth century had bequeathed to the twentieth. The crash tangled other wires besides those which concerned the defence of coffee in Brazil.

The "defesa do café" aimed at regulating access to the market, and thus keeping up the price of coffee. No Brazilian ever contemplated the possibility that the very existence of the market might be threatened; that, for instance, the German market and the Austrian market might be closed to them by a blockade. Now, however, such a market crisis had come. Whither, then, was Brazil to export her coffee? Could France and Italy make good for the loss of Germany and Austria? Worse still, not only were the Central Powers blockaded by the Allies, but the Allies themselves were blockaded by the German submarine campaign. For a time, neutrals likewise were outside the market, the trade with Denmark and Sweden, to name two of the most important consumers of Brazilian coffee, coming to an end.

The Allies now turned to account this state of affairs that was so dangerous for Brazilian economics. In the year 1917 the French pledged themselves to buy two million sacks of Santos coffee. Simultaneously Washington purchased a million sacks for the American Expeditionary Force. Part of the bargain was that Brazil must declare war against Germany. To ship the requisite supplies, the Brazilians seized forty German steamships that were awaiting the end of the war in Brazilian ports. The loss of tonnage effected by the submarine campaign had greatly circumscribed the possibility of freightage. The temptation of playing upon Brazil's need in this way was too much for the Allies.

Had there been any warlike mood in Brazil? Nothing of the sort. Here begins the tragedy of a very remarkable man, Lauro Müller, the Brazilian minister for foreign affairs, a German by birth, who was forced, in his new home, to work against his native country.

Lauro Severiano Müller was born in 1863 of German parents in the

German colony of Itajahy. His grandfather owned a vineyard on the Moselle; his father Peter emigrated as a boy of fifteen, and in southern Brazil had married a woman named Anna Michels, from the Rhineland. The pair kept a small general store. Such were the mediocre circumstances amid which the man who was to be a noted statesman was reared. He became a student of engineering, and then, in his twenties, was involved in the storms of the revolution. In 1889, as Marshal Fonseca's aide-de-camp, he took part in the attack upon Emperor Pedro II's palace. The revolution having been successful, at the age of twenty-six he was appointed provisional governor of the province of Santa Catharina. In the National Assembly he was known by two nicknames, "Sabe tudo" (Know-All) and "Allemão-sinho" (the Little German).

Later, in 1902, he became minister of communications in the central government at Rio. Finding employment for the workers who were streaming into the capital from the plantations, he transformed the Brazilian metropolis to make of Rio de Janeiro the most magnificent seaport in the world. When Rio Branco, who had been minister for foreign affairs, died, Müller took over the vacant post. Two years afterwards, the great war began. At first the Germans in Brazil, who were very numerous in the province of Santa Catharina, tried to induce Lauro Müller to swing Brazil over to the German side. Müller, however, remained strongly in favour of Brazilian neutrality. His endeavours were fruitless, for coffee was stronger than he. Ninety per cent of the property in the country depended upon a market for this export. When, in April 1917, the United States declared war against Germany, the neutrality of Brazil became untenable, and Müller broke off relations with what had once been his fatherland. He probably hoped that matters would not go beyond this. But popular feeling was roused, the minister for foreign affairs was reviled as an "Allemão," and was threatened with personal violence. On May 2, 1917, he resigned office, to be succeeded by Nilo Peçanha, who declared war against Germany. In 1926, Müller died at Florianopolis, highly respected by many of the citizens of his adopted country, but regarded harshly by others. His diary has never been published. Some day, perhaps, it will give a clue to much that has remained obscure in the Brazilian history of those days.

Thus Lauro Müller's personal honour was tarnished by the coffee interests. But what did the individual matter? The country had once more been saved. Purchases of coffee by the Allies, financed in Paris and New York, gave Brazil a breathing-space. The stocks on hand having been cleared away, nature must now help to prevent a new glut. The Brazilian coffee-barons put their trust in the famous nocturnal frosts, which are, however, rare in Brazil. This time they came to the rescue, occurring at the right moment to nip the blossoms and destroy the expected harvest. The lean year coincided with the epoch when, after the war, European consumption was reviving, so that the planters were able to sell what coffee they garnered at prices far more favourable than had prevailed for a long time. They recognized again that, as the newspapers declared, "God was a Brazilian."

Then came the year 1920. Was God a Brazilian after all? In 1919, when the harvest had been so scanty, the coffee-shrubs were granted a rest, with the result that they now showed a fertility unexampled since 1906. Who was going to consume these mountains of coffee? The news from Europe was that of Job's comforters. In 1920 the "victorious" Allies began to recognize that not Germany and Austria alone had lost the war, but that the supposed conquerors on the field of battle were nevertheless financially defeated. Europe's indebtedness to America had a disastrous effect in the markets. No wholesalers were inclined to buy coffee, for the consumption of the masses in all European countries was greatly reduced.

Coffee-substitutes were still being used to a disquieting extent. Where the necessities of life are bought and sold there is no restriction upon distortion, so those who wished to depress prices told coffee home-truths which that commodity had not listened to for centuries. Throughout Germany it was bruited abroad that the Black Apollo was an assassin, and that a beverage prepared from malt or from figs was wholesomer as well as cheaper.

Great was the disturbance in coffee-consuming countries, with a consequent fall in prices. Once more the Brazilian government had to come to the help of the planters. This time a miracle contributed to their salvation. The miracle was wrought by the Big Brother in the North, the only country where money was not tight. Prohibition was inaugurated in the United States by the eighteenth amendment to the constitution. Coffee rushed into the field that alcohol had been compelled to evacuate.

The long-lasting and fierce campaign in the American Union against the evils of alcoholism at length proved victorious. The Woman's Christian Temperance Union, by making common cause with the churches, had secured the governmental suppression of all beverages containing over one-half of one per cent of alcohol. The cult of Bacchus in North America was not of ancient date, but was vigorous. Whereas in Europe grapes will not ripen north of the fiftieth parallel of latitude, in America the limit is as low as the forty-fifth parallel, on the east coast it is even lower, and the Virginia Company, which in 1620 made the first experiments in vine-growing, had no success. Then, in 1769, French Canadians, driven south, tried their hand in Illinois, which is crossed by the fortieth parallel; but there, likewise, failure resulted. Not until the year 1820 did an army officer named Adlun succeed in growing satisfactory vines on a large scale. From this date, the Americans began to drink home-grown wines, and of these for decades the Isabella wine of Ohio was the best known. Today there is a good deal of viticulture in the United States, especially in California, New Mexico, and Arizona. (Of course vine-growing was interrupted during the prohibition years.) Nevertheless, down to the passing of the eighteenth amendment, and after it illicitly, the import of Rhenish wines, claret, and champagne continued.

The American temperance movement was directed, not so much against wine as against beer and spirits. Neither Bacchus nor Gambrinus could withstand its onslaught. There existed a number of "dry" states before 1920, but in that year the whole of the Union went dry. In name, at least, for illicit drinking was widespread until, in December 1932, the ranks of the prohibitionists were broken when Congress authorized the consumption of beer with an alcoholic content of 3.2 per cent.

Besides the illicit traders, the "bootleggers," who, like their prototypes in history, made their profit out of defeating the aims of the puritans (since human nature is such that people will spare neither trouble nor expense in the endeavour to secure forbidden fruit), the coffee-barons reaped the advantages of prohibition. Smuggled liquor was expensive, and the synthetic product often dangerous; so during the prohibition years, coffee became the chief beverage in the United States. In the gigantic manufacturing enterprises of New York, Chicago, Pittsburgh, San Francisco, and elsewhere, it had long been prized as an accelerator, as a potion that could enhance muscular and nervous energy, and therefore increase output. But now, when the eighteenth amendment was in force, the population drank more and more, coffee because they liked it, and not simply because they found it useful. True, coffee did not, in the American Union, give a peculiar stamp to the civilization of the country, did not fertilize intellectual life as it had done in Venice, in Paris, and in Vienna. The fundamental characteristics of Americans forbade this effect. Even while drinking coffee for pleasure, they did not forget, in the unconscious at least, that the main use of the beverage was to promote energy.

But it is time to return to the effect of the eighteenth amendment upon Brazil. Promptly the United States became the chief recipient of the most important Brazilian export.

Whereas in 1913 the United States imported, in round figures, six and a half million sacks of coffee, ten years later the amount rose to nearly eleven millions. This signified a great relief to a vastly overburdened Brazil.

But what was the nature of that burden? Merely overproduction of coffee? No; it was, rather, the mentality of the planters; their selfish misunderstanding, their cupidity. Instead of being grateful to the state authorities, who, again and again, had saved them by valorization purchases, they repeatedly broke their word.

Obviously, in valorization, the state took all the risks. If the valorization system had gone bankrupt, the State would have gone bankrupt as well. For making this immense sacrifice, this unprecedented venture, the state asked the planters to pledge themselves, in return, not to extend their plantations. But the coffee-barons did not keep the pledge. They were getting good prices for their produce; what did it matter to them whether it was from the state or from private merchants in their own or in foreign lands? Without restriction, therefore, they continued to play a game of roulette with the soil. They ignored the prohibition against extended planting, and in an unintegrated country sixteen times as large as France control was impossible. Besides, in many cases, without actually breaking new ground, they weeded, manured, and pruned their coffee-bushes more carefully than before, thus multiplying the output.

When, in 1924, there was a disastrously large harvest, and the clamour for governmental intervention was renewed, the state, warned by experience, modified its economic policy. Finding that its partners, the coffee-barons, were unteachable, it refused to go on carrying the burden alone. It conceived the excellent idea of transferring the risk to the shoulders of the producers. Instead of buying the crops, it prescribed the quantity of coffee that might be daily transported to the coast. Only a definite number of sacks were to be sent from the interior to the ports. The Instituto do Café, which had developed out of the Sociedad Promotura da Defesa do Café, became the new central authority of Brazilian economic policy. Its dictatorship, called for short the "Defesa," was wielded from the Rua Wenceslau Braz in São Paulo, and acquired worldwide importance.

In the economic life of the globe, "Rua Wenceslau Braz" became a name of power like "Quai d'Orsay" or "Downing Street" in world politics.

Valorization had always been instituted when a crisis was threatening or had already arrived. The aim of the Defesa was to prevent crises.

In the interior of the country, the Defesa established warehouses, known as "reguladores," in which the planters were obliged to store their coffee. According to the date of storage and the condition of the market, the Defesa allowed the delivery of coffee to a port of shipment. Thus supplies were kept equable throughout the year, and a crash in prices was prevented. As the most important feature of the system, the Defesa maintained strict secrecy concerning the number of sacks of coffee that were stored at a given time in the reguladores, the divulging of information about this matter being severely punished. No one could learn the amount of the Brazilian harvest; and, in course of time, speculators in Havre, London, Hamburg, and New York lost all inclination for gambling in a staple that could no longer offer surprises. The Defesa controlled the coffee-market of the world.

But the maintenance of this dictatorship was too costly. Although the Defesa did not, as the government had done, buy the crops, it had to make advances to the coffee-barons on the security of what they put in storage. Furthermore, it had to pay the salaries of its own officials, its countless watchmen and spies. Dictatorships are always costly.

Brazil was still abundantly supplied with capital from the financial world in general. The valorization of coffee had proved a great success. The state, acting as intermediary, sold its coffee at much higher prices than it had previously paid the planters. International financiers felt they had good reason for continuing to support "so well-advised a state." Above all they had to bear in mind that stored coffee was the security for their loans. If they called in their advances, thus forcing down the price of coffee, they would undermine the value of this security. In a word, to quote an old saying, they had to throw good money after bad.

Such was the mechanism, both financial and psychological, which for nearly five years made the Defesa invulnerable. It became a state within the state. People bowed before its executive authority; it was a department with ministerial powers, against which there was no appeal. Mario Tavares, A. B. de Salles, and other officials of São Paulo, held sway by turn in the Defesa.

The dagger-thrust was delivered at a weak spot in the armour. A planned economy—to say nothing of "State socialism"—was impossible, in the long run, where capitalism and anarchism were so closely linked. The character of the Brazilian planters recalls the peculiarities of a high explosive, combining as it does the unstable charm of the Portuguese and the hardness of the Indian aborigines, whose favourite word, "ita," stone, is found in so many place-names of Brazil. A Brazilian will make sacrifices for the common welfare in the showy form of war and of death upon the battlefield. But it is harder to live for the fatherland than to die for it, and hard to make sacrifices under stress of reasonable considerations!

The Achilles' heel of the Defesa was that it was not able to cope with the anarchy of production. It merely supervised distribution. Dictatorship notwithstanding, it could not enforce its veto upon expanded planting. As soon as the planters realized that the Defesa was maintaining prices, they perceived that extended plantations were more lucrative than gold-digging. Even more serious was the fact that, trade being good, the number of planters steadily increased. The result was something that resembled the "tulip mania" in seventeenth-century

Holland. Just as in those days all the Dutch, with a blind faith that the luxury price of tulips would be maintained, set to work cultivating these flowers, so now did every Brazilian, be he small shopkeeper, host of a tavern, apothecary, or sailor, take to coffee-planting—if no more than indirectly and as a means of investment for his savings. The result was that, while quantity increased, quality fell off. Coffee-planting is a fine art, and needs expert training. The influx of amateurs into the occupation, the growth of "private coffee-planting," led to so great a deterioration of the product that many consumers began to demand other coffee than Brazilian. They had been noticing for some time that Brazilian coffee was becoming acrid. It was lacking in aroma. Simultaneously there had been an increase in Central American production, stimulated by the measures of the Defesa though the administrators of that organization had had no such object in view. What Brazil had been doing for herself at a considerable financial sacrifice was a great advantage to Brazil's competitors in Central America.

While the "mild" coffees from Colombia, Nicaragua, and Costa Rica were comparatively easy to sell, in the interior of Brazil the quantities of "sharp" Brazilian coffee accumulating in the reguladores of the Defesa became so enormous that the time arrived when the fruits of anarchic over-production could no longer be marketed at any price.

In October 1929, Brazil's black day dawned. The Defesa collapsed. Thereupon the price of coffee, which had been artificially maintained for a quarter of a century, crashed.

The centre of Brazilian economic life, the Defesa do Café, had been destroyed. The planters had anarchically undermined their own buttresses.

To save itself, the state now had recourse to equally anarchic measures.

Breathless with astonishment and horror, the world watched the third phase of the Brazilian coffee-war.

The first phase began in 1906, when the state bought the crop in order to speculate with coffee for the advantage of the producers.

The second phase began eighteen years later, in 1924, when the state ceased to buy the crop, but advanced money on it, and regulated export.

Now, in 1931, the state began to destroy coffee.

24

Reason Becomes Nonsense—Bonfires of Coffee

D ON'T you smell something?" asked the pilot.
The windows of the fuselage were open. The pilot, entrusting the control to his mechanic, had left his seat to come in to speak to me. He closed the door behind him. Although we were not flying swiftly, this needed a good deal of exertion. The air was pressing heavily against the front of the machine.

"Can't you smell anything?" he repeated.

"No, I smell nothing," I replied.

"This is the place where it begins," he said, snuffing the breeze. "Last week, it began here."

"How high are we?" I inquired.

"Three thousand feet."

"What can one smell at such an altitude?"

I looked out of the window. During the last ten minutes, there had been a change in the landscape. The green coastline over which we were flying from north to south had become invisible. The breaking of the Atlantic rollers on the shore could no longer be seen. Vanished, too, the salmon-coloured rocks that showed from time to time above the green fringe, and around which the white sea-foam had been especially conspicuous.

We were passing over a stratum of clouds that looked like cotton-wool. Since we were not very high, the clouds must be close to the ground.

I grew weary of the view. Everything was shapeless, as it had been when we left Rio de Janeiro that morning, before dawn, in a fog. Lighted only by the flashes of the exhaust, we had risen steadily. Beneath us, at first, were the buildings of the capital; then we flew between cliffs to the outlet of a forest-valley. The right wing of our plane seemed almost to touch a ghostly monument of white stone. "That was the figure of Christ," said the pilot, shouting to drown the thunder of the engine. "He stands on the top of Mt. Corcovado, and is more than three hundred feet high." We issued from the valley, and the fog cleared. Soon we could distinguish the green coastline and the blue sea.

"Now we need merely follow the coast to Santos," explained Sutter, the pilot. From time to time he came to visit me in the cabin, for a talk. He had been a German officer, in the flying corps, and had gone to Rio as soon as the war was over to become a professional airman there. He was pilot of the *Fraternidado*, one of the Condor Syndicate's air-fleet. Once a week he flew south, to Santos and Florianopolis; and once a week north, to Bahia, Pernambuco, and Natal.

I pointed to the cottony clouds: "Oughtn't we to be in sight of Santos by now?"

No answer. But the smell he had spoken of assailed my nostrils. An aromatic yet pungent odour was rising from beneath and permeated the cabin. Stronger than the wind, and swifter than our speed. It was the smell of burning coffee, a smell so concentrated that it dulled the senses, and was at the same time actually painful.

The ship volplaned down to fifteen hundred feet. The clouds divided. Between the parted masses we saw green land, with here and there bright yellow patches, from which smoke rose.

"Those are fires," I said.

"Yes, they are burning coffee!" replied airman Sutter, wrathfully.

The smell by now had become intolerable, and the fumes had produced a ringing in my ears. It seemed to sap my strength. For a while I felt as if we were flying through the noise made by a gigantic alarm-clock. Then we passed the fire-zone, and fresh air blew in through the windows once more. We could see the hills that surround the harbour of Santos, and the rows of neat, white houses in the town.

"Well, I must make the landing myself," said Sutter. Through the speaking-tube he called to the mechanic, a Portuguese half-breed, who thereupon left the driver's seat. Sutter took the man's place, and five minutes later we settled down softly upon the waters of the harbour.

We were seated on a terrace overlooking the sea. Above us shone an arc-lamp, thickly surrounded by swarms of flying creatures, beetles, ants, and moths.

The sea was groaning rather than roaring. Very dark, like the ocean of a nightmare, it stretched away towards the east. The restlessness of the water communicated itself to the land. How sultry was this starless night! Sutter and I were reclining in a pair of folding long-chairs. The wood and the linen seemed to sweat. Sutter was smoking, and this helped to keep off the insects. I wanted to remove the atmosphere of depression by a comforting dose of whisky and soda. A bottle of a well-known brand stood on the table, a tower filled with fluid repose and radiating British phlegm. After we had clinked glasses and drunk, we felt more at ease.

"Well, what do you think of this coffee-burning business? Would you have believed such a thing to be possible?" asked Sutter.

"I read about it before I left Europe," was my answer, "but, I may tell you frankly, it seemed to me incredible. How large an area was covered by the bonfires?"

"What we flew over today? Ten kilometres, at least. It may have been fifteen."

"Past belief!"

"Well, you know, from Santos alone they brought millions of sacks, emptied them, and fired the whole lot. Disgusting. It has been going on for months."

I took another drink.

"It's no concern of mine, after all," said Sutter, in an outburst. "I was brought up as a soldier, and now I am a professional air-pilot. But what gets my goat is the illogicality of the whole thing. Here they are burning coffee to rid themselves of it, while in Europe many poor devils of starvelings cannot afford to buy themselves a cup of coffee!"

"You think that the coffee ought to be given away to those who are in need?"

"I'm not such a dunderhead as that," answered Sutter. "Before the coffee could be given away in Europe, someone would have to pay for the transportation. How could the cost be defrayed except by the coffee itself, by coffee becoming a saleable commodity once more, instead of being a drug in the market?"

"Yes," said I, "man's sublimest power, that of bestowing gifts, has no place in economic life. What is given away freely has, thereby, lost its value as a saleable commodity."

"Can you understand that?" asked Sutter, in astonishment.

" 'Understand' is not the right word. All I know is that such is the fact."

The air-pilot emitted two or three puffs of smoke. Next he took a pull at his glass of whisky and soda.

I laughed. Then a whimsical thought came into my head. "Do you remember the witches' multiplication-table in the first part of *Faust?*"

He nodded. "More or less. 'Twice one is four, and carry two makes seven. Add one is ten, you'll all be rich men.' Something of that sort, wasn't it?"

"More or less," I said, with a laugh. "Well, listen carefully. That's the multiplication-table that they use today in the world markets—a perfectly logical one. No difficulty, now, in understanding why there are bonfires of coffee here at Santos."

He sat up and stared at me, saying: "Are you drunk?"

"Not so fast. I only wanted to show you that you were wrong when you said that the illogicality of the coffee-burning business revolted you. It is disgusting, as you say, but perfectly logical."

"I suppose," said Sutter sarcastically, "that you are going to quote old Hegel next. 'Whatever is, is rational'?"

"Unfortunately Hegel was right. Let me tell you a story, a fable, rather, that is told in Europe today to all students of economics. They call it the 'law of marginal utility.' "

"Go ahead," said Sutter. "But you're not going to pull my leg, are you?"

"Oh, no, my fable is perfectly serious."

"Well, let me hear it," said the pilot.

"A man has five sacks of grain. He uses the first to appease the pangs of hunger; the second, to produce complete satiety; the third, as fodder for cattle; the fourth, to make strong drinks; the fifth, to feed race-horses. Has each sack the same value? If the man reflects a little, he will realize that every sack has a different value, a value that varies according to its use. The value of the first sack, which was used to allay the pangs of hunger, may be indicated by the figure five; that of the second sack, by four; that of the last sack by one. But since the man has all five sacks simultaneously at his disposal, he estimates their value as equal, and at the value of the last sack, at the value of what is called 'marginal utility.' Each sack, therefore, is worth one. All the sacks taken together are worth five times one. That is to say five."

"Well, isn't that true?" asked Sutter. "Do you mean to say that five times one is not five?"

"Not in all circumstances. I shall make that clear to you in a moment. Suppose that the man in our fable loses one of his sacks? What will he do? He will stop keeping race-horses. The remaining four sacks have risen in value, to the marginal value of the sack used for making strong drinks, which was worth two. Now the four sacks together have the value of four times two, which is eight. Thus the quantity of grain has diminished, but its value has increased."

"The devil it has!" said Sutter. "My head is swimming. Is that really true?"

"It is really true! Now, surely you can understand, however much you may dislike the fact, why the value of coffee increases when large quantities of coffee are ruthlessly destroyed!"

The airman's sides shook with laughter. "Yes, but what about the air, the air, the air?"

"What has the air got to do with the matter?" I inquired.

"Why, if what you say is true of coffee, do you mean to imply that man's chief good, air, has no economic value? Certainly it has no value when the supply of it is unrestricted. But when there is a shortage, as for instance in a submarine, it becomes valuable, doesn't it? It grows more valuable the less there is of it." He smacked his thigh in his amusement.

"I congratulate you, Herr Sutter! You have grasped the root of the matter."

"And is that the sort of stuff they teach students of economics?"

"Yes. More than fifty years ago, a psychological trend came to the front in political economy. The leaders were Gossen, a German, and William Jevons, an Englishman. Then the Austrians took a hand in the game, Karl Menger, Böhm-Bawerk, and Friedrich von Wieser contributing so notably to the development of the theory that one speaks now of the 'Austrian School.'"

"And what are the teachings of this Austrian School?"

"The theory of marginal utility. A diminution of quantity signifies an increase in value. Four sacks of grain are worth more than five, because . . . but need I repeat?"

Sutter, the air-pilot, struck the table, so that the whisky-bottle tottered and the glasses jingled. "No, you do not need to say it all over again, for I have had enough!" he said angrily. "What the professors teach may be extremely reasonable. But at the same time it is rank nonsense, because it ignores the common sense and the morality of the plain man. Those who sharpen their wits too much, lose them. To be over-subtle is to be stupid, my dear sir. The world at large will never be the fenced precinct or the desert island of the professors of economics."

Out of the sultry seacoast air of Santos, I took a train next day to the plateau of São Paulo. There it was as bright and fresh as it had been when we were flying high on the way from Rio to Santos. That evening, while the jazz-band was braying in the hotel lounge—where the company looked as smart as in Paris or Trouville or St. Moritz, though their skins were somewhat darker—the head-porter asked me, in a whisper: "Would you like to see a quemada?"

"A quemada? What is that?"

"You know, sir, don't you, that coffee is being burned wholesale? I can get you a taxi, and you can see it yourself, at half an hour's drive from the town."

"Why are you making such a mystery of the matter? Are spectators forbidden?"

"No, sir, there is no prohibition. Still, the government is not best pleased for European visitors to see what is going on. I know well enough why. In Europe, coffee is dear, and foreigners grow angry to see us burn it here as worthless."

After thinking for a moment, I asked: "Are there many police there?"

"Not more than four or five gendarmes. The quemada do café is of no interest to us Brazilians."

"I should have thought," said I, astonished, "that there would have been people ready to carry off the coffee destined for the flames. It seems to me strange if there are not."

I was watching the porter's face, and saw that he regarded my observation as "strange." Whose thoughts were topsy-turvy, those of Brazilians, or those of Europeans? "None of us Brazilians take any interest in the matter." The whole thing was an enigma. The South American continent was an enigma with its perilous wealth which, if left unregulated, could transform itself into grievous poverty.

I accepted the porter's offer, and drove out to see the quemada. Our route led by a fine road through garden suburbs. We reached a square, the farther side of which was bounded by a big shed. The sort of shed you might have seen anywhere in Europe, with a tar-paper roof. From within came a sputtering and sizzling noise. There was a smell of burning, but no smell of coffee. I could not see any flame.

The chauffeur entered the shed and came out again accompanied by a gendarme. He told the latter that I wanted to see the burning. The gendarme looked at me indifferently, and said I might go a few paces inside. I paid off the chauffeur, who did not wish to wait, lest he might "get into trouble." The gendarme opened the door of the shed, and, pointing with his rifle, showed how far I could advance.

Thus I reached the edge of the quemada. The roof of the shed had been removed over the part where I now stood, and I looked into a vast space filled with smoke-wreaths—a Pythian space, which, for all one could see, might have extended for two kilometres or for twenty.

The fumes were not white only, but black and reddish as well. I stretched forward my hands. It was like thrusting them into an oven. The place was an inferno, although flames flickered only fitfully here and there. A sinister region, where doomed spirits hovered, talking in a tongue no mortal could understand.

Strange indeed was the noise. The note of the conflagration was not such a roar as one hears when a huge house is burning in the open, and the flames rise freely into the sky. Since above the vast heap of coffee there were no bellying fires, that sort of music was not to be heard. The auto-da-fé of the glutted coffee had something sinister about it, a smack of furtive malice. The sound of the burning reminded me of the noise made by bees when their hive is smoked; it was a crafty, whining, chattering noise. The glow hugged the ground, as if tormented by an uneasy conscience. Because combustion was not free, the odour was offensive, that of matter being charred until it becomes black and irrecognizable.

Not all the time, however. While I was standing in front of this forsaken pyre, suddenly the wind found entry, and blew the stinking vapours aside. Then there was an ethereal odour. That always happens when the flames attack a new heap. At first they roast the beans instead of destroying them. The necromantic smell of the oil liberated in the roasting process, this aroma of Araby, was what brought tears to my eyes and a lump into my throat. For, properly speaking, to roast coffee is to effect the first transformation through which it passes on the way to become something that comforts the human nervous system in so mysterious a fashion. Now, however, what I witnessed was a coffee-roasting that was only a prelude to destruction.

Here the odour had become Satanic. It was the odour that I had smelt for the first time when visiting the Berlin Industrial Exhibition of 1896, and that I have loved ever since. There a cylindrical machine, invented by John Arbuckle, was on show. Wonderful, to me, was this roasting-drum, in which, by opening a flap, one could watch how far the process had advanced. Some of the coffees that were being roasted were of very light colour, others were medium-brown, and others dark-brown. I envied the employees who were demonstrating the use of the machine, and who lived in the hot vapours that rose from the roasting beans. Now, however, I should have preferred that the coffee perish amid a hideous stench rather than amid this beloved aroma.

I had already turned to quit the shed, when a loud crackling arrested my attention. It sounded like a machine-gun. Were some rebels attacking the quemada? Oh, no, nothing of that sort. In one of the heaps of burning coffee, the beans were exploding. For a minute or two, sparks flew in every direction. They looked like fireflies, describing little parabolas athwart the greyish-black fumes. Soon it was all over, the last chemical revolt against destruction had been crushed. Now the beans had been reduced to charcoal; they had suffered the inevitable death whose germs slumber in all living creatures.

I took my departure. The street along which I walked ran between the high walls of gardens, walls overtopped by huge cactuses, by pines, and by eucalyptus trees. How cool the night was on this plateau. Where the coffee was burning, smoke had hidden the stars. Now they were sparkling abundantly in the clear sky. Yet not so abundantly as in our northern hemisphere; the fertility of the southern soil has not been communicated to the southern skies. I recognized some of the constellations: the Southern Cross, the Centaur, the Compasses.

Then, looking at the zenith, I descried the two dark areas that are known as the "coal-sacks." These are like black pits in the firmament, pits where no star shines.

An Indian passed me. He was wearing blue overalls, open in front down to the navel. The man went by without a greeting. He was lean of visage, and walked stiffly, barefooted, so that his feet made no sound.

I turned to follow him with my eyes, as he glided towards the shed. Was he the night-watchman's relief? His raiment and his bare feet suggested extreme poverty. Perhaps he hoped to steal some of the unburned coffee?

No, that was unlikely. Coffee was too cheap in Brazil to be worth stealing. Everyone could get as much as he wanted for nothing. What did it matter to the poor of Brazil that the poor of Europe could not buy coffee because the price was kept up by these bonfires?

Most Brazilians shrug their shoulders when you speak to them of the quemada. All the same, they look at this coffee-burning askance, for simple folk are not pleased by the destruction of commodities produced by their comrades' labour. The ill-feeling, however, does not take a violent form. I had been told that a very few policemen sufficed, in Santos, to guard the barges into which coffee is shovelled in order to be dumped out at sea.

"Nevertheless," I said in conversation next day, "there must be persons who disapprove of these bonfires and of this dumping? I do not mean poor folk, who are comparatively indifferent to what happens. I am thinking of members of the intelligentzia, who cannot fail to regard the destruction of the coffee crop by governmental action as a grave economic problem."

I was talking to Carlos Hennig, an elderly German merchant, who settled in Brazil forty years ago.

"Of course there are some such. For instance, the liberals, who are opposed on principle to state interference with the interplay of supply and demand. I may mention Alves de Lima. He is one of the wealthiest men in the country, belonging to the old Portuguese stock, and he has written a fierce invective against this form of state intervention."

"Do you think I could have a talk with him?"

"He runs a newspaper in São Paulo. I will ring him up on the phone."

In a few minutes Carlos Hennig came back to me. Alves de Lima was not in São Paulo. He had gone to his country house, which lay amid extensive coffee-plantations, not far from Campinas.

"Where is Campinas?" I asked, and was glad to learn from Hennig that I could get there without spending several days in an airplane. As distances go in Brazil, it was close at hand, only sixty-five miles northwest of São Paulo. I could reach it in an hour or two by rail.

Next day we took train across the "terra roxa." The railway ran among dark-green plantations. The coffee-shrubs looked to me like dwarf trees rather than big bushes. With their abundant foliage they formed a huge green carpet stretching to the horizon. The whole countryside was a green garden. Where roads crossed the green, one saw the earth, chocolate-red, sometimes almost violet in tint. Dark-green and dark-red were the "national colours" of the coffee-state São Paulo.

We reached Campinas. It was a busy little town, surrounding a central square, known in Portuguese as the "Praça." All these central squares are children of the Forum of ancient Rome. Pigeons were wheeling round the church, but in Brazil their iris pinions did not contrast with a Mediterranean sky. The birds disappeared beneath a pergola, under whose shelter three vigorous women were doing laundry-work in a stone basin. A couple of vultures lumbered across the marketplace. We were not in the Campagna, where civilization has prevailed for thousands of years, but in South America, subject to the unceasing menace of birds and beasts of prey.

Hiring a taxi in the square, we drove out through the plantations. The air was sultry-sweet, and the breeze that whistled past the windshield, rustling in the hood, was like the *Föhn* made odorous by jasmine and orange-blossom. The last building we passed as we left the outskirts of the town was the Botanical Institute, whose creation has been the life-work of an Austrian scientist named Dafert. It is one of the most important experimental stations for the study of sub-tropical agriculture,

Then, for a long time, there was nothing to be seen but coffee-trees. One forgot that they were trees. So bent and laden were they that they seemed, rather, an endless herd of cattle. We saw few men. They wore white shirts, wide open at the neck, and broad-brimmed straw hats. Their trousers were tucked into high boots.

"A defence against serpents," explained Hennig. "Many thousands of Brazilians die every year of snake-bite; it is extremely dangerous to go barefoot in this country!"

At length we reached the lodge, a roughly built frame-house. When we had left the taxi, two slender half-breeds, wearing clean, white raiment, conducted us by garden-paths to the planter's villa, a three-storied building. But for certain peculiarities of the colonial style of architecture, one might have thought it one of the fine country houses lying between Nice and Cannes.

The walls of the building were covered with a purple-flowering Bougainvillaea. Where barely half a century ago the primeval forest had stood intact, the power of money and of labour had charmed into existence a fragment of the Riviera.

Octaviano Alves de Lima was reclining in a long-chair on the veranda when we were announced. He knew what I had come to ask about, and sprang to his feet exclaiming: "There is no such thing as overproduction! O fantasma da superproducção não existe! Overproduction is a phantom of the imagination! The pundits at the Coffee Institute should read Henry George and learn that the Brazilian crisis is wholly due to protectionism. Free trade would instantly solve the coffee-problem!"

"Then you don't think that there is too much coffee?" I asked, in astonishment.

The white-clad millionaire waved his hand in the negative.

"O café reclama expansão, exige novos mercados consumidores. Coffee needs expansion, and new markets for its consumption."

I objected. "Surely the production of coffee needs to be restricted; at any rate until new coffee-consuming countries have been found."

"Per a derrubada da barreira alfandegeria!" exclaimed Octaviano Alves de Lima. "By throwing down tariff barriers! Why do the Russians drink no coffee? Could they not buy millions of sacks from us? There is no over-production; it is tariffs that are the root of the mischief."

"Do you want to go to war with Russia?" I inquired. "How are you going to compel the Russians to buy Brazilian coffee?"

"Easily enough," answered Octaviano. "The Russians want to export their own produce. Brazil need merely enter into a satisfactory commercial treaty with the Soviet Union. We shall willingly pledge ourselves to take Russian grain, if they will take Brazilian coffee in exchange."

"An excellent idea," said Hennig. "You scratch my back, and I will scratch yours! But it won't work so far as Russia is concerned."

"Why not?" asked the fazendeiro.

"Because consumption does not depend exclusively upon tariffs and prices. The Russians have their own habits. How can you compel people who have been accustomed to tea for centuries to drink coffee instead? Even if you abolish tariff barriers, you will still have this obstacle in your path. It is much easier to make tea than to make coffee. You put your tea in a teapot and pour boiling water upon it, and there you are. Lots more than that to do before you can make drinkable coffee! No one knows it better than you. Coffee is not for Russian peasants or for Chinese coolies."

Octaviano Alves de Lima made no answer. Our host and Hennig lighted cigarettes. A mulatto woman served us with coffee. After a while the fazendeiro ended the silence.

"All tariff barriers must be broken down," he repeated obstinately. "Free trade must become worldwide. Immediately. Yes, immediately."

That word "immediately" haunted me. I asked Senhor Alves de Lima how he thought free trade in coffee could be inaugurated "immediately."

He looked at me in astonishment. Where was the difficulty?

"If prices were left uncontrolled, if they were to be determined by nothing but the haggling of the market, would they not fall so low that the majority of planters would be compelled to close down?"

"Of course! So much the better. Thus you would get restricted planting, which is universally regarded as a desideratum."

"Then only those who could produce for a market in which knockdown prices prevailed would escape bankruptcy?"

Alves de Lima smiled.

"That is the fundamental law of economic life," he said. "The fittest survive. Anyone whose production is too costly is forced out of the running."

I suppressed the obvious retort that capital punishment was a rather harsh measure for producing at too high a cost. O fantasma da super-producção não existe? Certainly, if only a few survivors were left upon the battlefield, over-production would come to an end. Still, so merciless a "Darwinism" was uncongenial to me.

"The fittest." Who are the fittest? Octaviano was a Crœsus. Perhaps he was one of the few planters who would have been able to survive the crash; to keep his head above the waters of insolvency until, through ruthlessly reduced production, his coffee would again become marketable at a paying price. But what about the millions who would be slaughtered on the economic battlefield? Was this a solution?

The tropic night fell swiftly. The orange-coloured sun had dipped below the horizon. We strolled through the garden, our nostrils assailed by sweet scents. Flowers fertilized by night-flying insects were pouring forth their perfume as a nightingale pours forth song.

Our host's lovely garden was further beautified by the statues of Italian gods and goddesses. They were watching over a marble reservoir, filled with clear water.

Beside this reservoir we said farewell. In the quickly gathering darkness, Octaviano, wearing white drill, reminded me somehow of a Roman proconsul. His words had been reasonable enough, but the reasoning was that of an extremely rich man.

"Of course Octaviano is absolutely wrong," said Carlos, when we had taken our seats in the train for the journey back from Campinas to São Paulo. The brightness of the starry heavens showed that we were on a lofty plateau. As the train gathered speed, the wind blew chill through the window. "Octaviano is mistaken when he believes that, as soon as the Brazilian government ceased to maintain prices, most of the planters would abandon their plantations."

"Still," I said, "if prices were to fall as they must, the planters could not go on paying wages to their workers."

"All the same, very few of the fazendas would be abandoned. A man will stick to his land so long as he has a roof over his head, enough food to keep him from starving, and a little live-stock. Rather than quit his plantation, he would introduce a profit-sharing system."

"Profit-sharing?"

"Certainly. If the Chinese tin barons were able to work with their coolies on a profit-sharing system, the Brazilian coffee barons could do the same. In times of crisis, they could pay a portion of the profits instead of paying straight wages. We must not underestimate a planter's love for his land. The smaller the plantation, the greater the affection! The land has been secured at a heavy sacrifice. Will it be lightly forsaken?"

That seemed to me psychologically sound.

"Do you think," I asked, "that the owners of comparatively small plantations would grow rice and other cereals, without allowing their coffee-trees to perish? That they would hold on to coffee in the hope that prices would rise some day?"

"I am sure of it."

I was watching the coloured illuminated advertisements as we passed through the outskirts of São Paulo.

"There is another respect in which Alves de Lima misunderstands the situation. The advocate of free trade forgets that the Brazilian currency is bolstered up by the price of coffee. When the coffee-crash occurred in São Paulo, it coincided with the general crash in Wall Street. Because the international financiers were in it up to the neck, we could raise no more loans. The price of coffee having fallen too low, the balance of trade was against us. The milreis fell on the foreign exchanges, and we began to export our gold reserves. . . . No, it would be madness to let the price of coffee take its own course, as the free-traders demand. Brazilian exports would steadily diminish, and therewith our currency would be undermined. We must try and discover new forms for the state control of economic life. Only in that way can our country be saved from ruin."

25

Envoy

NEXT day, Hennig told me how the quemada system had been introduced. Like all cultured Brazilians, he hated the destruction of coffee in bonfires, and knew that it was preposterous. If any had a better plan to suggest, they must bring it before the Coffee Council.

As yet, however, nothing had been found to replace this detestable method.

I was tired and distrait. "A god is being burned," I should have liked to say. "The god and sustainer of most of the Brazilians. Are you burning him because he has become too great? Are you burning him because he has deceived his votaries? Is not this pure mythology?" But I kept my thoughts to myself.

Our conversation grew transcendental.

We were strolling hither and thither through the town. Suddenly Hennig broke off with the words: "Where had we got to? I mean, to what point in Brazilian economic history?"

"We had reached the collapse of the Defesa, in 1929. This is April 1932. Little is known in Europe as to what has happened in the interim. Nothing more than conflicting newspaper reports. It is impossible to form a clear picture from them."

"No, there is something better than that available," said Carlos Hennig. "The London and Cambridge Economic Service has published a memorandum about recent happenings. I will order a copy for you."

Next afternoon, the pamphlet was brought to me in the hotel. The author's name was I. W. F. Rowe.

From it I learned that when, in 1929, the Defesa collapsed, and there was imminent danger that a huge harvest would be poured into the market, a certain Charles Murray came forward with a proposal to solve the joint problem of "coffee and currency" at one stroke. His scheme was as simple as it was bold. The chief wonder was that no such proposal had ever been mooted before.

The export value of the coffee-crop, said Murray, was estimated in 1930 at one-third more than it had been in 1929. To maintain the old price would endanger the stability of the currency. "But," said Charles Murray, "besides that, if we keep the price of coffee at its former level, the whole crop will, once more, be extremely lucrative. This will lead to further plantation, and the situation will grow steadily worse. Now we find that consumption throughout the world is increasing, steadily though slowly. High prices, strangely enough, do not check the growth of consumption; whereas (and that is still more remarkable) low prices do not markedly stimulate consumption. Consumption, therefore, does not play the part attributed to it by free-trade philosophers. But that is a side-issue. Our immediate object must be to find means: first of bringing back the gold-price of coffee to its former level; and, nevertheless, secondly, of avoiding any stimulus to the planters to extend the area of plantation. On the contrary, it is indispensable that they should make so little out of their coffee as to incline them to reduce plantation. Apparently there must be discovered some effective way of diminishing supply, since it is excessive supply which forces down prices. Well and good; but how is all this to be managed?"

Murray's plan was that for the following two years every sack of coffee should pay an export tax of one hundred per cent ad valorem. In that case, he calculated, the gold price would, after six months, attain the level of the preceding year, whereas the planters would receive only the present lower price, and would, as a psychological consequence of this, proceed to restrict production. The revenue derived from this export tax would provide the government with funds for the purchase and destruction of the surplus crop. After the glut had been reduced by destruction of surplus coffee and after the production of coffee had been restricted, the export tax could be withdrawn, and the price of coffee be left to adjust itself freely in accordance with liberal principles. This scheme was to run for only two years.

When it was bruited abroad in Brazil that Charles Murray had suggested such a plan to the Coffee Institute, there was a storm of indignation. Everyone knew that, since the collapse of the Defesa, the Institute had been on the lookout for a new economic scheme—but this one would never do. The planters threatened revolution. To appease them, Whittaker, the new minister for finance, made an agreement with the United States to exchange Brazilian coffee for American wheat, and he was able to buy the harvest at a fairly good price.

But this expedient was successful for no more than another six months. The fundamental notion of Charles Murray had, at length, to be adopted. The government decided to compel the planters to deliver one-fifth of their total harvest in kind, and this fifth was to be destroyed. The planters raised a cry of fury. Were they to surrender one-fifth of their crops to the government for nothing? And were they, over and above this, to bear the cost of production and transport? No parliament would have approved the plan, and no police force could have carried it into execution. Since, however, something had to be done to prevent coffee becoming valueless, a compromise was reached. Charles Murray's scheme seemed not so bad after all. In April 1931, a congress from the coffee-growing provinces unanimously accepted the essence of it: the levying of an export duty whose proceeds were to be devoted to the purchase of coffee for destruction.

"Who, then," I asked, lifting my eyes from the Cambridge pamphlet, "really paid the expenses of the quemada?"

"The producer and the consumer have joined forces," replied Carlos Hennig. "First of all, the exporter pays, since upon every sack that is sent out of the country an export duty of ten shillings sterling is levied. The exporter does what he can to shift this burden upon the shoulders of the planter. The proceeds of the tax are used by the Brazilian government to finance the destruction of surplus coffee."

"How many sacks," I inquired, "does the government propose to destroy?"

"The Supreme Coffee Council in Rio has pledged itself to destroy within the year twelve million sacks. I believe, however, that this estimate will be exceeded. The coming crop is once more enormous; the planters must export coffee, and for each sack that is exported, ten shillings automatically drop into the treasury. Automatically, therefore, the process of destruction continues."

I was dumbfounded as I stared at Carlos Hennig. I found myself repeating the words which the German airman had used three days ago: "The plans of the Coffee Council may be extremely reasonable. All the same, they are preposterous, since they ignore the understanding, the morality, and the sentiment of the plain man."

Hennig dropped his eyeglass, and in his turn looked at me with astonishment. He nodded twice, as if in approval, and then restored the eyeglass to its place. For some reason, today, he looked to me extremely old, much older than he had looked the day before in Campinas. His eyebrows had worn thin, just as a fine piece of furniture will grow shabby during long years of use. But his countenance was placid, as if he felt glad that it was unlikely he would survive to witness the "regression of the world into simplicity."

"What hopeless anarchy!" I thought to myself, as I walked through the streets of São Paulo.

Yet there was nothing anarchical about the aspect of the town. It was a clean, tidy place, with its white buildings; much cleaner and tidier than most towns I have seen, the towns of southern Europe especially. Tropical cities have to keep themselves clean. Dirt in the tropics gives rise to epidemics. And tropical epidemics entail a very high mortality.

São Paulo, however, which is a good way south of the equator, on the tropic of Capricorn, does not resemble other tropical towns, at any rate in its central part. Its policemen and taxis, its restaurants and shops, are as spruce as those of a well-to-do town in the temperate zone; and, though the morning sun shone brightly, the atmosphere was pleasantly cool. We were fully three thousand feet above the sea, and at that altitude the tropical heat is tempered.

For the casual visitor in the business quarter of São Paulo, the errors of the coffee-dictatorship were as invisible as were the flaws of tropical life. The house in the Rua Wenceslau Braz, which since 1906 has been the headquarters of state intervention in the coffee-plantations (though, since the collapse of the Defesa, part of its powers has been surrendered to the Supreme Coffee Council in Rio de Janeiro), looked like an ordinary house of business. Schedules of one sort and another ornamented the walls of the room, and the courteous officials were seated at inoffensive-looking desks. Calendars were also posted up. Some of the employees were ticking away at typewriters. The work was done at an easy pace, as usual among the upper grades of employees in the tropics.

A good deal of their work obviously must be calculations, to ascertain how much coffee, during the next few weeks, had to be shovelled into bonfires or dumped into the sea. Fire and water were of equal importance as destroyers of the glut. Clerks were also drawing up plans for commercial treaties, organizing a system by which coffee could be exchanged for imports: for North American wheat, for coal from the Ruhr and German manufactures, for electrical machinery from Austria, for whatever Turkey could export—but the most dependable partners of these regulators of the coffee-market were two of the four primary elements, fire and water.

When I got back to the hotel, a queer type of fellow was awaiting me. Long and lean as Don Quixote, he was clad in white tropical raiment, which was however both ravelled and soiled. This was unusual here, for anyone who has pretensions to be a "gentleman," since the majority of such buy their coats and trousers by the dozen and put on a clean suit every morning.

"Good day to you," said this phenomenon in my native tongue. "I speak German, for my mother was German. My name is Gonçalves." Short pause, while he waited for me to reply. Since I said nothing, he went on: "My name is Simone Gonçalves, lieutenant-colonel on half pay."

I bowed. "What can I do for you?"

"The hotel porter, who is an acquaintance of mine, told me of your arrival. Is it true that you contribute to the newspapers over there?"

Over there. He uttered the words in a tone like that in which many people in Europe are apt to pronounce the name of America—in a tone of envy and respect. The tone made me prick up my ears.

"Won't you take a seat, colonel?"

"I'd rather stand," said he, "if you don't mind." He flushed a little. "I should probably get up again very soon."

He closed his eyes for a moment, and continued speaking furtively, almost in a whisper: "I have reason to suppose that you are being misinformed. All the Europeans who come here are humbugged. I suppose they have told you that the government is destroying twelve million sacks of coffee every year. Let me assure you, sir, that that is untrue. The government does not destroy six million, barely two million."

"I don't understand . . ." I murmured.

He looked at me with a distressful expression: "Let me tell you the facts. The coffee is secretly shipped away. It is simply stolen by the government; by these . . ."—vainly he sought a term of abuse strong enough for his liking—"who subsequently speculate with it!"

By this time I realized that my visitor was a lunatic. His delusion played with him as strings pull the limbs of a puppet. For a moment every nerve in him, every muscle, seemed to be twitching. He swallowed two or three times. Then he grew calmer, and sat down, unbidden.

"I see that you don't believe me. Of course I cannot prove what I am telling you; but you can see, at least, how probable it is that some hanky-panky is going on. Otherwise the government would not have recourse to so unserviceable an instrument as fire. . . ." He searched his pockets, produced a notebook, a corkscrew, a couple of handkerchiefs. His hands flew from one part of his coat to another, but he could not find that of which he was in search.

"I used to be a planter. In one of the years when prices fell almost to nothing, I was ruined, had to discharge my workers, and quit. My nearest neighbour, a fellow from Alagoas, bought my estate for a song. Now he goes on growing my coffee." The poor fellow stared thoughtfully into vacancy.

"Coffee is our national misfortune in Brazil. The government does not play straight. It is in league with the rich planters. Ah, here it is!" he said triumphantly. "It" was a small pasteboard box with a glass cover. He handed this to me, and a magnifying-glass as well.

"That is the broca do café."

"The coffee-borer?" I asked. "A noxious beetle, isn't it?"

"Yes, it made its first appearance about ten years ago. In the Campinas district alone it has destroyed a hundred thousand coffee-trees. But that is far too few, nothing at all."

"I have heard of it," said I, "and I have also been told what strong measures have been taken to fight the pest. I understand that every plantation has a disinfection-outfit provided at the cost of the state."

My interlocutor laughed scornfully, and said: "Senhores Lopes de Oliveira and Antonio de Queiroz Telles, two famous coleopterists, have actually prepared a motion-picture to warn everyone against the broca."

The story of the ruin of the plantations in Ceylon came into my mind. There have been great advances during the last fifty years. Means of defence are put into operation far more quickly. My thoughts wandered. As if from a great distance I heard the colonel saying: "Nothing should be done to resist the onslaught of the broca. If the government really wants to save the country, it will take up loads of the eggs of this beetle in airplanes, and strew them far and wide over the plantations."

"You don't say so!" I interposed, rising.

Stuttering in his haste, he said: "Let me beg you to write about this matter when you return to Europe."

Turning the door-handle to usher him out, I replied: "Certainly I will do what you ask."

The night-train to Rio was scheduled to start at ten o'clock. It was known as the "Cruzeiro do Sul," the Southern Cross. Its bright blue carriages revived memories of taking train to the Riviera. Soon I was on my way back towards the Atlantic, to Rio the hothouse, whence you see the sun rising out of the sea. We passed through Taubaté, where, in 1906, the three state presidents met in council. I asked the attendant to call me when the train reached Tuba Ton, at which place rocks and palm-trees begin.

As noon struck, I drove to Independencia Park, to see the monument to the independence of Brazil. It consists of stone figures of goddesses, warriors, and symbols of one sort and another. A pair of Indians in feathered robes participate in the commemoration of liberty. The whole is eloquently decorated with Portuguese inscriptions.

I sat down upon a bench at a convenient distance, gazing at the monument. My thoughts turned to Gonçalves, the lunatic who had called on me the previous day; and to what he had in his pocket.

Well, what had I got in my pocket? A coffee-twig! I had snapped it off one of the shrubs in Alves de Lima's plantation. I was keeping it as a memento. It bore a few withered flowers and some fruits.

Of all the wealth of coffee in the world, I owned no more than this twig. Nor should I ever own more than this, being neither planter nor merchant, neither speculator nor dealer, nor with talent for any of these professions. I had nothing but my vision of them all, and perhaps a gift for expression.

I was no more than a consumer; and, when I wanted to drink coffee, I had to pay for it like anyone else in the world.

The notion was so comical that I burst out laughing.

How strange! I picked a berry and pierced it with one of the blades of my pocket-knife. The outer envelope through which the point passed was what is called the epicarp. The next wrapping was the endocarp. Then came the pulp; then the silver-skin; then two seeds, grown together by their bellies, like Siamese twins. Inside all that I could dissect there was a kernel, that was certain. But what was the innermost nucleus of this kernel? An incomprehensible mystery, which no botanist could unravel.

I sat there like a sportive boy. I was holding something sticky between my fingers. The dissected coffee-berry looked at me and hypnotized me. A day-dream took possession of me.

I seemed to be making my way up a river, a very wide river, so wide that the farther bank was invisible. Nor could I make out the nature of the fluid in this river, except that it was yellow, and flowed swiftly. But the first dam that I saw was unquestionably the Murray scheme; and the second dam, over which the current flowed irresistibly like Niagara, was the Defesa policy. Above this the stream narrowed somewhat, so that I could see the farther bank. I made my way to a very early dam, and read on it the words "Convenio di Taubaté." This was the valorization of the year 1906. Now the channel narrowed yet more. I was no longer following up the course of a river, but was tracing back a current of human history; was studying well-known happenings, ranged in series. I saw towns full of coffee-houses, Napoleon's Continental System, Frederick the Great, old Paris and Versailles where dwelt Louis XIV, old Leipzig and Johann Sebastian Bach. On the flat shores of the Upper Adriatic stood Venetians wearing dominoes. Marseille appeared, capped in the baroque fashion by a huge wig, proper to a seventeenth-century physician. To the left lay the port of Amsterdam, whence the high-pooped sailing-ships set forth towards the East Indies; and London, where, beneath the shadow of St. Paul's, coffee had begun its fierce campaign against beer and brandy.

On the horizon lay Vienna, besieged by the Turks. The tower of St. Stephen's, with its fine traceries, rose into the sunshine above the smoke of artillery. Then I followed up the stream—yes, it was still a stream—to Constantinople, across the Bosporus into Asia Minor, and farther on into a fabled Araby. While my nostrils were assailed by a familiar aroma, I heard in my dream the voice of the old sheikh Abd el Kader:

> O Coffee, thou dispersest sorrow,
> Thou art the drink of the faithful,
> Thou givest health to those who labour,
> And enablest the good to find the truth.
> O Coffee, thou art our gold!
> There, where thou art offered,
> Men grow good and wise.
> May Allah overthrow thy calumniators
> And deliver thee from their wiles.

I came to myself and looked round me. Behind the National Monument the sky had turned orange. What would have happened if, near Shehodet Monastery, the goats had never eaten of the fruit of the coffee-shrub? If the imam had never discovered the sleep-dispelling energy of this marvellous plant, had never extracted its divine and demoniacal powers? What if this Prometheus among plants had never become known to man? "There are no plants, there is nothing material," I murmured. "If there be such things, they are brought into existence by our mythology, the mythology of raw materials."

It was time to turn in. But before I did so, I pencilled, to commit myself, the title of the opening chapter of my book:

"Night in the Land of Yemen."

Postscript

Aᴄᴛᴇʀ five years' study, I bring this saga to a close. Besides the aid of books, I am indebted to the stimulating assistance of friends: first of all to that of Dr. Kurt Schechner of Vienna; next to that of Dr. Eckener, of the Zeppelin aerodrome at Friedrichshafen. These two gentlemen have enabled me to undertake a personal study of coffee culture in South America.

From the literary point of view, I have suffered the fate common to so many authors. As soon as my book was on the way, I was overwhelmed with letters, data, all kinds of information. New springs were continually welling up.

No doubt many historical facts must have been overlooked. Much that I had intended to include has slipped through the meshes of my net, because its inclusion would have confused the general impression, and because it was a refractory element. Not every interesting fact can be woven into a comprehensive survey like the present. Here is one example among many. If Francis Bacon, lord chancellor, and pioneer in the field of scientific method, compares the influence of coffee on the brain to the influence of opium, this is not a medical error (had it been such, I should have indicated the fact in the text); but evidence that in 1620 coffee as a beverage was unknown in London, and that one of the leading intelligences in the England of that day knew of it only from hearsay. Here is a historical fact from which inferences can be drawn, but one which has nothing to do with Bacon himself.

There are other obvious lacunæ. It might have been well to investigate Balzac's attitude towards coffee, which was sometimes puritanical, sometimes one of intemperate use; or to ask why Fontenelle, in his hundredth year, had come to believe that coffee promotes longevity. A chapter might have been devoted to the great importance assumed by "eleven o'clock coffee" among the huge army of commercial employees in every modern great town. From this might be deduced the need for reducing the import duties on coffee in almost all European States.

Much, however, has been intentionally omitted. Friends in Warsaw have written to ask whether I am unaware that the proper spelling of Kolshitsky is Kulczycki. I don't wish to take sides too obviously in so delicate a matter, but it is questionable whether the valiant Kolshitsky was, after all, a Pole! The best and oldest authorities describe him as a Rascian. Rascia is in Serbia, and in Banat Serbs are often called Rascians. If Kolshitsky was a Serb and not a Pole, that explains a good deal. Then, the "Sambor" which is said to have been his birthplace was not the Sambor near Lemberg in Galicia, but "Sombor" in Jugoslavia, a town whose population is today still a mixed one, consisting of Serbs, Hungarians, and Germans. Like all Banat, Sombor was in those days under Turkish rule. This would explain how it was that Kolshitsky could speak Turkish as a second mother-tongue. His servant, Georg Mihailovich, was unquestionably a Serb. Ruthenians contend that Kolshitsky was a Ukrainian, and that his name was really Kolshetshko. The Viennese always spell it Kolschitzky; but Kolshitsky will do for the English-speaking world, the question being one of phonetics rather than of an indeterminable orthography and racial origin.

The sources of the history of coffee are in a queer condition. Where we should like them to be abundant, they are inclined to dry up. On the other hand, matters of trifling importance are confirmed by a wealth of identical testimony. Hitherto, moreover, there have only been monographs, and works in which coffee is incidentally mentioned; no attempt at an inclusive treatment of the subject. For data concerning the early use of coffee in France, and down to the days of the revolution of 1789, an excellent authority is Alfred Franklin's *Vie privée d'autrefois*, in "*Arts et métiers des Parisiens du XIIe au XVIIIe siècle.*" As to the English "coffeo-mania," consult Westerfrölke's monograph; as to the Viennese coffee-houses, the *Festschrift des Gremiums der Kaffeehausbesitzer in Wien*. Uker's *All about Coffee* contains trustworthy information upon the history of coffee in America. There are monographs by Dr. Hans Roth, Dr. Hermann Kurth, and Dr. Klara Ratzka-Ernst on the economic history of coffee in Brazil during the nineteenth century, and the latest problems of the coffee industry: over-production and the world market, sequestration, and valorization.

Bibliography

BOOK ONE

ALBANUS, Prosper: De plantis Ægypti liber, Venice, 1592. BOER, de: Geschichte der Philosophie im Islam, 1901. BROCKELMANN: Geschichte der Arabischen Literatur, 1897–1902. BUNGE, Gustav von: Lehrbuch der physiologischen und pathologischen Chemie, Leipzig, 1894. BURCKHARDT, I. L.: Travels in Arabia, London, 1829. DEFLERS, A.: Voyage au Yemen, Paris, 1889. GOLDZIHER, Ignaz: Abhandlungen zur arabischen Philologie, Leyden, 1899. GROHMANN, A.: Süd-Arabien als Wirtschaftsgebiet, Vienna, 1922. HAMMER-PURGSTALL, Joseph Freiherr von: Geschichte des Osmanischen Reiches, 1835, *and* Literaturgeschichte der Araber, Vienna, 1856. HERBERT, Sir Thomas: A Description of the Persian Monarchy, 1634, reissued with additions as Some Yeares Travels into Africa and Asia the Great, 1638. HORMAYR, Joseph: Wien, seine Geschichte und Denkwürdigkeiten, Vienna, 1823–4. KAEMPFER, Engelbrecht: Amoenitatum exoticarum, Lemgo, 1712. KOENIG: Chemie der menschlichen Nahrungs- und Genussmittel, Berlin, 1823. (KOLSHITSKY, F. G.) Warhaffte Erzehlung welcher gestallt in der änstlichen Türkischen Belägerung der kayserl. Haupt- und Residentzstadt Wien in Österreich durch das feindliche Lager gedrungen und die erste Kundschafft zur kayserlichen Haupt-Armee, wie auch von da glücklich wieder zuruck gebracht worden, 1683. KLAGES, Ludwig: Vom kosmogonischen Eros, Munich, 1922. LECLERC: Histoire de la médecine arabe, Paris, 1875–6. LEWIN, Louis: Phantastica, die betäubenden und erregenden Genussmittel, Berlin, 1924. MANZONI, R.: El Yemen, Rome, 1884. MAYER, Hans and Gottlieb: Die experimentelle Pharmakologie als Grundlage der Arzneibehandlung, Berlin, 1930. MOHAMMED, the Prophet: The Koran. MÜLLER, August: Der Islam, 1885–7. MULLER, Edgar: Arabiens Vermächtnis, Hamburg, 1931. NAIRON, Antonius Faustus: De saluberrima potione cahue seu cafe nuncupata discursus, Rome, 1671. NIEBUHR, Karsten: Reisebeschreibung von Arabien, Copenhagen, 1774. NIETZSCHE, Friedrich: Die Geburt der Tragödie aus dem Geiste der Musik, 1872. NOORDEN, von, and SALOMON: Handbuch der Ernährungslehre, Berlin, 1920. PAULITSCHKE: Harrar, Leipzig, 1888. POLAK, I. E.: Persien, Leipzig, 1865. PRESCOTT, Samuel C.: Report of an Investigation of Coffee, New York, 1927. RAUWOLF, Leonhard: Eigentliche Beschreibung der Raisz so er vor diser Zeit gegen Auffgang in die Morgenländer vollbracht, Laugingen, 1582. RENNER, Victor von: Wien im Jahre 1683, Vienna, 1883. RITTER, Carl: Vergleichende Erdkunde von Arabien, Berlin, 1846. ROHDE, Erwin: Psyche. Seelenkult und Unsterblichkeitsglaube der Griechen, 1890–4. SILVESTRE DE SACY, Antoine: Chrestomathie arabe, Paris, 1826. SNOUCK HURGRONJE, C.: Mekkanische Sprichwörter, The Hague, 1886, *and* Mekka,

The Hague, 1888–9. SPENGLER, Oswald: Der Untergang des Abendlandes, Munich, 1922. SPENGER, A.: Das Leben und die Lehre des Mahommed, 1868–9. SCHMIDT, W.: Das südwestliche Arabien, Frankfort-on-Main, 1913. SCHWEIN-FURTH, Georg: Arabische Pflanzennamen, 1912. TORNAUW, N. von: Das moslemische Recht, St. Petersburg, 1856. TRAPPEN, I. E. van der: Specimen historico-medicum de Coffea, Utrecht, 1843. VAELKEREN: Vienna a Turcis obsessa, Vienna, 1863. VALLE, Pietro della: Viaggi, Brighton, 1843. WELTER: Essai sur l'histoire du café, Paris, 1868.

BOOK TWO

ANDERSON, Adam: Historical and Chronological Deduction of the Origin of Commerce from Earliest Accounts to the Present Time, 1762. AUDIGER: La maison réglée, Paris, 1692. BRANDES, Georg: Shakespeare, 1898. BRODE, Reinhold: Friedrich der Grosse und der Conflict mit seinem Vater, Leipzig, 1904. Capitular des deutschen Hauses in Venedig, edited by Thomas, Berlin, 1874. BÜNTEKUH, Cornelius: Korte verhandeling van 't menschenleven, Amsterdam, 1684. CHARLES-ROUX, I.: Aigues-Mortes, Paris, 1910. DAWSON, Warren R.: The Treasures of Lloyds, London, 1930. DROYSEN, J. G.: Der Staat des Grossen Kurfürsten, Leipzig, 1872. DUFOUR, Sylvestre: Traitez nouveaux et curieux du café, du thé et du chocolat, Lyons, 1685. ELLIS, John: An Historical Account of the Coffee, London, 1774. ENNEN: Die Stadt Köln und das Kaufhaus der Deutschen in Venedig. (In the first annual number of the *Monatschriften für rheinisch-westphälische Geschichtsforschung und Altertumskunde*.) ERD-MANNSDOERFER: De commercio quod inter Venetos et Germaniae civitates aevo medio intercessit, Leipzig, 1858. GALLAND, Antoine: De l'origine et du progrès du café, Caen, 1699. GARNETT, R.: The Age of Dryden, London, 1897. GURLITT, Cornelius: August der Starke, Dresden, 1924. HAENDCKE, Berthold: Deutsche Kultur im Zeitalter des 30-jährigen Krieges, Leipzig, 1906. HAHN, Ludwig: Geschichte des preussischen Vaterlandes, Berlin, 1893. HASCHE: Diplomatische Geschichte Dresdens, von seiner Entdeckung bis auf unsere Tage, Dresden, 1816. HEYD, Wilhelm: Abhandlungen über das Haus der deutschen Kaufleute in Sybels historischer Zeitschrift, 1874, *and* Geschichte des Levantehandels im Mittelalter, Stuttgart, 1879. HETTNER, Hermann: Literaturgeschichte des 18. Jahrhunderts. KIESSELBACH, Arnold: Die wirtschaftlichen Grundlagen der deutschen Hanse und die Handelsstellung Hamburgs, Berlin, 1907. KNACKFUSS, H.: Tizian, Leipzig, 1907. LENTHÉRIC, Charles: Le Rhône, Paris, 1905. MACAULAY, Thomas Babington: Complete Works, London, 1898. MICHEL, Karl: Beiträge zur Entwicklungsgeschichte der Bierbrauerei, Munich, 1906. MONE: Der Süddeutsche Handel mit Venedig (in seiner Zeitschrift). MOSELEY, B.: A Treatise concerning the Properties and Effects of Coffee, London, 1792. OLEARIUS (Oelschläger), Adam: Beschreibung der Newen Orientalischen Reise, Schleswig, 1647. ROBINSON, E. F.: The Early History of Coffee-Houses in England, London, 1893. ROQUE, de la: Voyage de l'Arabie Heureuse, Amsterdam, 1716, *and* Voyage de Syrie et du Mont Liban, 1723. SCHÄFFLER: König Waldemar und die Hansestädte, Jena, 1879. SCHÜCK: Brandenburg-Preussens Kolonialpolitik. STRIEDER, Jakob: Levantinische Handelsfahrten deutscher Kaufleute des 16. Jahrhunderts, Berlin, 1919. THÉVENOT, Jean de: Relation d'un voyage fait au Levant, Paris, 1665. TISSOT: Von der Gesundheit der Gelehrten, Leipzig, 1769. WARD, Edward: The Humours of a Coffee-House, London, 1709. WESTERFRÖLKE, Hermann: Englische Kaffeehäuser als Sammelpunkte der literarischen Welt im Zeitalter von Dryden und Addison, Jena, 1924. WESTER-MAYER: Jacobus Balde, sein Leben und seine Werke, Munich, 1868. WICQUE-

FORT: Relation du voyage d'Adam Olearius en Moscovie, Tartarie et Perse, traduit de l'Allemand, Paris, 1666.

BOOK THREE

ARGENSON, B. L. de: Journal et mémoires, Paris, 1859–67. ARNETH, Alfred, Ritter von: Maria Theresias letzte Regierungszeit, Vienna, 1879. BAUDIL-LAT, H.: Histoire du luxe, Paris, 1878. BERGER, Heinrich: Friedrich der Grosse als Kolonisator, Giessen, 1896. BERTRAND: Louis XIV, 1924. BOCKELMANN, A. von: Wirtschaftsgeographie von niederländisch Ost-Indien, Halle, 1904. BONN: Spaniens Niedergang, Stuttgart, 1896. BORRMANN, Martin: Sunda, eine Reise durch Sumatra, Frankfort-on-thé-Main, 1925. BOSCH, van den: Nederlandsche bezittingen in Azie, America en Afrika. BOURETTE: La muse limonadière, Paris, 1755. BRESSON: Histoire financière de la France. BURMEISTER, Friedrich Karl: Der Merkantilismus im Lande Braunschweig-Wolfenbüttel im 16. und 18. Jahrhundert. BURSTNER, Fritz: Die Kaffee-Ersatzmittel vor und während der Kriegswirtschaft, Berlin, 1918. CASPARY, Adolf: Wirtschaftsstrategie und Kriegführung, Berlin, 1932. CAUER, Edouard: Zur Geschichte und Charakteristik Friedrichs des Grossen, Breslau, 1883. CHEVRIER, F.: Les ridicules du siècle, 1752. CLIEU, de: Lettre à Fréron dans L'Année littéraire, 1774. CLEMENT, Pierre: Lettres, instructions et mémoires de Colbert, Paris, 1860, and Histoire de Colbert et de son administration, Paris, 1892. COGNEL, F.: La vie parisienne sous Louis XVI. CORTI, Egon Caesar, conte: Die trockene Trunkenheit. Ursprung, Kampf und Triumph des Rauchens, Leipzig, 1930. DEPPING: Correspondance administrative sous Louis XIV. DUCROS, L.: Les encyclopédistes, Paris, 1900. DU DEFFAND: Correspondance, Paris, 1877. DULAURE, I. A.: Histoire physique, civile et morale de Paris, Paris, 1823. DUMREICHER: Ueber den französischen Wohlstand als Werk der Erziehung, Vienna, 1879. DIDEROT and d'ALEMBERT (editors): L'encyclopédie, 1751–80. ELIZABETH CHARLOTTE OF THE PALATINATE: Briefe, 1867. Encyclopädia van Nederl. Ost-Indie, The Hague, 1921. Etrennes à tous les amateurs de café, Paris, 1790. FICHTE, J. G.: Der geschlossene Handelsstaat, 1800. FLOSSMANN: Picander, Leipzig, 1899. FÖRSTER, Christian Gottlieb: Geschichte von der Erfindung und Einführung des Zichorienkaffees, Bremen, 1773. FRANKLIN, Alfred: Le café, le thé et le chocolat. (In "Arts et métiers des Parisiens du XIIe au XVIIIe siècle," Paris, 1893. FRÉRON, E. C.: L'Année littéraire, Paris, 1754. FUNCK-BRENTANO, E.: Les nouvellistes, Paris, 1905. GONCOURT, E. and J.: La femme au XVIIIe siècle, Paris, 1862. GRIMM, F. M.: Correspondance, 1877–82. HAECKEL, Ernst: Aus Insulinde, Malaiische Reisebriefe, Bonn, 1901. HECHT, Gustav Heinrich: Colberts politische und volkswirtschaftliche Grundanschauungen, Freiburg i. B., 1898. HERSCH, Heinrich: Friedrich der Grosse als Kronprinz im Briefwechsel mit Voltaire, Halle, undated. HINTZE, O.: Die Industrialisierungpolitik Friedrichs des Grossen, Danzig, 1903. HITZIGRATH: Hamburg und die Kontinentalsperre, 1900. HURTAUT and MAGNY: Dictionnaire historique de Paris. Imperial Decree from the Minutes of the State-Secretariat, Berlin, November 21, 1806. KARMASCH: Geschichte der Technologie, Munich, 1872. KELLER, F. E.: Der preussische Staat, Berlin, 1873. KIELSTRA: Die niederländischen Kolonien in Süd-Ostasien im Weltverkehr, Jena, 1922. KOSER, Reinhold: Friedrich der Grosse, Berlin, 1904–5. LECOMTE: Le capitaine de Clieu ou le premier pied du café aux Antilles, 1862. LEPAGE, A.: Les cafés politiques et littéraires de Paris, Paris, 1885. LE SAGE, Alain René: La valise trouvée, 1740. LUDWIG, Emil: Napoleon, London and New York, 1926. LUMBROSO: Napoleone e l'Inghilterra, 1897. MACK, H.: Geschichte der Mumme, insbesondere des Mummehandels im

17. Jahrhundert, "Braunschweig. Magazin," 1911. MATSCHOSS: Friedrich der Grosse als Beförderer des Gewerbefleisses, Berlin, 1912. Mémoires de l'Académie des Sciences, Paris, 1716. MERCIER, L. S.: Le tableau de Paris, Paris, 1781–8. MICHELET, Jules: La régence, 1874. MONTESQUIEU: Les lettres persanes, Amsterdam, 1721. NEMEITZ, J. C.: Séjour de Paris, c'est à dire instructions fidèles pour les voyageurs de condition, Leipzig, 1726. ONCKEN, Wilhelm: Das Zeitalter Friedrichs des Grossen, Berlin, 1881. PEEZ, von, and DEHN: Englands Vorherrschaft, Vol. I, Aus der Zeit der Kontinentalsperre, 1912. PHILIPPSON: Das Zeitalter Ludwigs XIV, 1890. PRUDHOMME: Miroir de l'ancien et du nouveau Paris. PUJOULSE, J. B.: Paris à la fin du XVIIIᵉ siècle. REIMANN, E. P.: Der brandenburgisch-preussische Staatshaushalt in den beiden letzten Jahrhunderten, Berlin, 1866. ROCKE: Die Kontinentalsperre, reprinted from *Der Weltmarkt*, Hanover, 1919. SAVARY: Dictionnaire du commerce, 1723. SCHMOLLER, Gustav: Studien über die wirtschaftliche Politik Friedrichs des Grossen und Preussens, 1680–1786, *Jahrbuch für Gesetzgebung und Verwaltung*, vols. VIII, X, and XI. SONNENFELS, Josef von: Grundsätze der Polizey, Handlung und Finanzwissenschaft, Munich, 1787. SPARSCHUH, Henricus: Potus coffeae, Upsala, 1761. SPITTA, Philipp: Johann Sebastian Bach, 1873–80. STORCH, Heinrich: Russland unter Alexander dem Ersten, St. Petersburg, 1805. TAINE, Hippolyte: Les origines de la France contemporaine. THIBAUDEAU, Clair Antoine: Le consulat et l'empire, Paris, 1834. TÓTH, Karl: Weib und Rococo in Frankreich, Vienna, 1924. VALLENTIN, Berthold: Napoleon, Berlin, 1923. VOIGT, Erich: Wirtschaftsgeschichte niederländ. Indiens, Leipzig, 1931. VOLTAIRE: Oeuvres. WAHL, A.: Vorgeschichte der französischen Revolution, Berlin, 1905–7. WALTZ, Gustav Adolf: Die Staatsidee des Rationalismus und der Romantik und die Staatsphilosophie Fichtes, Berlin, 1928. WARNKÖNIG and STEIN: Französische Staats- und Rechtsgeschichte, 1846–8. WEBER, Max: Der Nationalstaat und die volkswirtschaftpolitik, Freiburg, 1895. WITH, Karl: Brahmanische und Buddhistische Architektur auf Java, Hagen i. W., 1920. WUSTMANN, G.: Aus Leipzigs Vergangenheit, 1885–1909. ZIMMER: Zachariae und sein Renommist, Leipzig, 1892.

BOOK FOUR

ARNHOLD, Erna: Goethes berliner Beziehungen, Gotha, 1925. BAB, Julius, and HANDL, Willi: Wien und Berlin, Vergleichendes zur Kulturgeschichte, Berlin, 1918. BERMANN: Alt- und Neu-Wien, Vienna, 1879. BOEHN, Max von: Modespiegel, Berlin and Brunswick, 1919. BRIAN-CHANINOV: Alexander I, Paris, 1934. CAPEFIGUE: Histoire de la restauration, Paris, undated. CASTELLI, Ignaz Franz: Wiener Lebensbilder, Vienna, 1848. CLOETER, Hermine: Häuser und Menschen von Wien, Vienna, 1917. ECKER, Victor Ludwig: 250 Jahre Wiener Kaffeehaus, Festschrift des Gremiums der Kaffeehausbesitzer, Vienna, 1933. FALKE, Jakob von: Aus alter und neuer Zeit, Berlin, 1895. FINDEISEN, Franz: Der Kaffeehandel, Halle, 1917. GEIGER, Ludwig: Berlin von 1688 bis 1840, Geschichte des geistigen Lebens, Berlin, 1892–5. GLEICHEN-RUSSWURM, Alexander von: Geselligkeit, Stuttgart, 1912. HICKMANN: Wien im 19. Jahrhundert, Vienna, 1903. HOUBEN, H. H.: Gutzkow-Funde, Berlin, 1901. IMBERT DE SAINT-AMAND: La cour de Louis XVIII, Paris, 1890. KASTAN, I.: Berlin, wie es war, Berlin, 1925. KURTH, Hermann: Die Lage des Kaffeeweltmarktes und die Kaffeevalorisation, Jena, 1909. LACRETELLE, J. C.: Histoire de la France depuis la restauration, Paris, 1829–35. LUCAS-OUBRETON: Louis XVIII, Paris, 1925. MARTIGNAC: Essai historique sur les révolutions d'Espagne,

Paris, 1832. MUNCH, Ernst: Allgemeine Geschichte der neuesten Zeit, Leipzig, 1834. NICOLAI, F.: Beschreibung einer Reise durch Deutschland und die Schweiz im Jahre 1781, Berlin, 1783–97. OSTWALD, Hans: Kultur- und Sittengeschichte Berlins, Berlin, undated. PERIGNY: Storia di Verona dal 1790 al 1822, Verona, 1873–85. RATZA-ERNST, Klara: Welthandelsartikel und ihre Preise, Munich, 1912. RODENBERG, Julius: Bilder aus dem berliner Leben, Berlin, 1891. ROTH, Hans: Die Ueberzeugung in der Welthandelsware Kaffee im Zeitraum von 1790 bis 1929, Jena, 1929. SCHEFFLER, Karl: Berlin, Berlin, 1910. SCHIEMANN, Theodor: Kaiser Alexander I und die Ergebnisse seiner Lebensarbeit, Berlin, 1904. STRECKFUSS: Berlin im 19. Jahrhundert, Berlin, 1867–9. TIETZE, Hans: Wien, Leipzig, 1931. Uhlands Leben, von seiner Wittwe, Stuttgart, 1874. VARNHAGEN VON ENSE, Karl August: Rahel, ein Buch des Andenkens für ihre Freunde, 1834. VILLEMAIN: Chateaubriand. Ses écrits, son influence littéraire et politique, Paris, 1858. WILHEIM, S.: Wiener Wandelbilder, Vienna, undated. ZOHNER, Alfred: Das junge Wien (in Castle's Deutsch-Oesterreichischer Literaturgeschichte, Vienna, 1934).

BOOK FIVE

ALVES DE LIMA, Octaviano: Revulcão economico-social, São Paulo, 1931. BARBOSA, Ruy: Queda do Imperio, Rio de Janeiro, 1921. BEER, Adolf: Geschichte des Welthandels im 19. Jahrhundert, 1864–80. BIBRA, E. von: Die narkotischen Genussmittel und der Mensch. BÖHM-BAWERK, Eugen von: Kapital und Kapitalzins, 1884–9. BRANDENBURGER, Clemens: Brasilien zu Ausgang der Kolonialzeit, São Leopoldo, 1922. BROUGIER, Adolf: Der Kaffee, dessen Kultur und Handel, Munich, 1897. BÜRGER, Otto: Brasilien, Leipzig, 1926. CIUPKA, Paul: Taschenbuch des Kaffeefachmanns, Hamburg, 1931. Coffee, published by the Coffee Institute of São Paulo, 1928. DAFERT, F. W.: Ueber die gegenwärtige Lage des Kaffeebaus in Brasilien. A Lecture delivered in Amsterdam on March 18, 1898. DECKER: Lebensbilder aus der Flora Brasiliens, São Leopoldo, 1931. DUMONT VILLARES, Jorge: O Café, cultura, producão e commercio, São Paulo, 1927. FINDEISEN, Franz: Der Kaffeehandel, Halle, 1917. FUCHS: Der Warenterminhandel, seine Technik und volkswirtschaftliche Bedeutung, fifteenth issue, Jahrbuch für Gesetzgebung, Leipzig, 1891, GRUNTZEL, Josef: Allgemeine Volkswirtschaftslehre, Vienna, 1929. HAHN, Lilly: Die Kaffeestatistik, ihre Bedeutung für den Welthandelsartikel, Vienna, 1934. HELLWIG, Karl: Organisacão bancaria e financeira do Brasil, São Paulo, 1930. KERNER VON MARILAUN, Anton: Pflanzenleben, Leipzig, 1896. KURTH, Hermann: Die Lage des Kaffeeweltmarkts und die Kaffeevalorisation, Jena, 1909. LEITE, Antonio José: Resumo da historia da defesa do café, São Paulo, 1932. LÜCKER, Albert: Neue Probleme in der Frage der brasilianischen Kaffeevalorisation, Crefeld, 1925. MAULL, Otto: Brasilien, eine geopolitische Studie. (In Haushofer's Bausteine zur Geopolitik, Berlin, 1928). MENGER, Karl: Grundsätze der Volkswirtschaftslehre, 1871. MESSNER, Franz: Der Kaffeebau im Staate São Paulo, a Dissertation, Vienna, 1934. MISES, Ludwig von: Liberalismus, Vienna, 1927, and Kritik des Interventionismus, Vienna, 1929. MÜLLER, Edgar: Kaffee und Rösten, Hamburg, 1929. OBERPARLEITER, Karl: Der Londoner Kaffeemarkt, Vienna, 1912, and Funktionen und Risiken des Warenhandels, Vienna, 1930. OLIVEIRA, Lima: O Imperio Brazileiro, 1822–89; São Paulo, 1927. PIERIS: Ceylon, its History, People, Commerce, Industries, and Resources, Colombo, 1924. RATZKA-ERNST, Klara: Welthandelsartikel und ihre Preise, Munich, 1912. REINHARDT, L.: Kulturgeschichte der Nutzpflanzen, Munich, 1911. RITTER, Karl: Die Erdkunde im Verhältnis zur Natur und zur Geschichte des Menschen. Berlin, 1817–8.

ROTH, Hans: Die Ueberzeugung in der Welthandelsware Kaffee im Zeitraum von 1790 bis 1929, Jena, 1929. ROWE, I. W. F.: Brazilian Coffee, London and Cambridge Economic Service, 1932. SEMLER, Heinrich: Tropische Agricultur, Wismar, 1897. SIEGMANN, Heinz: Der Kaffeeweltmarkt, Frankfort-on-Main, 1931. SONNDORFER, R.: Die Technik des Welthandels, Vienna, 1922. SCHER-RER, Hans: Die Kaffeevalorisation und Valorisationsversuche in anderen Welthandelsartikeln, *Weltwirtschaftliche Archiv*, vol. XIV, 1919. SCHÖFFER, C. H.: Der Kaffeehandel, Amsterdam, 1868. SCHÖNFELD, Karl: Der Kaffee-Engroshandel Hamburgs, Heidelberg, 1903. SCHÜLER, Heinrich: Brasilien, ein Land der Zukunft, Stuttgart, 1921. TAVARES, Mario: The Coffee Institute of the State of São Paulo, São Paulo, 1926. UKERS, William H.: All about Coffee, New York, 1922. WERTHER, Paul: Der Hamburger Kaffeemarkt, in the *Hamburger Ueberseejahrbuch*, 1929. WIESER, Friedrich von: Theorie der gesellschaftlichen Wirtschaft, 1914. *Wirtschaftsdienst*, Hamburg, annual issues from 1924 to 1934 inclusive.

Index